CATALÀ-ROCA
BARCELONA
ARQUITECTURA

An Accidental Masterpiece

An Accidental Masterpiece
Mies van der Rohe's Barcelona Pavilion

Dietrich Neumann
with David Caralt

Birkhäuser
Basel

Abbreviations

AA	Politisches Archiv des Auswärtigen Amtes, Berlin
ACB	Arxiu Contemporani de Barcelona
ANC	Arxiu Nacional de Catalunya
AHCB	Arxiu Històric de la Ciutat de Barcelona
AMAB	Arxiu Municipal Administratiu de Barcelona.
BArchL	Bundesarchiv Lichterfelde, Berlin
BG	Berlinische Galerie
CCA	Centre Canadien d'Architecture / Canadian Centre for Architecture, Montréal, CA
GKM	Georg Kolbe Museum
GStA PK	Geheimes Staatsarchiv Preussicher Kulturbesitz, Berlin
HHSA	Hessisches Hauptstaatsarchiv
HoeA WaB	Firmenarchiv der Hoechst GmbH, Friedrichsdorf
MoMA	Museum of Modern Art, New York
LArchB	Landesarchiv Berlin
LoC	Library of Congress, Washington, D.C.

Introduction

"The work in Barcelona was a luminous moment in my life."[1]

Ludwig Mies van der Rohe, 1957

On June 11, 1929, Ludwig Mies van der Rohe and his partner, Lilly Reich, left Barcelona by train from the vast iron vaults of the new Franca station, never to return. Exhausted and in desperate need of a vacation—Reich was running a high fever[2]—they did not take the train straight back to Berlin, but headed west to the seaside resorts of Biarritz and San Sebastian for a two-week vacation. During this period of recuperation Mies must have thought, with rather mixed feelings, about the building they had left behind in Barcelona.

The previous months had been the most dramatic and chaotic period of Mies's professional career. Reich and Mies had designed all of the sections representing German industry at the Barcelona International Exposition, spread across eight different palaces, with a separate structure for the electrical industries. The separate national pavilion was intended as the centerpiece and summation of Germany's exhibition. Mies had long been undecided about the design and delayed its presentation to the commissioner until early February. The task was unfamiliar to him and his solution reflected his current occupations with innovative exhibition stands and residential architecture. Money had run out at a crucial moment in mid-March, just as construction was about to begin, and the project of a pavilion was officially abandoned. Spain's proto-Fascist dictator, Miguel Primo de Rivera, personally intervened to express his displeasure, prompting a scramble for additional funds in Berlin, which arrived some sixteen days later, and work began on site ten days after that, on April 14. But the hiatus meant that none of the official maps would show the pavilion's location, and most visitors missed the German information section, which had been hastily relocated to the second floor of the Machinery Hall. The delay also meant that the construction of the entire pavilion, from the excavation of the foundations to its completion, had to be accomplished in a mere six weeks. There were night and evening shifts, agonizing delays in the delivery of materials, and a shortage of workers, disagreements with the German commissioner about the use of funds, and angry altercations between members of Mies's team. Partly due to this accelerated schedule, but mostly because of the brazen extravagance of cladding the entire structure in travertine and polished marble, it was by far the costliest pavilion at the exposition, as well as the most expensive building Mies had ever designed. When it opened on May 27, 1929 (one week after the expo's official inauguration), a number of details remained unfinished and some compromises were obvious. Painted stucco stood in for polished stone in the back, and the small structure on the southeastern end was not yet accessible, its front covered with sheets of drywall. Inside, the wall-high dark-red velvet curtain, a key piece of the interior concept, had not been delivered in time, and the luminous glass wall, the only source of light at night, did not work. Most importantly, the inscription "Alemania"—the single word needed to identify the national pavilion's role and purpose—was missing from the facade, perhaps held back by the disgruntled German commissioner, who had provided the money for the pavilion himself when additional government funds were not forthcoming.

But still, the general concept was clearly visible: on an oblong podium, expansive walls of marble and glass and eight cruciform, nickel-clad columns formed a sequence of freely connected spaces, some underneath a thin continuous roof slab, others open to the sky, by turns luminous and dark, mysterious and inviting. The arresting center of an otherwise empty building was marked by a freestanding onyx wall, a huge black carpet, and a few pieces of custom-designed furniture. There were two shallow

1 Mies van der Rohe, letter to the magazine *Arquitectura*, Madrid 1957. Quoted from: Josep Quetglas, *Fear of Glass*. (Basel, Birkhäuser, 2001): 181.

2 Anon. (probably a General Director Kauffmann),"Bericht über meinen Besuch der Internationalen Weltausstellung Barcelona 1929, May 19, 1929," HoeA, WaB 1929–1930, 11. See also Lilly Reich to Elisabeth Hahn and Grete Uhland, 26 June 1929, MoMA, MvdR Papers, Barcelona Pavilion, Folder 8.

water basins, the larger one outside flanked by a long wall and travertine bench, the smaller one in an interior court adorned with a female figure by the sculptor Georg Kolbe. Nothing remotely comparable had ever served as a national pavilion at an international exposition.

At the brief opening ceremony on an overcast Monday morning, Mies had to endure the mockery of King Alfonso XIII, who joked that he had anxiously driven by the building site every day to check on its progress until it dawned on him that the Germans had purposely delayed construction in order to show the world just how much they could accomplish in a week. The low, upholstered leather chairs on flat chromium steel springs that Mies had designed for the king and queen of Spain (and had flown in at the last minute at great expense) were ignored by the royal couple.[3] The general public at the exposition seems to have been similarly unmoved. Most visitors did not know what the structure was; some mistook it for an advertising kiosk for the marble industry, while others approached the German representative and asked what it was all supposed to mean.

In his own speech at the opening, however, German commissioner Georg von Schnitzler began to frame a narrative that would become the foundation for many future interpretations. He presented the clarity and simplicity of the German sections and this building as a deliberate reflection on the young Weimar Republic's economic woes and its humble desire for sincerity and openness (indeed, this facile equation of the pavilion's forms with political and moral ambitions has enjoyed a long afterlife, even surviving to the present day). Von Schnitzler had both a general and a very personal interest in a positive reception of the pavilion at home, since he hoped to recoup from the government some of the money he had invested in its construction–an ambition supported by several of his friends, who placed glowing reviews in major newspapers and journals.

Mies himself appears to have been less certain of the building's success. Contrary to his usual habit, he did not commission any professional photographs of it. At the end of June, weeks after Mies had left Spain, and in the absence of any other imagery, a professional photographer, Sasha Stone, documented its exhibits at the behest of the German silk industry. Stone also photographed the pavilion and sold his images to a news agency in Berlin. Rigorously composed around a horizontal symmetrical axis, the images lent the pavilion a stark gravitas, presenting it as a mysteriously beautiful, abstract composition of horizontal and vertical planes–its formal purity enhanced by the complete absence of visitors. Restrictions on official photography meant that these images remained almost the only ones available of the pavilion, and as such they illustrated and influenced many articles in newspapers and architectural journals over the following months.

The almost unanimous enthusiasm of these reports must have genuinely surprised Mies. But his uneasiness about the project and its painful genesis remained. When von Schnitzler invited Mies to attend the expo's "German Week" in October 1929 to see the pavilion again, now with all its details in place, and to attend several festivities planned there, he politely demurred. He would not get another opportunity, as three months later the building was dismantled, its metal frame scrapped, and the marble and travertine slabs shipped to Hamburg, where they were eventually used in building projects for the state.

What happened next is one of the most unusual success stories in the history of architecture: despite its short existence, and thanks in part to Stone's brilliant photographs, the building's reputation grew steadily over the following decades. Before long, it was considered a built manifesto for the modern movement, with its spatial and "spiritual" ambitions, and "one of the milestones of modern architecture."[4] The pavilion itself was proclaimed "one of the great works of art of all time,"[5] "a virtual *ur*-hut" or "temple"[6] of modernity, a true archetype akin to Bramante's Tempietto in Rome, which holds a comparable emblematic position for the Renaissance. At the same time, architects the world over adopted the pavilion's formal and spatial vocabulary, which became a central strand of Mid-Century Modern's DNA from California to postwar Germany and is still vividly palpable today. Mies himself applied the pavilion's essential language only to two subsequent structures—the Tugendhat House in Brno of 1930 and the House for a Childless Couple shown at the Berlin Building Exposition of 1931—but it reverberated, hauntingly, through his sketches and studio exercises all the way into the 1940s. From the 1960s on, reflecting the growing discontent with the modern movement, more critical and complex readings of the pavilion emerged, both in defense of it or as symbol of its shortcomings. Italian critics in particular probed the political intentions of its designer.

Known for more than half a century only through Stone's black-and-white photographs, the pavilion was rebuilt at its former location, just in time to commemorate the 1986 centenary of Mies's birth. However, given the almost complete absence of original construction documents, the new building is at best an approximation, and provoked a spirited debate about the value of reconstructions and the importance of authenticity. "How fundamentally does it differ from Disney?"[7] Rem Koolhaas asked, while Alison and Peter Smithson wondered if, deprived of "its revolutionary intent," it would become "merely a tourist attraction."[8]

But even those uneasy with this "replica," "facsimile," or "parody" had to admit that the experience of the building in color and three dimensions offers rich new insights into its architectural concept. Its reincarnation also coincided with—and was probably helped by—wider changes in the discourse about historical architecture, notably, the rediscovery of a "Presence of the Past," as Paolo Portoghesi titled the first Venice Architecture Biennale in 1980, and the rise of a postmodern architecture. In this context, the very real, physical, presence of the reborn Barcelona Pavilion paradoxically helped to rekindle a renewed interest in the architecture of the modern movement, which postmodernism had ostensibly set out to replace. And while the pavilion certainly never regained the political connotations it carried in the 1920s or foreshadowed in the postwar period (when Mies's architecture and that of his peers returned to Europe, supposedly as an architecture of democracy and freedom), its careful execution, play with light and shade, and open spatial sequences have had a lasting impact on generation after generation of architects and critics. In the process it has become the single most written about building of the modern movement.

Apart from descriptions in virtually every history of modern architecture and lengthy chapters in any biography of Mies, eight monographs on the pavilion have already appeared.[9] Why, then,

3 Letter from Erich von Kettler to Georg von Schnitzler, 5 July 1929, HoeA, WaB 1929–1930.

4 Philip Johnson, *Mies van der Rohe*, exh. cat. Museum of Modern Art (New York: Museum of Modern Art, 1947), 58, 60.

5 Peter Blake, "Afterword: Conversation at 23 Beekman Place: Interview with Paul Rudolph (1996)," in Roberto de Alba, *Paul Rudolph: The Late Work* (New York: Princeton Architectural Press, 2003), 217.

6 See George Dodds, "Body in Pieces: Desiring the Barcelona Pavilion," *Res* 39 (2001): 173; and Vincent Scully, *Modern Architecture: The Architecture of Democracy* (New York: George Braziller, 1961), 27.

7 Less is More," in Rem Koolhaas and Bruce Mau, S.M.L.XL. (New York: Monacelli Press, 1995): 48–61.

8 Alison Smithson, La Vanguardia (November 15, 1985): 44.

9 Rosa Maria Subirana i Torrent (Ed.), *Mies van der Rohe's German Pavilion in Barcelona 1929–1986*, Barcelona 1987; Ignasi de Solà-Morales, Cristian Cirici, Fernando Ramos, *Mies: El Pabellón de Barcelona*, Barcelona 1993; Josep Quetglas, *Der gläserne Schrecken: Mies van der Rohes Pavillon in Barcelona*, Basel 2001; Lluís Casals, Josep M. Rovira i Gimeno, *Mies van der Rohe: Pavilion: Reflections*, Barcelona 2002; George Dodds, *Building Desire: On the Barcelona Pavilion*, London, New York 2005; Ursel Berger, Thomas Pavel (Hrsg.), *Barcelona-Pavillon. Mies van der Rohe & Kolbe: Architektur und Plastik*, Berlin 2006; José Vela Castillo, *(De)gustaciones gratuitas: de la deconstrucción, la fotografía, Mies van der Rohe y el Pabellón de Barcelona*, Madrid 2010; Valentin Trillo Martinez, *Mies en Barcelona: Arquitectura, Representacion y Memoria*, Sevilla 2017; Juanjo Lahuerta, Celia Marín Vega (Ed.), *Mies in Barcelona*, 1929, Barcelona 2017.

another book on the building? One immediate answer is that this volume presents new findings from US, Spanish, and German archives that shed light on the context of the building's creation in greater detail than before.[10] The emergence of several crucial protagonists besides the architects, for example, complicates questions of authorship. And while almost no design or construction drawings have survived in the archives, there is abundant correspondence regarding the political process, the building's financing and genesis, and rich collections of contemporary critical voices. As a result, the building can now be placed with greater certainty in its multiple contexts. The following chapters present the political conditions in Germany and Spain, contemporary debates about the building type, the trajectory of Mies's work, the financing, design, and construction of the pavilion, events during its short-lived existence, and its documentation through photography. Finally, we chronicle the long path to its reconstruction from the 1950s to the mid-1980s.

In an artistic intervention at the rebuilt pavilion in 2010 Catalan artist Antoni Muntadas underscored the "reciprocal dependence between the built structure and its other, paper-based condition—its memory as embodied by the archive, in its multiple publications and documents," which he made perceptible through archival material in the pavilion and "the olfactory experience of printed, stored paper."[11] Beatriz Colomina noted at that occasion that "the smell of Mies is the smell of documents."[12] Indeed, as another historian, Marco de Michelis, has suggested, what connects the powerful contemporary reconstruction with the lost original building—these two distant and different stages of its story—are "the documents that enable us to tell it again today."[13]

Buildings such as Mies's Barcelona Pavilion, Le Corbusier's Villa Savoye, or Wright's Fallingwater acquire their notoriety not just as an automatic result of intrinsic, outstanding qualities, but rather emerge from complicated, often accidental relationships and sometimes from carefully orchestrated campaigns.[14] Our appreciation of any building is inseparable from the evolution of its reception over time. While something like a textbook reading of the Barcelona Pavilion emerged early on and is usually found in publications for the general reader, additional, often contradictory, readings coexisted from the beginning and continue to emerge, in particular since the pavilion's rebuilding in 1986.[15]

A separately published anthology of 100 texts on the pavilion offers access to the astonishingly varied approaches and viewpoints over the past nine decades and thus complements our analysis. Our detailed account of the pavilion's genesis and political context might help to separate the more plausible interpretations from misunderstandings or overly speculative approaches and suggest a reading that is less heroic, but more realistic, *sachlich* even, as it acknowledges the complex conditions of architectural production, of accidents and circumstance.

10 Most important are the Mies van der Rohe Papers at the Museum of Modern Art in New York and at the Library of Congress in Washington, the Archive of the Hoechst AG in Friedrichsdorf near Frankfurt, the Political Archive of the Foreign Ministry in Berlin, the GStA PK in Berlin, the Bundesarchiv Berlin, the Arxiu Nacional de Catalunya, Arxiu Històric de la Ciutat de Barcelona, and Arxiu Municipal Administratiu de Barcelona. In addition, the recent digitization of historical newspapers, such as *ABC*, *La Vanguardia*, *Vossische Zeitung*, and architecture journals such as *Wasmuths Monatshefte für Baukunst*, *Die Form*, and many others has considerably facilitated our access to the contemporary discourse.

11 Xavier Costa, "The Pavilion and Its Archive," in *Muntadas: On Translation: Paper BP/MVDR*, ed. Xavier Costa (Barcelona: Fundació Mies van der Rohe, 2010), 14–19.

12 Beatriz Colomina, "The Smell of Mies," in Costa, *Muntadas*, 20–27 (see note 12).

13 Marco de Michelis, "The Smells of History," in Costa, *Muntadas*, 28–31 (see note 12).

14 Beatriz Colomina has frequently pointed to the important role that media have played in our relationship with the architecture of Mies van der Rohe and others, most recently in *Manifesto Architecture: The Ghost of Mies* (Berlin: Sternberg Press, 2014).

15 In Rafael Moneo's words, these "hackneyed interpretations" are "invariably centered on spatial flow, on the presence of neoplasticism, on the distinction to be made between structural and merely formal elements, on the rareness and the quality of the materials, and so on. According to these interpretations, the Barcelona Pavilion is the paradigm of pure, abstract architecture, making the principles of modern architecture manifest with that very clarity with which Alberti's church of Sant'Andrea at Mantua once displayed the principles of Renaissance architecture." Rafael Moneo, introduction to Quetglas, *Fear of Glass*, 9–13 (see note 9).

Barcelona 1929

On September 13, 1923, the citizens of Barcelona woke to alarming news: the head of the city's military command, General Miguel Primo de Rivera (1870–1930) **FIG. 1**, had rallied his troops and staged an overnight coup. The governor of the province of Catalonia had been deposed, and the army now controlled the telephone and telegraph office and all government agencies. In a well-orchestrated campaign, similar coups had been staged simultaneously all over Spain. That morning, Primo de Rivera announced that the liberal Prime Minister, Manuel García-Prieto, had been relieved of his post and the military was taking over the running of the country. He unveiled a long list of ambitions, promising to restore law and order, eliminate corruption, suppress Communist and separatist tendencies, help the working classes, and bring the Rif War in Morocco to a victorious end.[1]

Soon afterward King Alfonso XIII **FIG. 2** pledged his support to the junta and named Primo de Rivera prime minister. Most of the population also accepted the situation, if somewhat wearily, hoping for a period of calm and economic recovery after the instability and bloodshed caused by the Second Moroccan War. Fired up by his recent encounter with the Italian dictator Benito Mussolini, whose own coup had shaken Rome the year before, Primo de Rivera proceeded to dissolve the parliament, suspend the constitution, introduce censorship and martial law, eliminate town councils, and close political and literary associations.

But Primo de Rivera did not hold on to his initial support for long, even though the economy showed signs of improvement and the military conflict with the Berber leader Abd-el-Krim in northern Morocco was finally resolved in Spain's favor in 1927, thanks to massive French military support. The dictator turned out to be an inept politician endowed neither with a clear vision nor with any organizational and strategic talent. His major public works projects, funded by increasing the money supply, initially reduced unemployment but in the long term fueled inflation. And his heavy-handed efforts to suppress Catalan moves toward independence led to simmering unrest in the region, which ignited into a major wave of strikes and public protests in 1928, when he raised taxes on low-wage workers while providing tax relief for the rich.[2]

Primo de Rivera's most visible, most expensive undertaking of all was the 1929 International Exposition in Barcelona and Seville. As his political fortunes waned in the latter half of the 1920s, he pinned his hopes for redemption on the success of the Expo—in vain: his fate was sealed by his mismanagement of the country's economy and by the worldwide economic collapse heralded by the US stock market crash in October 1929. Having lost the support of both the king and the population at large, Primo de Rivera was forced to resign as soon as the Exposition closed its gates in January 1930; he would die a few weeks later. His hapless regime had energized and radicalized Spanish society, and in the following elections, in the spring of 1931, republicans achieved landslide victories throughout Spain, effectively putting an end to 1,200 years of monarchic rule on the Iberian peninsula. King Alfonso fled the country and settled in Rome. Unfortunately for the Spanish, Primo de Rivera's seven-year dictatorship was a prelude of much worse to come. From 1936 on, General Francisco Franco fought and ultimately defeated the Republican forces in the Spanish Civil War, and suppressed the values they had long promoted: regional autonomy, liberal or social democracy, free

1 The sudden developments in Spain caused great concern all over Europe. See "Die Spanische Militär-Rebellion: Alle Provinzen ergriffen," *Vossische Zeitung*, September 14, 1923 (morning edition), 1.

2 See "Der Streik in Barcelona," *Vossische Zeitung*, February 2, 1928 (morning edition), 4; and "Streik-Ende in Barcelona," *Vossische Zeitung*, February 14, 1928 (evening edition), 1. Under continuing threats of losing their jobs, the striking workers finally capitulated after two weeks.

1

2

3

1 General Miguel Primo de Rivera (1870-1930)

2 King Alfonso XIII of Spain (1886-1941)
Photographer: Antonio Cánovas del Castillo, aka Dalton Kaulak (1862-1933)

3 Exhibition grounds ca. 1920 with the Victoria Eugenie and Alfonso XIII exhibition halls in place, as well as the four central columns

4 Aerial view of the national palace and new exhibition halls under construction in 1927

elections, and women's rights. His fascistic dictatorship lasted until his death in 1975.

The idea for an international exposition did not originate with Primo de Rivera. Barcelona's previous universal exposition in 1888 had been an enormous success, not only making a substantial profit but generating urban development, such as the improvement of the city's tram lines and the creation of the Ciutadella park north of the medieval city center.[3] Less than twenty years later, in 1905, the prominent Catalan architect and politician Josep Puig i Cadafalch began to promote the idea of another fair,[4] hoping for a repeated boost to urban growth.[5] In these turn-of-the-century years Catalonia enjoyed extraordinary prosperity as Barcelona, Spain's second largest city, emerged as a major Mediterranean metropolis and trading center. At the same time, and unsurprisingly, the region's desire for autonomy became resurgent. In 1913 Puig's campaign succeeded. Montjuïc, a prominent hill southwest of the city center–then a mix of farmland and defensive fortifications–was named as the site for a future international exposition, with 291 acres earmarked for development.

Puig i Cadafalch, Lluís Domènech i Montaner, and other architects proceeded to draw up detailed–and astonishingly retrograde–plans for an exhibition site at the foot of the hill.[6] Although the outbreak of the First World War thwarted plans for a major international fair in 1917, work on the site went ahead as Spain, a neutral territory, was only marginally affected by the conflict. Two major exhibition palaces by Puig i Cadafalch, named for King Alfonso XIII and Queen Victoria Eugenie, were finished in time for an international furniture exhibition in 1923.[7] **FIG. 3** Both had expansive skylights and plain, windowless walls embellished by sgraffito ornaments of turned baroque columns. Planning for another international exposition was briefly halted after the military coup, but Primo de Rivera decided to press ahead with the

4

fair, recognizing its propaganda value. **FIG. 4** While projecting to the world an image of stability and prosperity under his new rule, it would also, he hoped, create a unifying, common cause to counter domestic unrest and growing separatist movements. For many homeless who had settled in slums on Montjuïc **FIG. 5** and downtown near the church of Santa Maria del Mar, more than two thousand *casas baratas* (affordable housing units) were built along the Bezos River, north of the city center.[8]

But to involve more than one Spanish region, as well as to avoid the impression of a Catalan exceptionalism, Primo de Rivera divided the fair into two sections—one in Seville, where Portugal, Latin America, and the United States would be represented, and the other in Barcelona, for Europe as a whole. A Barcelona businessman and aristocrat, Mariano de Foronda y González Bravo, Marqués de Foronda (1873–1961), was named director of the exhibition.[9] As head of the city's tram network, he was familiar with large and complex infrastructure projects, and immediately made the new subway system one of his priorities (a first segment was opened to great fanfare in 1924). Other developments included the redesign of the Catalunya square **FIG. 6** in the city center and the demolition of large areas on the southern end of the Gran Via for the creation of a monumental new square at the main entrance to the fair next to the existing Moorish bullfighting ring, Plaça de toros de les Arenes. The new square, Plaça d'Espanya, was conceived as a celebration of Spain's diverse geography centered around Josep Maria Jujol's fountain depicting the seas surrounding the Iberian Peninsula and its main rivers the Ebro, Tagus, and Guadalquivir. **FIG. 6**

The chief planner of the fairgrounds, Puig i Cadafalch, was relieved of his post as soon as the new regime took over, not because of his planning approach, but for the simple reason that Puig was one of the most vocal advocates for Catalan independence (for several years he had been president of the regional

3 For a history of the 1888 Universal Exposition, see *Exposició Universal de Barcelona* (1888): *Catálogo general oficial* (Barcelona: Impr. de los Sucesores de N. Ramírez, 1888); and *Exposició Universal de Barcelona: Llibre del centenari, 1888–1988* (Barcelona: L'Avenç, 1988).

4 Josep Puig i Cadafalch, "A votar per l'Exposició Universal," *La Veu de Catalunya*, November 1, 1905, 3.

5 French planner Léon Jaussely had proposed an urban framework for growth, which the city adopted in 1907.

6 For the transformation of the mountain, see J. Oriol Granados, Jordi Calafell, and Rafel Torrella, *Montjuïc 1915, primera mirada* (Barcelona: Arxiu Fotogràfic-Institut de Cultura de Barcelona, 2007); and Rafel Torrella, *El registre fotogràfic de Montjuïc, 1915–1923: La Metamorfosi d'una muntanya* (Barcelona: Arxiu Històric de la Ciutat de Barcelona, 2008). Laura Lizondo Sevilla has convincingly argued that the layout was influenced by Otto Wagner's Artibus Project for Vienna. See Laura Lizondo Sevilla, "Mies's Opaque Cube: The Electric Utilities Pavilion at the 1929 Barcelona International Exposition," *Journal of the Society of Architectural Historians* 76, no. 2 (June 2017): 197–217, here 201.

7 For a detailed account of the prehistory of the 1929 International Exposition and its architectural and urbanistic designs, see Ignasi de Solà-Morales, *La Exposición Internacional de Barcelona 1914–1929: Arquitectura y Ciudad* (Feria de Barcelona, 1985).

8 See "El Patronato de la Habitación de Barcelona," *ABC*, June 22, 1928, 12; and "Visita a los grupos de casas construídas," *La Vanguardia*, October 20, 1929, 12.

9 For a biographical sketch, see his obituary: "Ha Muerto el Marqués de Foronda: Fue comisario regio en la Exposición Internacional de Barcelona en 1929," *ABC*, July 10, 1961, 49–50.

5

5 Slums at the bottom of Montjuïc before the construction of the International Exposition grounds

6 Plaça d'Espanya 1929

7 The toppling of the four columns in the center of the exposition grounds, autumn 1928

8 Poble Espanyol

parliament, Mancomunitat, which was dissolved when Primo de Rivera seized power).[10] But while Puig's coherent, if somewhat overwrought, concept for the fairgrounds was officially abandoned, many of its central ideas survived, notably his preference for the somewhat dull classicism of Noucentisme, which became Barcelona's dominant style in the 1920s, as the city turned away from a highly inventive, richly ornamented Modernisme and sought to assert its Mediterranean connections through a neoclassicist, neo-Renaissance architectural language.

Such stylistic subtleties were lost on Primo de Rivera, who had a weak grasp of most cultural and artistic questions. Rather than signaling his commitment to modernity and progress, the final layout and aesthetic choices on Montjuïc turned out to be as predictable and conventional as Puig's had been. A competition for a new National Palace was won by the architects Eugeni Cendoya, Enric Catà, and Pere Domènech i Roura, whose domed structure bore a distinct similarity to the one envisaged by Puig. In the hands of the architects Ramon Reventós i Farrarons and Francesc Folguera, the two towers flanking the entrance to the exhibition grounds became a dual rendering of Venice's Campanile. Combined with the columnar embrace of the Plaça d'Espanya, reminiscent of St. Peter's in Rome, this made for an odd mix of Italian references.

The most successful part of the fair's site would be the Poble Espanyol (Spanish Village), on the northeastern edge of the grounds, also designed by Reventós i Farrarons.[11] **FIG. 8** In the mold of similar installations at previous world's fairs, such as the temporary Rue du Caire or Ville de Paris at the 1889 and 1900 Paris expositions, or the surviving Castello e Borgo Medievale from Turin's 1911 fair, this was a walled enclosure containing an assemblage of 115 interconnected vernacular buildings from every region in Spain, joined by a Romanesque monastery immediately outside. Carefully selected buildings had been measured and photographed at their original locations and their replicas in Barcelona became part of a picturesque sequence of narrow streets surrounding a central square, while craft shops and restaurants offered sights and tastes from different Spanish provinces. Puig i Cadafalch had originally conceived the village as Iberona (emphasizing shared geographical rather than cultural characteristics), but under Primo de Rivera it was renamed Poble Espanyol and turned into a brilliant piece of propaganda art demonstrating the diversity and coherence of Spanish culture as a spirited rebuttal to separatist tendencies. While providing refuge from the busy city and exhibition grounds, the Poble Espanyol also endeavored, according to contemporary observers, to

6

7

8

"erase the memory of the recent past"–the riots and protests against Primo de Rivera's dictatorship and for Catalan independence.[12] It was one of the most visited and commented-on parts of the exhibition, and one of the few sections complete on the day of the inauguration. An enormous display about the "Art of Spain" in the National Palace fulfilled a similar function and also opened on May 19, 1929.

In the center of the exhibition grounds Puig i Cadafalch had erected four Ionic columns **FIG. 3** whose meaning was obvious to every Catalan: they stood for the four red stripes on yellow ground in the Catalan flag, the Senyera–a reference to the bloody traces purportedly left by the fingers of King Charles the Bald on the golden shield of Wilfred the Hairy, Count of Barcelona, who was mortally wounded during the battle against Lobo Ibn Mohammed in 897. According to a fourteenth-century legend, the king dipped his fingers in the count's blood, creating what is believed to be the first-ever heraldic sign. But the use of the Senyera was outlawed under Primo de Rivera, and the new director of the fairgrounds, Jaume Bayó i Font, insisted the columns had to be demolished, ostensibly to make way for an enormous central fountain. **FIG. 7** The demolition of the columns came so late that some brochures advertising the exposition had already been printed and had to be hastily reissued with a corrected cover. **FIG. 9** Acutely aware of the symbolism of the act, Mies van der Rohe and the architects of the Italian and Swedish pavilions, Piero Portaluppi and Peder Clason, protested against the destruction of the columns, without success.[13] While the four columns were indeed taken down, they were also rebuilt four times over, partly reusing the original stones, in two rows of eight shorter columns on either side of the oblong Plaza de Bellas Artes, at whose center they had stood before. While it is tempting to read this quadrupling of the columns as a sly gesture of defiance, columnar screens were used frequently on the fairground as a tool to provide coherence and delineate sections.

10 Established in 1913, it exerted partial rule over the four Catalan provinces.

11 See Jordana Mendelson, *Documenting Spain: Artists, Exhibition Culture, and the Modern Nation, 1929–1939* (University Park: Pennsylvania State University Press, 2005), 3–38.

12 Ibid., 29.

13 Bonaventura Bassegoda, "Comentaris d'arquitectura," *Ciència: Revista catalana de ciència i tecnologia* 4, no. 36 (1930): 538–52; http://revistes.iec.cat/revistes224/ index.php/ciencia/article/viewFile/85074/84778.

9

9 Two versions of an exhibition brochure with and without the four columns, 1928

At the eastern end of the plaza, toward the old city center, the columns screened the exhibition palace of the City of Barcelona (architect, Josep Goday i Casals). **FIG. 12** The western end, toward Madrid, which was empty for a long time (another piece of symbolism that would not escape most Catalans), became the location of the German Pavilion. The open area framed by these sixteen columns offered respite from the hectic activity of the fairgrounds. A grove of trees—soon joined by rows of luminous stelae—lined its edges, and the center was occupied by the Font Màgica, a spectacular illuminated fountain.[14] **FIGS. 10, 11**

Intent on turning the fair into a superb nocturnal spectacle (by then a tradition at large industrial exhibitions), the organizers invested in a $250,000 custom-made lighting system from the American Westinghouse Corporation, which synchronized the color changes of 850 floodlight projectors. The park's architectural lighting was complemented by a sequence of 50 fountains and cascades, lit from underneath in a well-coordinated symphony of colored light orchestrated by the Catalan "magician of light," Carles Buïgas i Sans. These illuminations were on "a scale several times larger than any similar display hitherto produced."[15] **FIG. 13**

As support for Primo de Rivera began to erode, the political climate in Barcelona turned increasingly volatile, with the dictator barely escaping an assassination attempt on a visit to the city in July 1926. In the months leading up to the exposition's opening, there were frequent and sometimes violent demonstrations at the universities of Barcelona, resulting in their being shut down in March 1929. In protest, Ortega y Gasset—by now deeply disillusioned with the dictatorship he had initially welcomed—moved his lectures to a movie theater in the Calle Mayor and invited the public to attend.[16] Alfonso XIII signaled his own growing discontent with the dictator (as well as his eagerness to ingratiate himself with the public) when he signed a decree ordering the

10

11

10 Fontana Magica at the exposition grounds
Photographer: Emili Godes

11 Exhibition grounds by night
Photographer: Sebastian Jordi

12 Exhibition Palace of the City of Barcelona, 1929
Architect: José Goday

12

14 While the sixteen columns were later taken down again, the original four were reinstated in 2010, only a few meters from their original location.

15 C. J. Stahl, "The Colored Floodlighting of the International Exposition at Barcelona, Spain," *Transactions of the Illuminating Engineering Society* 24, no. 9 (1929): 876–89. On the lighting of the Barcelona Fair, see David Caralt, *Agualuz: De Pirotecnias a mundos flotantes: Visiones de Carles Buigas* (Madrid: Ediciones Siruela, 2010), 75–90; and Dietrich Neumann, *Architecture of the Night* (Munich: Prestel, 2002), 138–39.

16 Andrew Dobson, *An Introduction to the Politics and Philosophy of José Ortega y Gasset* (Cambridge: Cambridge University Press, 1989), 31.

13

14

13 Exhibition grounds by night

14 Apartment house, Barcelona, Calle Muntaner 342-348 (1929-1931) Architects: Josep Lluís Sert

15 Barcelona, Casa Vilaró, 1929 Architect: Sixte Illescas

16 Barcelona in the Future (Tudurí)

reopening of the universities on the day of the exposition's inauguration.[17]

But while the city of Barcelona was being readied for the expected flood of visitors to the exposition, it could hardly have been less prepared for the arrival of Mies van der Rohe's radical pavilion. The modern movement—in full swing north of the Alps and the Pyrenees—had barely a perceptible impact in Spain, even if a few modest skyscrapers spoke of Barcelona's metropolitan ambitions and American perspectives. But change was in the air: the simple, unornamented clarity of Le Corbusier's architecture had cast its spell over a number of young Spanish architects—in particular Josep Lluís Sert, who saw Le Corbusier's work on a trip to Paris in the spring of 1927 and invited him to speak in Barcelona.[18] In May 1928 the Swiss master gave two lectures to great public acclaim.[19] A few months later, Sert started working as an unpaid assistant in Le Corbusier's atelier in Paris and designed the first of two apartment buildings in Barcelona, financed by his mother.[20] **FIG. 14** In April 1929 he organized an exhibition, *New Architecture*, in the gallery of art dealer Josep Dalmau. The eleven participants (four of them still students) presented projects for modern typologies, such as an airport and a hotel, demonstrating a clear architectural allegiance to Le Corbusier.[21] Another member of the group, Sixte Illescas, then just three years out of architecture school, applied Le Corbusier's ideas to a built project: one of Barcelona's first modern villas, the Casa Vilaró, in the Tibidabo hills.[22] **FIG. 15** It is doubtful whether any of these young architects had even heard of Mies van der Rohe, or knew of his frantic efforts to finish his pavilion nearby.[23] In October 1930 the group traveled to Zaragoza for the inaugural meeting of the *Association of Spanish Architects and Technicians for Progress in Contemporary Architecture* (GATEPAC) and founded an affiliated Catalan group called GATCPAC.[24] Its magazine *AC* (*Documents d'Activitat Contemporània*), which appeared from 1931 onward, never once mentioned the Barcelona Pavilion, but would finally acknowl-

15

16

edge Mies some years later, in a 1934 report on the Tugendhat Villa in Brno and Mies's Berlin office.[25]

However, two important Barcelona modernists were not part of this group and were less dogmatic in their convictions: Ramon Reventós i Farrarons had designed a modern apartment block directly behind the exhibition grounds, which was almost finished when the exposition opened in 1929.[26] Stylistically promiscuous, he had also designed the Venetian towers at the main entrance to the fair **FIG. 6** and the acclaimed Poble Espanyol (with Francesc Folguera). His friend Nicolau M. Rubió i Tudurí was building another modernist structure at the time, a radio station on Barcelona's Tibidabo hill, which opened later that same year, and was also in charge of the garden design at Montjuïc, in collaboration with French urbanist and landscape designer Jean-Claude Nicolas Forestier. One of the few to remain unmoved by

17 Hans-Otto Glahn, "Die Ausstellungen von Sevilla und Barcelona," *Schwäbischer Merkur*, May 29, 1929, 105.

18 A Barcelona newspaper notes Sert's return from this trip, "De Sociedad. Notas informativas. Viajes," *La Vanguardia*, April 12, 1927, 15. Sert went on to become one of the most celebrated Spanish mid-century architects, practicing from 1939 to 1969 in the US, from 1953 on as chair of the Harvard Graduate School of Design.

19 For accounts of Le Corbusier's visit, see "Le Corbusier vendrá a Barcelona," *La Vanguardia*, May 2, 1928, 6; "Conferencias 'Le Corbusier,'" *La Vanguardia*, May 13, 1928, 6; "Conferencias Le Corbusier," *La Vanguardia*, May 15, 1928, 10; "El arquitecto Le Corbusier" *La Vanguardia*, May 16, 1928, 6; and "En la sala Mozart: Conferencia de M. Le Corbusier" *La Vanguardia*, May 16, 1928, 27-28.

20 For an account of the beginnings of modern architecture in Barcelona, see Josep M. Rovira, *José Luis Sert* (Milan: Electa, 2003), 14-27; and Josep M. Rovira, ed., *Sert 1928-1979: Medio siglo de arquitectura: Obra Completa* (Barcelona: Fundació Joan Miró, 2005). The Catalan magazines *Gaseta de les Arts* (1925-30), *Mirador* (1929-37), and *D'Aci i d'Allà* sometimes published articles on modern architecture. The newspaper *La Veu de Catalunya* had a section called "Pàgina de la construcció," where the critic Rafael Benet published several essays on Le Corbusier and German modern architecture. Spanish magazines such as *Arquitectura*, *Hogar propio*, and *La Construcción Moderna* also occasionally covered the International Style.

21 See *Arquitectura Nova*, exh. cat. Galerías Dalmau, Barcelona, April 13-27, 1929. The participants were: Antoni Puig Gairalt (a senior architect who had been invited to the show), Ricardo de Churruca, Francesc Fàbregas, Germán Rodríguez Arias, Cristòfol Alzamora, Enrique Pecourt, Pere Armengou, Francesc Perales, Sixte Illescas, Josep Lluís Sert, and Josep Torres Clavé.

22 See Albert Illescas and Manuel Brullet, eds., *Sixte Illescas Arquitecte (1903-1986), De l'avantguarda a l'oblit / de la vanguardia al olvido / From Vanguard to Obscurity* (Barcelona: Collegi d'Arquitectes de Catalunya, 2008), 296-327.

23 The Madrid-based journal *Arquitectura* had, in 1926, shown Mies's curvilinear glass tower and reported on the Weissenhof estate in 1927. See Paul Linder, "Tres ensayos sobre la nueva Arquitectura alemana: Los tectónicos (II)" *Arquitectura* 8, no. 86 (June 1926): 235-41; F. García Mercadal, "La Exposición de la Vivienda: Werkbundausstellung 'Die Wohnung,' Stuttgart, 1927," *Arquitectura* 9, no. 100 (August 1927): 295-98; and Paul Linder, "La Exposicion 'Werkbund Ausstellung' en Stuttgart" *Arquitectura* 9, no. 103 (November 1927): 383-98.

24 Group of Catalan Artists and Technicians for the Progress of Contemporary Architecture.

25 See "Villa en Brünn: Ludwig Mies van der Rohe, arquitecto," *AC*, no. 14 (1934): 30-33; and Isac Saporta, "La labor actual de Mies van der Rohe," *AC*, no. 14 (1934): 34; accessed August 15, 2015, http://www.numerossueltos.com/revistas/ac/ac-documentos-de-actividad-contemporanea-14.html.

26 It still stands at 11, Carrer de Lleida.

Le Corbusier's lectures in the city, Rubió openly challenged his formalist "Corbusian doctrine" as a "historicist style."[27] He never met Mies, but his work is more closely aligned with a Miesian approach, and he wrote a perceptive essay about the German Pavilion in a 1930 article for *Cahiers d'Art*.[28] But even Tudurí could not fully escape the tug of Le Corbusier's influence. Across the plaza from the Mies pavilion, in the building dedicated to the City of Barcelona, he exhibited a large diorama showing his vision for the city's future—a vision in the mold of the Plan Voisin, with rows and rows of housing projects and a new port at the mouth of the Llobregat River, framed by glass and steel towers and superhighways.[29] **FIG. 16**

If Barcelona's architects had little knowledge of the development of modernism in the rest of Europe, then most German visitors to the city were equally unaware of its own architectural tradition, despite the growth of Mediterranean tourism.[30] The one apparent exception was Antonio Gaudí, whose work was briefly discussed in the early 1920s because of its perceived affinity with Expressionist architecture, and indeed Mies had probably seen images of the Casa Milà or the Palau Güell in *Wasmuth's Monatshefte für Baukunst* or in the Expressionist journal *Frühlicht* (in which Mies's own work had also been published).[31] Bruno Taut, the editor, had requested material from Gaudí (whom he considered a soulmate) to include in *Frühlicht*, but never heard back.[32] In 1926 (coincidentally only weeks before Gaudí's death) the *Deutsche Bauzeitung* carried an extensive report about the construction of the Sagrada Familia.[33] **FIG. 17** But in reality the German press treated Gaudí's work more as a curiosity than as a serious architectural statement.[34] His most outspoken German critic was the prominent art historian Julius Meier-Graefe, who had seen Gaudí's work on a trip to Catalonia in 1908 and was so horrified by his formal exuberance that he referred to him henceforth simply as "the monster of Barcelona."[35] Mies knew Meier-Graefe from a visit to Paris in 1912 to solicit support for his Kröller-Müller project (and perhaps also to present himself as a suitable architect for the house the art historian was about to build in Berlin).[36] Walter Gropius had traveled to Barcelona in 1908 and met with Puig i Cadafalch, but not with Gaudí. His students Ernst Neufert and Paul Linder managed to meet Gaudí in 1920; they reported that he'd urged them to study Catalan Gothic architecture rather than his own work.[37] For most German architects, then, Barcelona remained a kind of terra incognita, while Spain as a whole continued to be seen as "Europe's most artistically conservative nation."[38]

17 La Sagrada Familia, Barcelona, in 1928
Architect: Antonio Gaudí (1852-1926)

17

27 N. M. Rubió i Tudurí, "Enfront de Le Corbusier," *La Nova Revista*, June 18, 1928, 163–64.

28 Nicolau M. Rubió i Tudurí, "Le Pavillon de l'Allemagne à l'Exposition de Barcelone par Mies van der Rohe," Cahiers d'Art, nos. 8/9 (August/September 1929): 408–11. In 1932 Mies (or possibly Lilly Reich, whom Tudurí might have mistaken for "Mrs. Mies van der Rohe") had, through an intermediary, expressed interest in Tudurí's architectural manifesto *Actar* of 1931. See Rubio Tudurí to Mrs. Mies van der Rohe, 20 December 1932 (Library of Congress, Mies van der Rohe papers).

29 See Francisco Cañadas, "Barcelona futura: Visiones Barcelonesas," *Diario Oficial de la Exposición Internacional Barcelona 1929* 1, no. 37 (November 16, 1929), 3–4; "Barcelona Futura," *Diario Oficial de la Exposición Internacional Barcelona 1929* 2, no. 46 (January 18, 1930); N. M. Rubió i Tudurí, "Al Pavelló Municipal de l'Exposició: La Barcelona Futura," *Mirador* 1, no. 44 (November 28, 1929); and "La Barcelona Futura," *Butlletí de la Cambra Mercantil* 9, no. 100 (July 1930).

30 "Spanische Reisen," *Vossische Zeitung*, May 25, 1924, "Literarische Umschau," 2; travel restrictions after the First World War were eased around this time, and tourism from Germany picked up again.

31 See "Beispiel jüngerer baukünstlerischer Bewegungen in Spanien," *Wasmuths Monatshefte für Baukunst* 5 (1920/21): 244; and "Neuere Baukunst in Spanien," *Frühlicht* 2, no. 3 (1922): 86. See also Wolfgang Weber, *Barcelona: Das Gesicht der Städte* (Berlin: Albertus-Verlag, 1928), a richly illustrated volume produced in anticipation of the international exposition. It also includes images of Gaudí's work.

32 Joaquin Medina Warmburg, "Gaudi am Bauhaus," in *Gaudí in Deutschland: Lyrik des Raums*, ed. Rainer Stamm and Daniel Schreiber (Cologne: Wienand Verlag, 2004), 30–43.

33 A. Lambert, "Die Kirche der 'Sagrada Familia' in Barcelona: Ein Werk von Antonio Gaudí, Architekt in Barcelona," *Deutsche Bauzeitung* 60, no. 39 (May 15, 1929): 321–27.

34 See, for instance. "Merkwürdige Architektur in Spanien: Ein mosaikbedecktes Wohnhaus im Knusperhäuschenstil in Barcelona," *Vossische Zeitung*, Zeitbilder, no. 22, May 30, 1926, 3, which showed a photograph of the entrance pavilion of the Parc Güell. The title translates as: "Curious architecture in Spain: A mosaic-covered residence in the gingerbread house style in Barcelona."

35 See Julius Meier-Graefe's text "Spanische Reise," in Stamm and Schreiber, *Gaudí in Deutschland*, 144–47 (see note 32).

36 Franz Schulze, *Mies van der Rohe: A Critical Biography* (Chicago: University of Chicago Press, 1985), 62–63.

37 Joaquin Medina Warmburg, "Gaudí am Bauhaus," in Stamm and Schreiber, *Gaudí in Deutschland*, 30–43 (see note 32).

38 Gustav Edmund Pazaurek, "Ist der Werkbund auf dem richtigen Wege?" *Münchner Neueste Nachrichten* 83, no. 308, November 12, 1930, 1.

Germany and the World's Fair

Invitations to take part in the 1929 International Exposition were sent out in February 1927, more than two years before the opening, and just after a new and inexperienced German government had been sworn in. The German reaction to the invitation was lukewarm and slow—it took half a year before the Spanish organizing committee heard back from Berlin, and even then the first exchanges were merely inquiries about details. A firm commitment only came about after prolonged hesitation and a considerable amount of arm-twisting.[1] From the outset, the Germans were urged to build a small "representative pavilion (300–700 square meters)"—national pavilions signaled international prestige and recognition and were considered essential to distinguish an exposition from a trade fair. As a form of inducement, the Spanish organizers reassured their German colleagues that land would be provided for free and that the cost of the pavilion need not exceed 70,000 Reichsmark.[2]

Much of this initial communication was channeled through Enrique Domínguez Rodiño (1887–1974), a cultural attaché at the Spanish Embassy in Berlin and holder of the honorary title Agent of the Barcelona Exposition in Germany. After a year of concerted effort, Rodiño finally managed to bring a small and somewhat reluctant delegation of German officials to Barcelona on February 22, 1928.[3] The Marqués de Foronda, director of the exhibition in Barcelona, personally invited the group to lunch.[4] Still, an official commitment to participate was not forthcoming.[5] Rodiño redoubled his efforts, appealing directly to influential industry leaders and placing ads on the front pages of the *Berliner Tageblatt* and *Hamburger Fremdenblatt*. An illuminated sign also materialized high up on the facade of Berlin's Tietz department store, proclaiming simply "1929."[6] These tactics had the desired effect, and the German government finally consented to take part. On April 27, 1928, Rodiño proudly reported home that there was "unanimous enthusiastic support for brilliant German participation" on "approximately 10,000 square meters." But he kept quiet about the important matter of Germany's pavilion—while agreeing to participate, the German Foreign Office had in fact categorically stated that a "pavilion was out of the question."[7]

The search for a German commissioner at the exhibition immediately then began. It had to be someone with organizational skills and experience, diplomatic talent, connections to different industries, and enough personal wealth to be able to do the job pro bono. Georg von Schnitzler (1884–1962), a forty-five-year-old Frankfurt industrialist, seemed to fit the bill. After some negotiations, he accepted the appointment on May 28, 1928.[8] **FIG. 1** He

1 Enrique Domínguez Rodiño had reported, impartially, from Germany for *La Vanguardia* during the First World War (as Spain's first foreign correspondent) before joining the Spanish Embassy in Berlin in 1925. See Josep Pla, "Records del periodisme," In *Notes disperses* (Barcelona: Destino, 2001). The Executive Committee of the Exhibition to E. D. Rodiño, 31 August 1927, Arxiu Municipal Administratiu de Barcelona, Z102 Exposició Internacional de Barcelona 1913-34 (hereafter AMAB, Z102), Box 47132: Expediente relativo a la designación de D. Enrique Domínguez Rodiño como Agente de la Exposición en Alemania (Rodiño file), folder 1927. Rodiño was rewarded for his efforts with a silver cigar box at a breakfast in Berlin's Hotel Kaiserhof in early December 1930. Rodiño to Ministerialdirektor Koepke at the Foreign Office, 4 December, Politisches Archiv des Auswärtigen Amts, Bestand R 240.031, AA, Abteilung II, R.901, 40031, "Einzelausstellungen Spanien. Internationale Ausstellung Barcelona 1929," vol. 5, 91.

2 See Santiago Trias to Enrique Domínguez Rodiño, 8 November 1927, AMAB, Z102, Box 47132, Rodiño file, folder 1927; Trias to Rodiño 12 December 1927, ibid.; and Trias to Rodiño, 3 February 1928, ibid., folder 1928.

3 Enrique Domínguez Rodiño to the Marqués de Foronda, 17 February 1928, AMAB, Z102, Box 47132, Rodiño file, folder 1928. Members of the delegation were Dr. Peter Mathies, Ernst Wagemann, Advisor to the Ministry of Foreign Affairs, and Director General Fritz Ter Meer, representing the German industry.

4 "La Participación de Alemania en la Exposición de Barcelona," *ABC*, February 24, 1928, 26.

5 AMAB, Z102, Box 47040: Exposició 1929, Copias, Junta Directiva Actas, Folder 25/2/1928: "Visit of the German delegates to inquire about the exhibition [...] stating their good impression."

6 Santiago Trias to Enrique Domínguez Rodiño, 14, 17, and 24 April 1928, AMAB, Z102, Box 47132, Rodiño file, folder 1928.

7 Bundesarchiv Berlin Lichterfelde (henceforth BArch L), Ausstellung Barcelona, AA, Abteilung II, R 9.01, 40027, no. 174, 175, Dr. Mathies (Government Commissary for Exhibitions and Trade Fairs) February 25, 1928, report of visit to exhibition grounds.

8 The runner-up had been Friedrich von Bülow (1889–1984), a high-ranking manager at the Krupp Corporation in Essen. See BArchL, Ausstellung Barcelona, AA, Abteilung II, R 9.01, 40027, no. 229, list of May 4, 1928. Internally, the name had been confirmed as early as May 14, as we know from a confidential telegram from Enrique Domínguez Rodiño to Madrid, 14 May 1928, ibid. Mies signed a separate contract with the German silk industry on June 2, 1928, for the design of the section for the Deutsche Seide. See Christiane Lange, *Ludwig Mies van der Rohe: Architektur für die Seidenindustrie* (Berlin: Nicolaische Verlagsbuchhandlung, 2011), 83. Note about meeting on June 2, 4-6 pm, between Mr. Rosenbaum, Mies van der Rohe, and Lilly Reich regarding the costs of the participation of the silk industry in Barcelona. MoMA, MvdR Papers, Barcelona Pavilion, folder with newly purchased material (Reuters), no pagination. Mies was given a stipend to travel to Barcelona.

1

2

1 Georg von Schnitzler (1884-1962)

2 Lilly von Schnitzler (1889-1981)

3 Ludwig Mies van der Rohe (1886-1969)
Photograph: Werner Rohde

4 Lilly Reich (1885-1947)
Photograph: G. Engelhardt

had been trained as a banker and lawyer and four years earlier had joined the board of directors at Farbwerke Höchst, which soon integrated into IG Farben (the world's largest drug, chemical, and dye conglomerate), where he became vice president for pigment production.[9] Von Schnitzler had recently immersed himself in the process of building a new headquarters for IG Farben in Frankfurt and initiated an open competition, which was won in August 1928 by Hans Poelzig.[10] Von Schnitzler remained involved in the building process until its completion in 1931. His wife, Lilly, was responsible for art inside the building and commissioned Max Beckmann's master student Georg Heck (1897–1982) with a large fresco in the building's "Red Salon."[11]

Von Schnitzler quickly appointed Ludwig Mies van der Rohe (1886–1969) and Lilly Reich (1885–1947) **FIGS. 3, 4** artistic directors of the German section. The decision was almost certainly down to the influence of von Schnitzler's wife, Lilly, a grande dame of Frankfurt society who presided over a salon that brought together prominent businessmen, politicians, actors, writers, artists—and the occasional architect. **FIG. 2** On first meeting Mies in 1925, she was immediately struck by the force of his personality. Three years later, she urged her husband to hire him: "I said to him, 'Mies is our most important architect, the Le Corbusier of Germany.' [...] Then he got the job, and requested to bring Lilly Reich along as his collaborator."[12]

Surviving correspondence reveals how von Schnitzler's thinking about the question of a separate pavilion then evolved, and the care he took to conceal his intentions from the government which was dead set against it. On June 1, von Schnitzler wrote to his colleagues at IG Farben of his appointment. His letter mentions that a "German House" was not being considered, since other countries, and in particular France, were not having a national building either.[13] Soon after, Mies and von Schnitzler traveled to Barcelona to get a firsthand look at the fairgrounds.[14] There they

3

4

discovered that France and several other countries had agreed to build pavilions after all. Surely, Germany could not lag behind.

But the political climate in Germany was volatile. The centrist coalition under Chancellor Wilhelm Marx had collapsed, and a general election held on May 20, 1928–the week before von Schnitzler's appointment as commissioner–had brought great gains for the Social Democrats (SPD).[15] With Hermann Müller as Chancellor, the SPD formed a grand coalition with the Center (Zentrum), the German Democratic Party (DDP), and an unlikely ally, the conservative German People's Party (DVP). The new government was less inclined than its predecessor to support industry and businesses and instead placed greater emphasis on domestic social programs. And it was even less enthusiastic about participating in the Barcelona International Exposition. The two ministers most closely involved were the Foreign Minister, Gustav Stresemann (a member of the German Werkbund), and the Minister of Economic Affairs, Julius Curtius, both of the DVP, which had close ties to industry and stood decidedly right-of-center. While the previous government had tentatively allocated a budget of two million Reichsmark for Germany's participation, the new administration slashed this to 350,000 Reichsmark.[16]

In early July 1928 Mies told his colleagues at the Werkbund, where he served as second director, that he had been commissioned to design "the industrial sections" and "a German representational space."[17] This could be understood as either a gathering space inside one of the palaces or a separate pavilion. One

9 "Again and again Germany has itself represented abroad by the old aristocracy," the socialist journalist Kurt Lenz griped about this choice. Kurt Lenz, "Die Weltausstellung von Barcelona," *Salzburger Wacht*, August 3, 1929, 6.

10 Participants were Paul Bonatz, Fritz Höger, Jacob Koerfer, Hans Poelzig, Ernst May, and Martin Elsaesser, in addition to six designs from IG Farben's planning department. Peter Cachola Schmal, "Der Kunde ist König: Zum Einfluß des Bauherrn I.G. Farbenindustrie AG auf die Entstehung der 'Grüneburg,'" in *Der Poelzig-Bau: Vom IG-Farben-Haus zur Goethe-Universität*, ed. Werner Meißner, Dieter Rebentisch, and Wilfried Wang (Frankfurt: S. Fischer, 1999), 47–59.

11 Christiane Schillig, "Ein Wandgemälde in Frankfurt's Universität: Das übertünchte Arkadien" *Monumente*, 2007, https://www.monumente-online.de/de/ausgaben/2007/5/das-uebertuenchte-arkadien.php#.XHFqeuj0lEY.

12 Interview, Ludwig Glaeser with Lilly von Schnitzler, September 6, 1974, 2. Canadian Centre for Architecture (henceforth CCA), Ludwig Glaeser Archive, Box 3, no. 5.

13 Confidential letter, Georg von Schnitzler to board of directors of Union Quimica y Lluch S.A., Barcelona, 1 June 1929, HoeA, WaB 1927–1928.

14 In a telegram of May 30 to the Spanish organizers, Mies was named as the architect responsible and his visit to Barcelona announced for June 7. See Ignasi de Solà-Morales, *Mies van der Rohe: El Pabellón de Barcelona* (Barcelona: Gustavo Gili, 1993), 8n7.

15 The previous government under Chancellor Wilhelm Marx of the Zentrum Party had been in charge from February 1, 1927, to June 28, 1928. It consisted of members of the Zentrum (Center), DVP (German People's Party), DNVP (German National People's Party), and the smaller parties DDP (German Democratic Party), and BVP (Bayerische Volkspartei). This right-of-center coalition was more business-friendly than the grand coalition under chancellor Müller that followed, which included the Social Democratic Party as a major player.

16 GStA PK, HA Rep 120 Ministerium für Handel und Gewerbe E XVI No 413, 1911–1929, 184; Note from the Fair Committee at the Prussian Ministry of Trade (Messefachausschuss des Preussischen Handelsministerium), February 9, 1928.

17 "Protokoll der Vorstands- und Ausschussitzung des Deutschen Werkbundes vom 5 Juli 1928 in München," MoMA, MvdR Papers, Barcelona Pavilion, Folder 1.

week later, a typewritten letter from von Schnitzler to Curtius contains a telling detail. Von Schnitzler wrote that he had commissioned Mies to design a "representative space" ("eines würdigen Raumes"), but then changed this by hand to a "representative framework" ("eines würdigen Rahmens").[18] He seemed at pains to make the planned space sound as inconspicuous as possible. In mid-August, the Spanish organizing committee got impatient. Bypassing von Schnitzler, it urged the German ambassador to pursue the matter with Curtius, and asked Rodiño to follow up with him in Berlin.[19] The result was the opposite of what it had intended: an assistant secretary at the Foreign Ministry wrote to inform the Spanish ambassador that "the question of a German pavilion [...] has long been dismissed as impractical," as there was no funding for it, and furthermore "the remaining eight months would be in no way sufficient" to build "anything remotely comparable" to the other pavilions in the exhibition.[20] In mid-September von Schnitzler returned to Barcelona with Dr. Peter Mathies, who was in charge of the Reich's exhibitions and trade fairs, and a Dr. Maiwald from the Ministry of Economic Affairs, along with Mies and Lilly Reich.[21] At a "gentlemen's breakfast" on June 22, 1928, at the Hotel Ritz von Schnitzler promised the mayor of Barcelona, Barón de Viver, and the exhibition's director, the Marqués de Foronda, that a "a representative pavilion of his country in the exhibition, of a size of 200–300 square meters" would indeed be built. He probably believed that he would easily secure the consent of politicians keen not to be outdone by Germany's "archenemy," France.[22]

After the official announcement in early October, the exposition newsletter noted jubilantly: "All of the details relative to the German contribution to the upcoming exposition have been finalized. Work will begin shortly on the construction of the magnificent Pavilion of Germany and on the installation of diverse contributions of the industry and economy of said country."[23] Barcelona's *La Vanguardia* reported that the pavilion would be in "modern style, particularly adapted to the general characteristics of modern architecture in our country." Greatly relieved, the organizing committee honored the German visitors with a banquet.[24]

It is worth dwelling for a moment on this particular step and the risks it involved. Berlin had sent a very clear directive *not* to build a pavilion, and the budget certainly did not allow for one. We can only speculate on von Schnitzler's motives for making this extraordinary commitment. He might have promised Mies the opportunity for a separate building early on, realizing that a photogenic pavilion by an avant-garde architect would do more for Germany's reputation than a series of industrial exhibits, or he might have succumbed to pressure from the Spanish organizers, who were eager for their major trading partner to have a prominent presence at the fair. In any event, von Schnitzler clearly underestimated the difficulties involved in raising the remaining money. His experience as a high-ranking manager at IG Farben had not prepared him for the complicated decision-making processes of a young parliamentary democracy. Used to telling others what to do, he had little regard for the directives of politicians, especially since the volatile political climate of the Weimar Republic had produced sixteen different governments over the previous nine years. Perhaps he assumed that the fluxing allegiances in the Reichstag would eventually settle in his favor, and that by establishing contractual obligations he would force the government to find the necessary funds.

When von Schnitzler returned home in mid-October, contract in hand, Privy Councilor Dr. Mathies cautioned him that his intended program was unlikely to succeed.[25] Unimpressed, von Schnitzler requested an additional 750,000 Reichsmark from the government. The Finance Minister, Rudolf Hilferding, politely agreed to include the amount in a forthcoming budget proposal.[26] By this time, the projected costs of Germany's participation in Barcelona had risen to 1.1 million Reichsmark. This included the cost of the—never officially approved—pavilion, now estimated at 150,000 Reichsmark. Von Schnitzler, still confident of success, assured potential participants on October 27 that "fortunately the financial basis for the German participation [...] can be considered secure."[27] In the meantime, discussions had begun with Mies van der Rohe about the details of his contract—to be based on that between Hans Poelzig and the IG Farben for the building of their headquarters in Frankfurt. Mies turned out to be a shrewd negotiator. He requested 10 percent of the overall sum, much higher than the usual 6.4–6.8 percent, based on the argument that he would do additional work on behalf of the different industries. Behind the scenes there were worries: Friedrich Rüggeberg, the German Consul in Barcelona, and Erich von Kettler wrote to von Schnitzler of their "fear that Mr. Mies van der Rohe—in particular under the influence of Mrs. Reich—might go too far in some artistic respects, in particular since we have looked closely at the two artists' recent work in Stuttgart." While they considered Mies "the calmer one of the two" they were convinced that Lilly Reich "pushes him toward artistic experiments, which he, however, always denies."[28] The two observers recommended the contract contain a clause that gave von Schnitzler a measure of control over any artistic decisions.

On November 12, 1928—and still without news of the success or failure of his application—von Schnitzler signed a generous contract with Mies van der Rohe and Lilly Reich on the basis of a revised cost estimate of 1.35 million Reichsmark—200,000 more than his most recent budget request. Some of the funding, he assumed, would be provided by the exhibiting industries. Despite Rüggeberg and von Kettler's misgivings, Mies and Reich were granted complete artistic autonomy and a generous honorarium of 125,000 Reichsmark plus all expenses paid for them and their team.[29] Lilly Reich clearly expected this to be an all-consuming job. She was being considered for the directorship of a new fashion institute in Munich, but declined on October 6, 1928, due to her commitment to the work in Barcelona.[30]

Besides the financing, one other crucial issue remained unresolved: the pavilion's location. The other national pavilions had long been assigned sites in the international section, next to the National Palace on Montjuïc. Only latecomers France and Germany still needed to find a spot. France ended up with the somewhat awkward inner corner of the two wings of the Palacio Alfonso XIII, facing the Plaza de los Bellos Officios. This plaza would fill up with a melee of commercial pavilions, food stands, and advertising kiosks, and the small cube of the French pavilion was never able to compete with the attention-seeking structures in front of it.

18 George von Schnitzler to Julius Curtius, 14 July 1928, HoeA, WaB 1927–1928.

19 Santiago Trias to Enrique Domínguez Rodiño, 17 August 1928, HoeA, WaB 1927–1928: "It is very urgent that Germany decides to build a pavilion at the Barcelona exhibition. In this regard, we have written to the German ambassador and hope V. will make the efforts to get what we want."

20 Letter from Hans Posse, assistant secretary at the Foreign Ministry, in response to an inquiry from the Spanish ambassador through his press attaché Enrique Domínguez Rodiño, August 17, 1928. BArchL, Ausstellung Barcelona, AA, Abteilung II, R 9.01, 40028, 49, 50.

21 "La participación de Alemania en la Exposición de Barcelona," *ABC*, September 16, 1928, 37.

22 See opening remarks in the contract between Georg von Schnitzler and the chair of the executive committee of the exhibition in Barcelona, Santiago Trias (October 1928), in BArchL, Ausstellung Barcelona, AA, Abteilung II, R 9.01, 40028, 122, preliminary contract between von Schnitzler and the chair of the executive committee of the exhibition in Barcelona, Santiago Trias, September 26, 1928, HoeA, WaB 1927–1928. Final version of October 1928, in BArchL, Ausstellung Barcelona, AA, Abteilung II, R 9.01, 40028, 125; and "Herrenfrühstück im Hotel Ritz," Saturday, June 22, 1928, HoeA, WaB 1927–1928.

23 *Memoria Diaria*, Año 1928 (October 16, 1928), AMAB, Z102, Box 47102.

24 "Gacetillas," *La Vanguardia*, October 11, 1928, 10.

25 Dr. Peter Mathies to Georg von Schnitzler, 13 October 1928, HoeA, WaB 1927–1928.

26 Dr. Peter Mathies to Georg von Schnitzler, 19 October 1928, HoeA, WaB 1927–1928.

27 Georg von Schnitzler to representatives of the German industry, 27 October 1928, BArchL, Ausstellung Barcelona, AA, Abteilung II, R 9.01, 40028, 127–30.

28 Friedrich Rüggeberg to Georg von Schnitzler, 5 November, 1928, HoeA, WaB 1927–1928.

29 Georg von Schnitzler to Mies van der Rohe, 12 November 1928, BArchL, Ausstellung Barcelona, AA, Abteilung II, R 9.01, 40030, 101–3; von Schnitzler promised to pay up to 150,000 Reichsmark of his personal funds to cover all expenses in connection with his role as German commissioner of the exhibition, such as the offices in Berlin and Barcelona. In the build-up to the fateful government discussion about funds on March 2 and 3, 1929, von Schnitzler expected to be asked by the government to reduce Mies's fee (which by then had increased to RM 160,000) and hoped to discuss this with him. Von Schnitzler to Dr. Maiwald, 2 March 1929, HoeA, WaB 1929–1930.

30 Magdalena Droste, "Lilly Reich: Her Career as an Artist," in *Lilly Reich: Designer and Architect*, ed. Matilda McQuaid (New York: Museum of Modern Art/Harry N. Abrams, 1996), 47–59, here 55.

5

6

The German delegation was offered the equivalent on the other side, at the inner corner of the two wings of the Victoria Eugenie Palace. It comes as no surprise that neither Mies nor von Schnitzler showed much enthusiasm. They urged the organizers to consider releasing the western end of the adjacent, much larger Plaza de Bellas Artes for construction. In Puig's original plan, both ends of the plaza formed a semicircular exedra, framed by low walls and planting. **FIGS. 5-7** Under the new master plan, the eastern end had been given over to the City of Barcelona's exhibition palace, while the western end remained empty and still contained its original, semicircular walls and planting, divided by a broad path and staircase in the center. This path was of strategic importance, as it would lead up to the Poble Espanyol, which was expected to be one of the biggest draws for the visitors. The potential of both sites thus differed enormously: while the inner corner of the palace only allowed for a small building of 200–300m^2 (roughly the size of the French pavilion), the larger plot at the western end of the Plaza de Bellas Artes accommodated a much larger footprint (Mies's design ended up using 1,400m^2). While the site on the Plaza de los Bellos Officios would be in the midst of the hubbub of the exhibition grounds, necessarily passed by everyone, the calmer, more distant alternative overlooked the vast Plaza de Bellas Artes with its enormous magical fountain.

Approval could not be given immediately, and so the official contract simply stated Germany's strong preference for the site at the

7

5-7 Plaza de los Bellos Officios, Barcelona, 1926
Photograph: Perez de Rozas

Plaza de Bellas Artes. The go-ahead was given at Mies's next visit to Barcelona, on November 25, 1928—exactly six months before the opening.[31] It was an extraordinarily generous concession, as it impeded one of the major circulation routes of the fair. In all likelihood Mies was given the site on the condition that he preserved access to the existing footpath and staircase. While several later reports claimed that Mies had selected the pavilion's site himself (German critic Walther Genzmer even called it "the architect's most important creative act"[32]), we have to bear in mind that only two locations were left at that point. The final decision lay in the hands of the Spanish organizers,[33] who—Mies later complained—"failed to designate the definitive space for the pavilion in time."[34] By then, most of the official maps had gone to print and

31 Mies had left again for Barcelona on November 18, 1928. See Erich von Kettler to Georg von Schnitzler, 19 November 1928; and Dr. Maiwald to Georg von Schnitzler, 26 November 1928, HoeA, WaB 1927–1928.

32 Walther Genzmer, "Der Deutsche Reichspavillon auf der Internationalen Ausstellung in Barcelona," *Die Baugilde* 11, no. 20 (October 1929): 1654–55.

33 The allocation of the sites had in general been a complicated and much delayed process. The site for the Italian pavilion, for example, was only dedicated in mid-December. See Rubén Domínguez Méndez, "El fascismo italiano y la Exposición Internacional de Barcelona de 1929," *Diacronie: Studi di Storia Contemporanea*, no. 14 (2013), accessed August 8, 2017, dialnet.unirioja.es/descarga/articulo/4495575.pdf.

34 Mies van der Rohe to Georg von Schnitzler, 24 March 1930, MoMA, MvdR papers, Barcelona Pavilion, Folder 2010 addition from Eduard Ludwig estate.

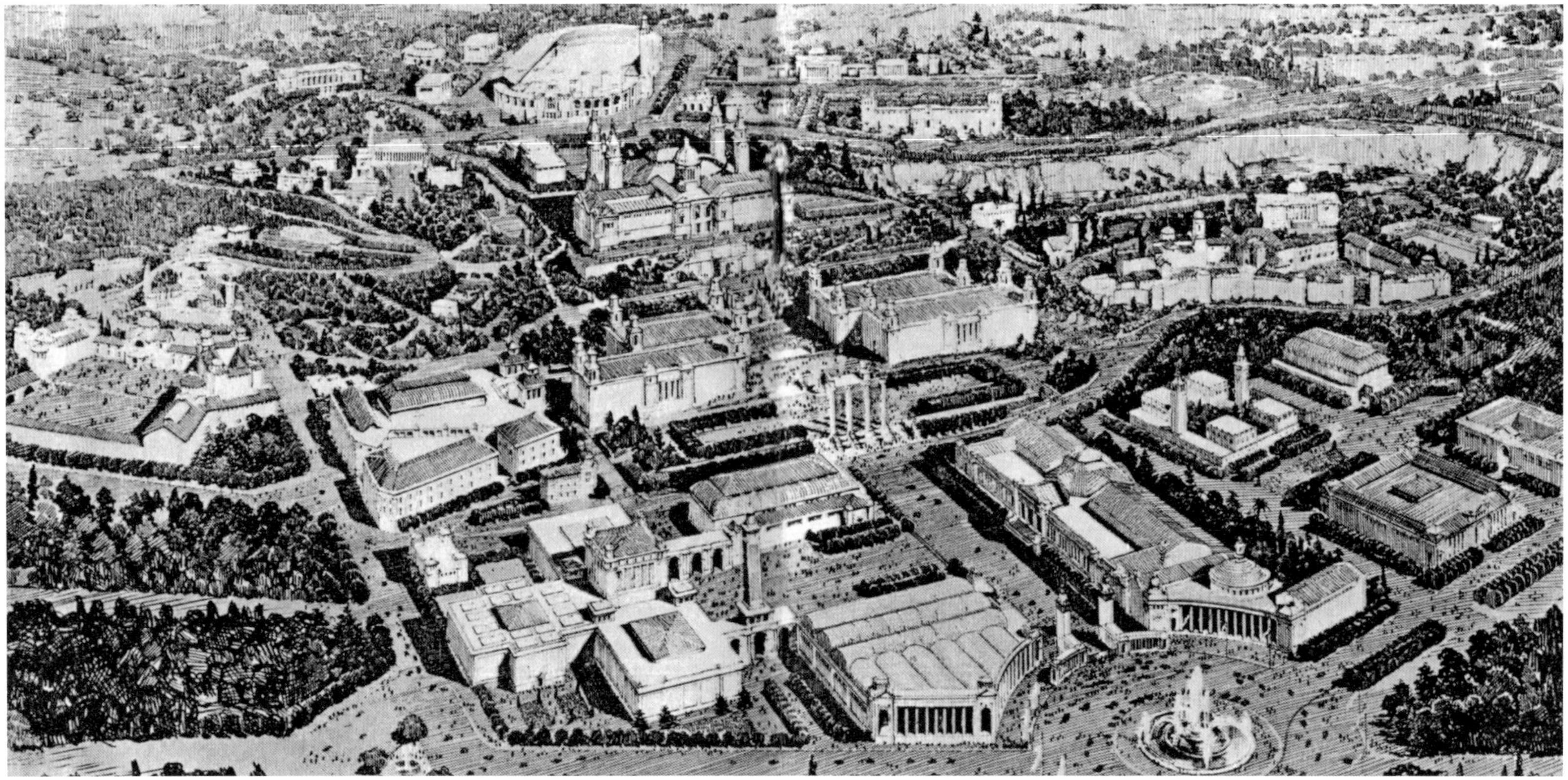

8

did not include the pavilion. **FIG. 8** At the end of January, when his design had progressed sufficiently, Mies traveled once more to Barcelona to negotiate the enlargement of his site toward the south and east.[35] We can assume that Lilly von Schnitzler, who had quickly developed a close friendship with the Marqués de Foronda, the head of the expo's organizing committee, helped to broker this extraordinary deal. In a small ceremony on February 7, 1929, the German flag was raised on the site, and it was officially handed over to the German government. Lilly von Schnitzler was hugely disappointed not to be able to attend, due to a bout of bronchitis, but the marquis assured her in a telegram that her memory would accompany him at the flag-raising ceremony.[36]

Georg von Schnitzler had submitted his request for an additional 750,000 Reichsmark in October 1928.[37] But the Finance Minister, Rudolf Hilferding, belonged to the Marxist wing of the SPD and would not have been naturally sympathetic to the project, which he may have considered an industrialist's vanity piece with no

9

8 Official bird's eye view of the exposition grounds, without the German Pavilion

9 "A lively meeting of the Reichstag Finance Committee," 1929 Photograph: Erich Salomon

obvious benefit for the working class. We do not know whether the long delay in submitting the request to the Reichstag's Finance Committee was attributable to his political differences with von Schnitzler, or to the fact that he was, according to several party colleagues, a "notorious lazybones."[38] In any event, when von Schnitzler's request finally reached the committee four months later, on February 26, 1929, it caused a great deal of consternation and was immediately put on the agenda for the next meeting. Von Schnitzler heard through the grapevine of the parliamentarians' misgivings and, in a panic, sent anxious telegrams to several politicians he knew in the Reichstag. He claimed (wrongly) that monies that had been promised to him were now being withheld and pointed out that any lack of additional funds would destroy the German participation in Barcelona and have severe consequences for the economic relationship with Spain, who had, he claimed, delayed the introduction of additional customs duties in order to facilitate the German participation.[39] Von Schnitzler's last-minute plea did not help—the deliberations on March 1 and 2, 1929, in the Finance Committee could hardly have been more dramatic: committee members did not hold back with their criticism of von Schnitzler's brazen disregard for earlier agreements and explicit financial limits, and angrily noted the lateness of his request and the sloppiness of his documentation.[40] Despite personal appearances and appeals by both the Minister of Economic Affairs, Julius Curtius, and von Schnitzler himself,[41] the two days of heated deliberations did not end well. **FIG. 9** While the Social Democrats and Communists were vehemently opposed to giving von Schnitzler any additional support, the representatives of the DVP (German People's Party, the party von Schnitzler was closest to) pleaded that the contracts he had signed in Spain had to be honored. The compromise solution, brokered by the right-wing Bayerische Volkspartei (Bavarian People's Party) and the DVP, was to grant von Schnitzler an additional 150,000 Reichsmark, raising the overall budget to 500,000 Reichsmark, far short of the 1.1 million he had asked for.[42]

35 Dr. Maiwald to Georg von Schnitzler, 11 January 1929, HoeA, WaB 1927–1928.

36 Marqués de Foronda to Lilly von Schnitzler, 7 February 1929, private archive.

37 Dr. Peter Mathies to Georg von Schnitzler, 19 October 1928, HoeA, WaB 1927–1928.

38 Hagen Schulze, *Weimar: Deutschland 1917–1933* (Munich: Siedler Verlag, 1982), 305.

39 Georg von Schnitzler to Lammers, von Raumer, Kalle, Hummel, 26 February 1929, HoeA, WaB 1929–1930.

40 Report of the meeting of the parliamentary budget committee, March 1, 1929, BArchL, Ausstellung Barcelona, AA, Abteilung II, R 9.01, 40028, 265–68, 275, 278–79; "Die Weltausstellung in Barcelona," *Vossische Zeitung*, March 2, 1929. Mies left again for Barcelona on November 18, 1928. See von Kettler to von Schnitzler, 19 November 1928 (see note 31).

41 Mies had been asked to attend this crucial meeting as well, but did not appear; see Erich von Kettler to Georg von Schnitzler, 25 February 1929, von Schnitzler Correspondence, HoeA, WaB 1929–1930.

42 Memorandum of March 4, 1929, from the Finance Ministry to the Economic Affairs Ministry. BArchL, Ausstellung Barcelona, AA, Abteilung II, R 9.01, 40028, 275; the entire discussion in the parliamentary budget committee is preserved in the BArchL. See also "Der Parteienstreit um Barcelona 1929," *Berliner Börsen Zeitung*, March 2, 1929; "Die Beteiligung Deutschlands an der Ausstellung in Barcelona," *Frankfurter Zeitung*, March 2 1929 (first morning edition); "Blinder Eifer," in *Nationalliberale Correspondenz*; and *Pressedienst der Deutschen Volkspartei* 56, no. 48 (March 5, 1929): 1. The respected economic journal *Der Deutsche Volkswirt* convincingly argued that the Reichstag would have had to sign off on any additional funds that von Schnitzler promised to spend in Spain. "Diese Woche," *Der Deutsche Volkswirt: Zeitschrift für Politik und Wirtschaft*, no. 23 (March 8, 1929), 1–2.

This represented a fatal blow to von Schnitzler's plans. He angrily tendered his immediate resignation, but Curtius talked him into staying.[43] In a memorandum of March 4, 1929, von Schnitzler then presented a greatly reduced program, and cancelled the pavilion: "As difficult as it is for me personally to abandon the pavilion, it is the only possible way to honor the budget committee's decision and still secure Germany's participation."[44] Germany's lack of funds and commitment would be embarrassingly obvious to an international public, he lamented, and about 100,000 Reichsmark worth of materials had already been ordered for the pavilion and would have to be paid for anyway. Mies informed his colleagues at the Werkbund that "the representational pavilion and the section about the Werkbund will probably not be executed."[45] What he did not say was that his design was already far behind schedule, and while some earth had been moved from the site's southern end for the small office and the street in front had been relocated 7 meters east and repaved, construction work for the pavilion proper had not yet begun. Its site now lay idle in the midst of the hectic construction efforts at the fair. As a result, Mies and Reich had to rethink the overall organization. If there were plans for a general German information section inside the pavilion, then the decision to relocate this crucial installation must have been made at that moment. While critics would later applaud the fact that the pavilion was left entirely empty, this important conceptual strategy was never mentioned in any of the correspondence. It is perfectly possible that it was a decision born from necessity rather than a preconceived idea.

Sixteen days later, finally, on the evening of March 20, 1929, a telegram arrived from Berlin: "Execution of pavilion secured. Spanish embassy notified."[46] The Foreign Office and the Minister of Economic Affairs had provided a loan of more than 250,000 Reichsmark to secure the continuation of the work.[47] The main reason for this change of heart was an urgent telegram from the German ambassador in Madrid: he had been approached by the Spanish government and told in no uncertain terms that dictator Primo de Rivera would be personally offended by the sight of an abandoned building site in the center of the exhibition grounds—the symbol of a broken promise on the part of the Germans.[48] Anxious to restore goodwill with its major trading partners in Europe after the catastrophe of the war, the German government relented.

Though several German sections had been cancelled (including the entire Werkbund section), or reduced in size (a large area of 1,000m² earmarked for Germany in the International Palace remained entirely empty), the newly released funds went entirely toward the pavilion. Work restarted, but the reordering of materials and equipment and the rehiring of workers took fourteen precious days. Reportedly, Mies had used the March hiatus for a vacation in San Sebastian, which contributed to the delay.[49] When it became apparent that the official inauguration date of May 19 was unrealistic, a new date was set first for Saturday, May 25 and then, finally, for Monday, May 27, the only other time when the participation of the king and queen could be secured.[50] With just six weeks remaining, the work pace would be grueling, with constant night and weekend shifts.

But while construction progressed, von Schnitzler's worries were far from over. The new funds ran out much faster than expected, and after three weeks, on April 8, he confessed that the pavilion was again in peril: "The financing for the pavilion is currently nonexistent. I have a noose around my neck."[51] With great indignation he reported in a personal letter how Dr. Mathies of the Ministry of Economics had suggested to him that he should travel at once to Barcelona to try to already sell the pavilion to the Spaniards for it to remain permanently in the exhibition grounds—an absurd idea, he pointed out, at a moment when its model had not even been seen by the Spaniards (let alone the built pavilion). Von Schnitzler urged his representative in Barcelona to sternly remind Mies of the tight financial constraints (since, he pointed out, "we know how Mies and Mrs. Reich deal with the finances—as artistically and generally competent they might be")[52] and desperately applied for a personal loan at the Reichskreditbank for an additional 150,000 Reichsmark, offering the pavilion itself as collateral. From this correspondence, we learn that he had entirely prefinanced the pavilion out of his own pocket. The bank confirmed that he was, together with the contractor, the pavilion's "sole owner."[53]

43 "Generalkommissar von Schnitzler will zurücktreten," *Vossische Zeitung*, March 2, 1929 (evening edition).

44 Memorandum of March 4, Von Schnitzler, BArchL, Ausstellung Barcelona, AA, Abteilung II, R 9.01, 40029, 11.

45 Protokoll der Vorstandssitzung des DWB vom 4 März 1929 in Berlin, MoMA, MvdR Papers, Barcelona Pavilion, Folder 4.

46 The possibility of a solution was already signaled, confidentially, on March 10. At that point 700,000 Reichsmark had been made available as a loan, but more was still sought by the government to also make the pavilion possible. See Erich von Kettler to Georg von Schnitzler, 10 March 1929, HoeA, WaB 1929–1930; and telegram from Foreign Office Berlin to the German Consulate in Barcelona, 20 March 1929, BArchL, Ausstellung Barcelona, AA, Abteilung II, R 9.01, 40029, 30.

47 Georg von Schnitzler to Ministerialdirektor Ritter at the Foreign Office, 25 July 1929, BArchL, Ausstellung Barcelona, AA, Abteilung II, R 9.01, 40029, 204–7.

48 Telegram from the German ambassador in Madrid, 6 March 1929, BArchL, Ausstellung Barcelona, AA, Abteilung II, R 9.01, 40029, 14. See also Georg von Schnitzler to Julius Curtius, 5 April 1929, BArchL, Ausstellung Barcelona, AA, Abteilung II, R 9.01, 40029, 61.

49 Interview with Wilhelm Niemann, Werkbund Archiv Berlin, ca. 1970, 13–14. I would like to thank Matthias Horstmann for providing me with a copy of this document.

50 Georg von Schnitzler to Count Welczeck, 29 April 1929, HoeA, WaB 1929–1930. The move from Saturday, May 25 to Monday, May 27, which brought a welcome reprieve of two days to Mies and his team, was the result of planning difficulties of the Spanish King. Count Welczeck to Georg von Schnitzler, 7 May 1929, HoeA, WaB 1929–1930.

51 Georg von Schnitzler to Erich von Kettler, 8 April 1929, HoeA, WaB 1929–1930: "Die finanzielle Sicherung für den Pavillon-Bau ist im Augenblick nicht vorhanden. Den Kopf halte ich persönlich in der Schlinge." Already at this point, plans were discussed to sell the pavilion to the Spanish government in order to generate further funds, but the idea was soon dropped. According to a questionnaire of 1946, von Schnitzler had earned 300,000 Reichsmark in 1930, slightly less in the following and preceding years. *Meldebogen auf Grund des Gesetzes zur Befreiung von Nationalsozialismus und Militarismus vom 5.3.1946*, Hessisches Hauptstaatsarchiv Wiesbaden.

52 Georg von Schnitzler to Dr. Maiwald, 8 April 1929, HoeA, WaB 1929–1930.

53 "We understand that the credit will be paid back by you out of the future proceeds of the sale of the pavilion in Barcelona's Park de Montjuïc (currently still under construction), of which you are the sole owner." Reichskreditanstalt to Georg von Schnitzler, 23 April 1929, BArchL, Ausstellung Barcelona, AA, Abteilung II, R 9.01, 40029, 142–43.

Mies van der Rohe

Mies van der Rohe's career up to that point had hardly been a straightforward success story. From 1908 to 1925 his portfolio featured only a series of conventional suburban villas, which he built at a pace of about one a year, barely enough to keep his small office afloat. After separating from his family in the fall of 1921, his apartment also served as his office.[1] Building permit applications for a succession of unassuming house commissions that followed (for the Kempner, Eichstädt, and Feldmann residences) reveal his adoption of the name Mies (initially spelled Miës) van der Rohe, linking his surname to that of his mother.[2] The contrived "van der" had a vaguely Dutch ring to it, or to German ears an aristocratic association—a "pretentious fraud," as his daughter Dorothea later remarked.[3] Probably it was meant "to lend a visible sign of prestige" and enhance "his prospects of receiving commissions for conventional work from an upscale clientele."[4] Writing in 1927, Werner Hegemann joked that Mies had "awoken one morning as the Dutch nobleman van der Rohe. [...] Newly baptized," he had realized "that as a German Mies, one can build very decent houses with sloping roofs without attracting much attention, while with a Dutch name one only needs to design one very impractical, Dutch-style high-rise to gain both the enthusiasm of the young and the directorship at the 1927 Werkbund exhibition."[5] Apparently, Mies's aristocratic aspirations only intensified after he spent time with Georg and Lilly von Schnitzler and the Marqués de Foronda. His collaborator Sergius Ruegenberg noted that on his return from Barcelona, Mies began wearing a monocle and a golden watch on a long fob chain. He fired his housekeeper and hired a butler instead. Fellow architect Hans Scharoun called him a snob.[6]

While still working on relatively conventional house designs between 1922 and 1924, however, Mies also established himself as a commanding voice in avant-garde circles by producing five visionary projects that were widely exhibited and published.[7] Each one of these projects was an exemplary study in materials and building types: two glass skyscrapers, a concrete office building, and two country houses, one of brick, the other of concrete. **FIGS. 1-4** They also reflected his exposure to new sources of inspiration. While his conventional house designs had revealed the influence of architects such as Bruno Paul, Paul Mebes, and Alfred Messel, he now directed his gaze abroad. In December 1923, when he began working on the Brick Country House, Mies wrote to Hendrik Berlage asking for material on Frank Lloyd Wright.[8] And Mies was aware of the work of the De Stijl group, in particular Theo van Doesburg, whose architectural analyses and *counter-constructions* were much noticed and discussed. **FIG. 5**

The Brick Country House would come to be regarded as an important predecessor to the Barcelona Pavilion. Mies himself described how it was the first time he had "abandoned the usual concept of enclosed rooms in order to create a sequence of spatial effects instead of a series of individual spaces."[9] The three drawings (a floor plan, an elevation, and a sketch) shown at the 1924 staging of the annual Grosse Berlin Kunstausstellung (Great

1 Franz Schulze, *Mies van der Rohe: A Critical Biography* (Chicago: University of Chicago Press, 1985), 94.

2 Andreas Marx and Paul Weber, "From Ludwig Mies to Mies van der Rohe: The Apartment and Studio Am Karlsbad 24 (1915-39)," in *Mies and Modern Living: Interiors, Furniture, Photography*, ed. Helmut Reuter and Birgit Schulte (Ostfildern: Hatje Cantz, 2008), 36-37.

3 This did not prevent her from also claiming the name for herself. See Georgia van der Rohe, *La donna è mobile: Mein bedingungsloses Leben* (Berlin: Aufbau, 2001), 14.

4 Marx and Weber, "From Ludwig Mies to Mies van der Rohe," 36-37 (see note 2).

5 Werner Hegemann, "Schräges oder Flaches Dach," *Wasmuths Monatshefte für Baukunst* 11, no. 3 (1927): 120.

6 Sergius Ruegenberg, "Glashaus," undated manuscript, Berlinische Galerie, Ruegenberg Papers.

7 Dietrich Neumann, "Three Early Projects by Mies van der Rohe," *Perspecta: Journal of the Yale School of Architecture* 27 (1992): 76-97.

8 Mies van der Rohe to Hendrik Berlage, 13 December 1923, LoC, Mies Papers, Personal Correspondence 1923-40. The original letter is in the Berlage papers of the Het Nieuwe Instituut (formerly the Netherlandish Architecture Institute) in Rotterdam.

9 Ludwig Mies van der Rohe, "Lecture (June 19, 1924)," in Fritz Neumeyer, *The Artless Word: Mies van der Rohe on the Building Art* (Cambridge, MA: MIT Press, 1991), 250.

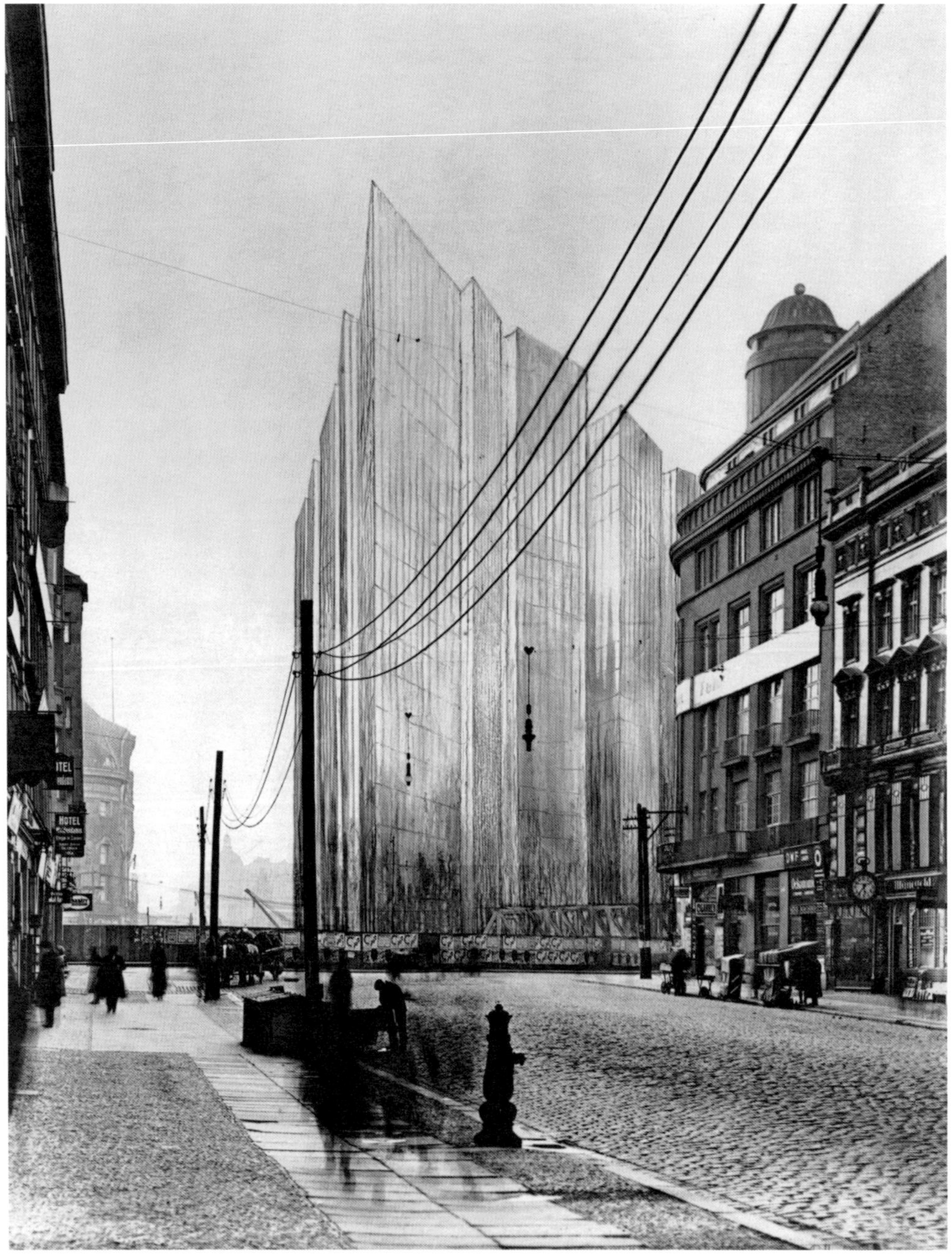

1

2

1 Skyscraper at Friedrichstrasse Railroad Station, 1922
Architect: Ludwig Mies van der Rohe

2 Glass skyscraper, 1922
Architect: Ludwig Mies van der Rohe

3 Concrete office building, 1923
Architect: Ludwig Mies van der Rohe

4 Concrete Country House 1923
Architect: Ludwig Mies van der Rohe

5 Theo van Doesburg, *Counter-Construction*, 1923

3

4

5

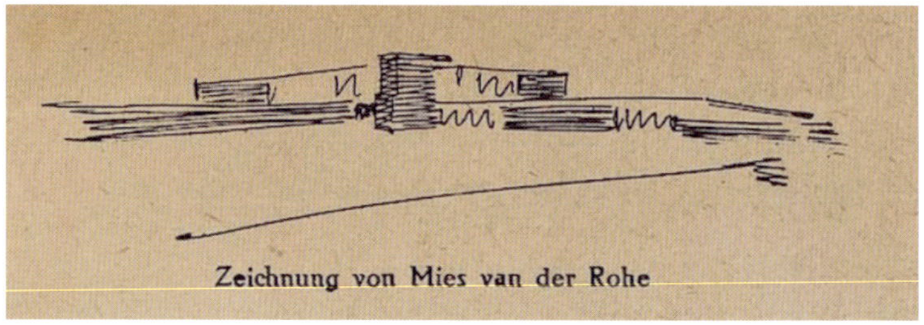

6

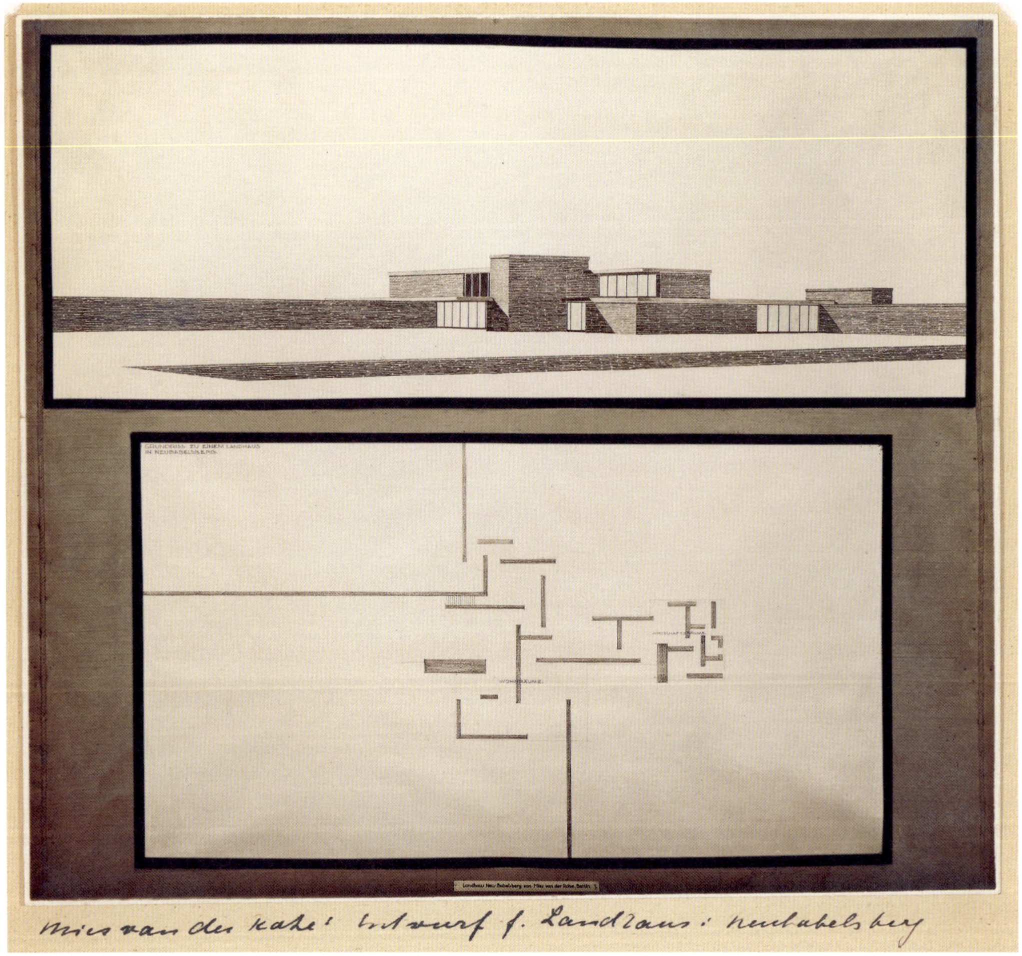

7

Berlin Art Exhibition) **FIGS. 6-7** brought him his greatest critical success to date, and it was here that the most significant trope of the later pavilion's analysis—its innovative handling of space through open interior connections—first emerged. Several writers had singled out the house's elegantly abstract and "tight floor plan uniting a group of rooms,"[10] which reminded Walter Curt Behrendt of a "machine product"; Hans Soeder called it "the strongest, most future-oriented project on display." Anticipating the elegies of later critics of the pavilion, Soeder wrote: "Here, on a higher plane, the path of rational calculations has been overcome, mathematics have been filled with music." Soeder confessed to being unable to "put his encounter with this design into words," and was instead content only to "see it, to be enchanted, to dream of it, and to admire the boldness of this spatial fugue."[11] Mies's friend Hans Richter responded a few months later (in a fawning celebration of Mies as the prototypical new "master builder") by redirecting the focus toward the building's function. The Brick Country House's floor plan, he argued, was "not a mathematical abstraction" but rather demonstrated the process of habitation, as it abandoned the "cozy corner" (*Wohnecke*) and separate rooms in favor of a "continuous dwelling complex."[12] Walter Curt Behrendt returned to the Brick Country House design in his 1927 book, *The Victory of the New Building Style*, and explained that the rooms in its floor plan "almost completely dissolve their borders by flowing into one another"[13]—the first time the notion of "flowing space" had been applied to Mies's architecture.

Alfred Barr would, in 1934, declare that Mies's Brick Country House was influenced by De Stijl, namely "a direct result of Doesburg's sojourn in Berlin in 1921 and 22." The source of inspiration, according to Barr, was Doesburg's 1918 painting *Rhythm of a Russian Dance*, **FIG. 8** which would later also frequently be claimed as an inspiration for the Barcelona Pavilion—thus seemingly confirming critics' association of Mies's plan with music and movement.[14] Mies would coolly dismiss this notion years later: "I think that was a mistake that the Museum of Modern Art made. [...] I never make a painting when I want to build a house. We like to draw our plans carefully and that is why they were taken as a kind of painting."[15]

Despite this considerable critical success, Mies still had few substantial commissions, and mostly watched from the sidelines when Germany experienced a building boom in the second half of the 1920s, thanks to American investments. Mies's first decidedly modern house—a home for hat manufacturers Erich and Elisabeth Wolf in Guben (today Gubin, Poland)—applied the connective principle suggested in his 1924 Brick Country House to a sequence of four rooms at the garden side of the house. **FIG. 9** The traditional enfilade of library, living room, and dining room, usually lined up along a central axis, was instead connected openly

6 Brick Country House, 1924
Architect: Ludwig Mies van der Rohe

7 Brick Country House, 1924
Architect: Ludwig Mies van der Rohe

8 Theo van Doesburg, *Rhythm of a Russian Dance*, 1918

8

10 Walter Curt Behrendt, "Die Architektur auf der Berliner Kunstausstellung 1924," *Kunst und Künstler 2*, no. 11 (1924): 351.
11 Hans Soeder, "Architektur auf der Berliner Kunstausstellung 1924," *Der Neubau* 6 (1924): 153–58.
12 Hans Richter, "Der Neue Baumeister," *Qualität* 4, nos. 1, 2 (January/February 1925): 3–9.
13 Walter Curt Behrendt, *The Victory of the New Building Style* (Los Angeles, Getty Research Institute, 2000), 134.
14 Alfred Barr, *Cubism and Modern Art* (New York: Museum of Modern Art, 1934), 156–57.
15 Peter Carter, *Mies van der Rohe at Work* (New York: Praeger, 1974), 180.

9

9 House for Erich and Elisabeth Wolf, Guben (Gubin), 1925-27
Architect: Ludwig Mies van der Rohe
Photographer: Arthur Köster

10-11 Werkbund Exhibition, Stuttgart, Weissenhof, 1927

and diagonally. While some roots of this idea can be found in earlier De Stijl designs and in the work of Frank Lloyd Wright, the house's exterior and material composition was indebted to projects by Dutch architects Willem Marinus Dudok and Johannes Bernardus van Loghem that had been recently published in Germany.[16] The Wolf House was in turn instrumental in securing two additional commissions, the Esters and Lange houses in Krefeld, which were under construction when the Barcelona Pavilion went up.

In the summer of 1925, Mies had met Lilly Reich, an exhibition designer and interior decorator, who would become his companion and close collaborator.[17] She had studied under Josef Hoffmann in Vienna in 1908 and had been asked to join the Werkbund in 1912. At Berlin's Fashion Week in 1920, she had organized the section on Craft in Fashion.[18] Several years before Mies was invited, she had become the first female board member of the Werkbund and was in charge of its first exhibition in the United States.[19] Between 1924 and 1926 she worked in Frankfurt at the city's Messeamt (Fair Office) and, before returning to Berlin, designed a major exhibition, *From Fiber to Textile*, at the Frankfurt Fair. Comparing the clarity of her own work before she met Mies to their joint efforts, it becomes quite obvious how much she brought into the partnership.

While commissions remained scarce, Mies maintained his visibility through his active participation in organizations such as the Ring, the Novembergruppe, and the Association of German Architects (BDA). He became vice president of the Deutscher Werkbund in 1925 and was put in charge of the 1927 Weissenhof exhibition in Stuttgart, where he brought together seventeen European architects (among them Le Corbusier, J. J. P. Oud, Hans Scharoun, and Peter Behrens). Of the twenty-one buildings constructed for the permanent exhibition, his own housing block **FIGS. 10, 11** was the largest and occupied a commanding central position. It was at the same time more dramatic and more carefully detailed and proportioned than other modern housing projects built by his peers in Berlin and Frankfurt. Still, further commissions for housing projects were not forthcoming. Mies was more successful with various exhibition stands, especially after 1926, thanks to his friendship and collaboration with Lilly Reich, even if Mies barely acknowledged his indebtedness to her. Their exhibition stands in Stuttgart, Berlin, and Leipzig, while hardly lucrative, allowed for creative expression and provided visibility. These designs represented the immediate predecessors of the Barcelona Pavilion.

10

11

16 Heinrich de Fries, ed., *Moderne Villen und Landhäuser* (Berlin: Wasmuth Verlag, 1924), vi.

17 The first surviving correspondence between Lilly Reich and Mies is from June 10, 1925. While Lilly Reich still addresses Mies with the formal "Sie," she mentions a potential future meeting. By November that year they seem to have become romantically involved, as Mies is selecting two handbags for her from a selection sent to him by Werkbund member Elizabeth Michahelles; Lilly Reich reciprocated with a yellow house jacket for Mies. see Lilly Reich to Mies van der Rohe, 10 June 1925, MoMA, MvdR Papers; and Elisabeth Michahelles to Mies van der Rohe, 21 November 1925, and John (Mies's office) to Elisabeth Michahelles, 26 November 1925, both LoC, Mies Papers, Private Correspondence 1923-40, Folder M. Lilly Reich to Mies, 2 December 1925. LoC, Mies Papers, Private Correspondence 1923-40, Folder R.

18 "Kunstnachrichten," *Vossische Zeitung*, December 5, 1919 (evening edition).

19 "Bericht über die 11. Jahresversammlung in Augsburg und München vom 29. Juni bis 1. Juli, 1922," *Die Form* 1, no. 4 (1922), 55. She had also been elected to the board of the Werkbundhaus in Frankfurt. "Deutsche Kunstgewerbe-Ausstellung in Amerika," *Die Voss*, May 7, 1921.

The first of the three, Mies's and Reich's Glasraum at the Stuttgart Werkbund exhibition in 1927, had been commissioned by the plate-glass industry to demonstrate the latest technological achievements and suggest new applications beyond display windows for department stores. It presented a sequence of openly connected spaces between wall-high clear and translucent glass plates in different shades of gray that served as walls, windows, screens, and space dividers. **FIG. 12** The Glasraum stood inside a large exhibition hall and was evenly lit via suspended lamps above a ceiling of stretched white canvas, with a colorful linoleum floor under foot. Sparsely furnished, the sequence of spaces had a vaguely domestic—but also rather unhomely—feeling. There

12

13

was a suggestion of indoor and outdoor areas (indicated by the absence of a canvas ceiling): a small courtyard contained a sculpture by Wilhelm Lehmbruck, while the living room looked onto a second courtyard populated by a rather ominous lineup of rubber plants. The most striking elements were the lightness of construction, the reflections and different degrees of transparency, and the eerie evenness of the light, as if one were experiencing the space on a bright but overcast day. Siegfried Kracauer, the prominent cultural critic, observed astutely, if somewhat skeptically: "In the exhibition halls we find a strange space, thought up by Mies van der Rohe and Lilly Reich. Its walls consist of opal and darkened plates of glass. A glass box, translucent, infiltrated by its adjacent spaces [...] any movement magically conjures up shadow plays on the wall, disembodied silhouettes, hovering in mid-air and getting mixed up with the reflections in the actual glass space. Conjuring up such an impalpable mirage, changing with the light reflections just like a kaleidoscope, demonstrates that the new domestic architecture is not yet the final word."[20] The use of terms like *mirage* and *kaleidoscope* equated the exhibit with a house of mirrors at an amusement park. Clearly, Kracauer disproved of such optical effects, deeming them self-indulgent.

In contrast, Mies's Dutch colleague Theo van Doesburg applauded what Mies and Reich had accomplished—an architecture of space and surface, and in his view the best example of interior architecture at the Werkbund exhibition, conquering "the material with all of its traits, such as weightiness, resistance, and

12 Glasraum, Stuttgart, 1927
Ludwig Mies van der Rohe and Lilly Reich

13 Café Samt und Seide, Berlin, 1927
Ludwig Mies van der Rohe and Lilly Reich

transience." This, according to van Doesburg, had broader implications: "Weighing the energy and character of materials against each other and proportioning them well, most certainly belongs to the essence of the new architecture. Only thus can modern architecture realize what it has to offer in involuntary beauty [...] the new ideal of an empty space and a pure surface comes closer to realization." It was here, too, that van Doesburg exposed a conceptual rift in Mies's architecture (which would confuse later reviewers of the pavilion), when he emphasized the importance in this project of surface over structure: "The development of the ultimate surface is essential, from the first stone to the last stroke of paint. Every architect having a visual sense for construction knows this, and with this glass display Mies van der Rohe proved to be on top of this new problem. [...] Only the surface is important. Man does not live within the construction or architectural skeleton, but touches architecture essentially through its ultimate surface [...] the new ideal of an empty space and a pure surface is all the time coming closer to realization."[21] Indeed, Mies and Reich had celebrated the surfaces of walls, windows, and ceilings while remaining unconcerned about the necessary structural means. This abstraction was such that Alexander Dorner discovered "obvious similarities" between the Glasraum and the Raum der Abstrakten (Space for Abstract Artists) that El Lissitzky had recently installed at the Hanover Museum.[22]

There was a similar emphasis on space and surface over structure in the German Silk section at the fashion exhibition *Die Mode der Dame* in Berlin later that year. There, open spaces were framed by silk curtains on horizontal metal rods, which were suspended by strong wires from the ceiling. The curtains were of different colors, heights, and widths: two of them formed semicircular enclosures, while others presented the equivalent of a freestanding wall—disconnected, independent, surrounded by open space on both ends. The stand contained new furniture designed by Mies and Reich for chairs and tables, which at times served as café seating.[23] **FIG. 13** The connections to the fashion industry led to two important commissions in the same year. Krefeld silk manufacturers Hermann Lange and Josef Esters asked Mies to design two large modern country houses on adjacent pieces of land in the Krefeld suburbs. **FIGS. 14, 15** Lange and Esters would be central to the German silk industry's engagement in Barcelona, and had hired Mies to design their section there long before he had signed the official contract with von Schnitzler.

The pavilion's closest relative in Mies's oeuvre, however, was a little-known installation for the linoleum industry at a Leipzig trade fair from March 3 to 13, 1929, whose development coincided with or even preceded the crucial design phase of the structure in Barcelona. The Leipzig fair's section on building materials and machinery was housed in the sensationally modern steel-and-glass Exhibition Hall 19 (designed by Leipzig architect Walter Gruner, with Berlin structural steel company Breest & Co.). Upon entering, visitors would spot from afar the inscription "Deutsche Linoleum-Werke" on the high front of Mies's pavilion.[24] Underneath the inscription were large display windows similar in size to those at the Barcelona Pavilion, two panes on the short and four on the long side, facing the center of the hall. The open entrance

20 Siegfried Kracauer, "Das neue Bauen: Zur Stuttgarter Werkbund-Ausstellung: Die Wohnung," *Frankfurter Zeitung*, July 31, 1927. Quoted in Siegfried Kracauer, *Schriften: Aufsätze: 1927–1931* (Frankfurt am Main: Suhrkamp, 1990), 68–74.

21 Theo van Doesburg, "'The Dwelling,' the famous Werkbund exhibition," *in On European Architecture: Complete Essays from Het Boubedrijf, 1924–1931* (Basel: Birkhäuser, 1986), 164–72.

22 Alexander Dorner, "Zur Abstrakten Malerei: Erklärung zum Raum der Abstrakten in der Hannoverschen Gemäldegalerie," *Die Form* 3, no. 4 (1928): 110–14.

23 See Christiane Lange, *Ludwig Mies van der Rohe: Architektur für die Seidenindustrie* (Cologne: Nicolaische Verlagsbuchhandlung GmbH, 2011), 71ff.

24 "Die Leipziger Frühjahrs-Baumesse 1929: Die Stände," *Deutsches Bauwesen* 5, no. 4 (April 1929): 90.

14

15

14 Josef Esters House, Krefeld, 1927-30
Architect: Ludwig Mies van der Rohe

15 Haus Hermann Lange, Krefeld, 1927-30
Architect: Ludwig Mies van der Rohe

16-18 Stand for the German Linoleum Works, Leipzig Building Fair, Spring 1929
Ludwig Mies van der Rohe and Lilly Reich

was roughly as wide as two of the glass panes.[25] Different types of colored linoleum covered the floors of the interior, as well as the walls, in the form of full-height samples. Mies's MR 10 and MR 20 chairs were grouped in two seating areas. Just like in Stuttgart, the lighting was provided by suspended lamps above a stretched white canvas ceiling. Most important, the stand contained the first examples of the cruciform, nickel-clad columns that would become a prominent element at the Barcelona Pavilion. **FIGS. 16-18** Their placement was more straightforward and their function more readable than at the pavilion—they carried the steel lintels above the display windows and the open entrance area.

Two additional projects occupied Mies during the crucial design phase for Barcelona, and both employ the same formal language. A first version of the design for the Tugendhat House in Brno had been discussed with the clients on December 31, 1928, and was undergoing a number of revisions while working drawings were being produced. In January 1929 Mies had also agreed to design a house for the prominent painter Emil Nolde on a plot of land in the affluent Berlin suburb of Dahlem. In early April 1929, just as the construction of the Barcelona Pavilion was getting under way, Mies hastily returned to Berlin for two weeks to submit the Nolde design and request a building permit.[26] Several key elements

16

17

18

developed for Barcelona were applied here: the freestanding wall, open spatial connections, floor-to-ceiling windows, and ten cruciform columns. The Nolde project shows how easily things could have gone wrong in Barcelona, for Mies committed similar transgressions—a cost projection twice as high as the agreed limit, a footprint far exceeding the zoning code, plans delivered much later than promised—but here the stars did not align in the most improbable fashion, as they had in Barcelona: the building permit was denied, the client could not afford the added cost, and the project remained unexecuted.

25 "Die Leipziger Baumesse," *Bauwelt*, no. 12 (1929): after 292, 1–3, and advertisements 17–18; compare also the (different) illustration in "L'Architecture et l'aménagement d'expositions," *La Cité* 8, no. 8 (February 1930): 126.

26 Mies returned from Barcelona to Berlin on April 5, submitted the application for the building permit on April 15, and on April 22 traveled back to Barcelona. See Georg von Schnitzler to the Marqués de Foronda, HoeA, WaB, 1929–1930.

The Building Type

In his later years Mies would often claim that no one knew what a German pavilion was supposed to look like, or indeed what role it should play: "You know, when I got the job from the government they said, 'We need a pavilion.' I replied, 'What do you mean by a pavilion?' He said, 'I don't know—we have so much money for it—build it. But please, not too much glass.'"[1] While this version made for a good story (and Mies's recollections may have been somewhat foggy decades later), it seems unlikely that Mies was unaware of the long-established building type of the exhibition pavilion and its important role in the architectural discourse of the day.[2] Exhibition pavilions had become one of the testing grounds for new architectural ideas, and several recent examples must be seen as important predecessors or counterparts to Mies's pavilion. Rather than being a building without a model, its design grew out of a rich tapestry of peers and precedents.

"Any country endeavoring to show the simplest but radically modern architecture would have created the greatest sensation, even if such an attempt were not entirely successful,"[3] art critic Julius Meier-Graefe had written in 1900 after reviewing the historicist buildings at the Paris Exposition. National pavilions at such occasions had customarily evoked historical structures with political or symbolic significance at home. Germany, for example, had erected buildings reminiscent of Gothic or Renaissance city halls at Chicago in 1893 and Paris in 1900. Four years after Meier-Graefe's admonition, Germany chose the domed central wing of Berlin's baroque Charlottenburg Palace as inspiration for the country's pavilion in St. Louis in 1904; it contained exhibition spaces, a lecture hall, and a restaurant.[4] **FIGS. 1, 2**

But change was in the air. At that same St. Louis World's Fair, Joseph Maria Olbrich's Summer House for an Art Lover created exactly the sensation that Meier-Graefe had been waiting for. **FIG. 3** An idealized residential structure, it contained several modern rooms by Olbrich and others around a courtyard whose water basins were flanked by a protruding roof on freestanding columns. A sculpture was placed on the main axis. According to the German commissioner, it "represented a domestic culture which had not hitherto existed"[5] and left a lasting impression: "The interior decorators of the United States are now talking about the Olbrich pavilion. It is already indicated as one of the things at the world's fair which will leave a permanent mark upon American life."[6] Mies was certainly familiar with this building, as his first teacher and employer in Berlin, Bruno Paul, had designed a study room inside. Olbrich's success might have helped to justify the concept to represent Germany in Barcelona by a structure whose size and layout evoked a small but exquisite residence.

At the next world's fair in Brussels in 1910—the immediate predecessor to Barcelona—another breakthrough occurred:[7] Germany's main building (the Deutsches Haus) by the Munich architect Emanuel von Seidl **FIG. 4** was decidedly contemporary, contributing, as critics noted, to the "general European desire for a twentieth-century style."[8] It vaguely resembled a so-called *Volkshaus*, a new building type in German cities providing meeting and

1 Verbatim transcript, Mies van der Rohe interview, ca. 1967, from *Mies* (documentary by Michael Blackwood and Franz Schulze, 1986); similarly, he told the journalist Katherine Kuh in a 1964 interview that he had been told: "'We need a pavilion. Design it, and not too much glass.' It was the most difficult work which ever confronted me, because I was my own client. I could do whatever I liked, but I did not know what a pavilion should be." Katharine Kuh, "Mies van der Rohe: Modern Classicist," *Saturday Review* 48, no. 4 (January 23, 1965): 22–23 and 61.

2 For a history of German pavilions at world's fairs, see Paul Sigel, *Exponiert: Deutsche Pavillons auf Weltausstellungen* (Berlin: Verlag Bauwesen, 2000).

3 Julius Meier-Graefe, *Die Weltausstellung in Paris 1900* (Leipzig: Verlag F. Krüger, 1900), 26.

4 Christoph Cornelißen, "Das Deutsche Reich auf den Weltausstellungen des 19. Jahrhunderts," *Wolkenkuckucksheim* 5, no. 1 (July 2000), accessed August 8, 2017, http://www.tu-cottbus.de/theoriederarchitektur/Wolke/deu/Themen/001/Cornelissen/cornelissen.htm.

5 Leo Nachtlicht, *Deutsches Kunstgewerbe St. Louis 1904* (Berlin: Ernst Wasmuth Verlag, 1904), 11.

6 "Germany's Wonderful New Art at the World's Fair: the Famous Olbrich Pavilion," *St. Louis Post-Dispatch Sunday Magazine*, June 5, 1904, 10.

7 Germany participated in another world's fair in Turin in 1911, but the German House was designed locally by an Italian architect.

8 Robert Breuer, *German Arts and Crafts at the Brussels Exhibition 1910* (Stuttgart: Julius Hoffmann, 1910) n.p.

1

3

1 The German House at the 1900 Paris Exposition
Architect: Johannes Radke

2 German House at the St. Louis World's Fair, 1904
Architect: Emil Boehl

3 Summer House for an Art Lover at the St. Louis World's Fair, 1904
Architect: Joseph Maria Olbrich

4 German House at the Brussels International Exposition, 1910
Architect: Emmanuel von Seidl

5 Leipzig Building Exhibition, Monument to Iron, 1913
Architect: Bruno Taut

6 Glass Pavilion, Werkbund Exhibition, Cologne, 1914
Architect: Bruno Taut

2

social spaces for the working class, and formed the nexus for a group of halls and pavilions showcasing German achievements in the arts and crafts, interior design, machinery, transport, etc.[9] Von Seidl, who was responsible for the overall appearance of the German contributions (the same role played by Mies and Reich in Barcelona), presented a unified and ambitious image of German design with a decided emphasis on industry. Two workers' cottages by Georg Metzendorf were on display, as well as exhibition halls by Mies's former teachers Bruno Paul and Peter Behrens. The three halls by the latter (for engineering, heavy machinery, and railways) came close on the heels of his famous Berlin Turbine Factory and were designed when Mies worked in Behrens's office. A German critic recognized "a style which is destined to conquer the world."[10]

4

5

6

But it was during the 1920s that exhibitions and trade fairs truly became important testing grounds for architectural experiments and stylistic innovation, in particular when those pavilions were not burdened with the task of representing an entire nation. Temporary pavilions allowed—almost like stage sets—radical and provocative approaches that signaled an industry's or a particular firm's aspirations to modernity and open-mindedness. A start had been made before the First World War, with Bruno Taut's Monument to Iron at the 1913 Leipzig Building Exposition or his 1914 Glass Pavilion at the Werkbund Exhibition in Cologne, which had represented the glass industry and was widely seen as a harbinger of a new architecture. **FIGS. 5, 6** At the same exhibition, Walter Gropius built a model factory with an early use of the glass curtain wall, and Henry van de Velde's theater demonstrated reinforced concrete's facility for sinuous curves.

In September 1924 Wilhelm Deffke, a graphic designer and aspiring architect who had worked occasionally with Mies in the early 1920s, designed an exhibition stand for the cigarette manufacturer TESMA at the Berlin Tobacco trade show. Under a thin protruding roof plate, the stand consisted of six full-height sheets of plate glass, offset against each other in order to create exhibition spaces between them. **FIG 7** This little-known stand anticipated some central ideas for Mies's Glasraum of 1927 and for his Barcelona Pavilion.[11]

The Belgian magazine *La Cité* devoted two issues in 1930 to a comparative study of recent exhibition pavilions and enthusiastically welcomed their inventiveness. Suddenly, the magazine stated, the former, conventional Beaux-Arts approach seemed out of place, in fact "absolutely foreign" vis-à-vis the striking new examples.[12] The images from exhibitions in Brussels, Brno, Barcelona, Poznan, Paris, and Milan demonstrated the enormous freedom of expression and unbridled creativity let loose on these occasions.

9 Sigel, *Exponiert*, 62–99 (see note 2).

10 Robert Breuer, "Deutschland auf der Brüsseler Weltausstellung," *Moderne Bauformen* 9, no. 7 (1910): 301–2. The German participation, dominated by key members of the German Werkbund, made the show the first representation of the group's ideas in an international context. On the role of the Werkbund at the Brussels International 1910, see Sigel, *Exponiert*, 97–99 (see note 2). See also Werner Durth and Paul Sigel, eds., *Baukultur: Spiegel gesellschaftlichen Wandels* (Berlin: Jovis, 2010), 93. A British newspaper conceded that the German exhibition "naturally advanced onto the first rank among nations," as it avoided "resplendent columns or architectural fanfares." *Daily Telegraph*, quoted in Durth and Sigel, *Baukultur*, 91.

11 About Wilhelm Deffke, the TESMA stand, and his collaboration with Mies, see Dietrich Neumann, "Mies's Concrete Office Building and Its Common Acquaintance," *AA Files* 74 (June 2017): 70–84.

12 See "Cahier Spécial sur l'Architecture et l'Aménagement d'Expositions," *La Cité: Urbanisme, Architecture, Art Public* 8, no. 7 (January 1930): 101–20; and "Second Cahier sur l'Architecture et L'Aménagement d'Expositions," *La Cité: Urbanisme, Architecture, Art Public* 8, no. 8 (February 1930): 121–32.

7

A prime example for such industrial fairs was the 1925 Exposition Internationale des Arts Décoratifs et Industriels Modernes in Paris, in which the participating countries (Germany was not among them) were asked to present "modern inspiration and real originality"[13] in the decorative arts. Josef Hoffmann's Austrian pavilion, for example, combined unusual stucco waves on its outside walls with a vivid interplay of interior and exterior spaces, ceiling-high openings, and freestanding columns, and certainly belongs to the family of predecessors and potential models with which Mies was familiar. **FIG. 8** (Lilly Reich had worked for Hoffmann in Vienna and remained interested in his work.) One of the best known and most sensational structures in Paris was Konstantin Melnikov's Soviet building, a two-story wooden exhibition hall with glass walls and a diagonal path slicing through it for dramatic effect. **FIG. 9** Its stairs ascended to the second floor in the center and then descended again. Alternating roof sections above pointed skyward, and a lattice tower carried the Soviet flag. It was "the first small building that gave clear evidence of the rebirth of our architecture," El Lissitzky claimed a few years later.[14] Here, as elsewhere in the exhibition, architectural and political ambitions went hand in hand—not least in the interior of a new workers' club by Alexander Rodchenko, which was prominently displayed. Le Corbusier's Pavillon de l'Esprit Nouveau—according to the architect a *succès de scandale*—presented one residential unit of his Immeuble-Villa housing complex, an important part of his envisioned Plan Voisin for the center of Paris, shown in a model and huge murals in the panoramic rotunda attached to the pavilion. The double-height living room was flanked by an open loggia and filled with Le Corbusier's furniture and purist paintings. **FIG. 10** The Danish architect Kay Fisker (in collaboration with a young Arne Jacobsen) provided another modern statement with his striated brick pavilion of four similar facades. **FIG. 11** The exhibition even offered space for those displays operating beyond the boundaries of a specific nation, notably Friedrich Kiesler, who showed a spectacular vision of a future city in space, the *Raumstadt*, whose three-dimensional model of vertical and horizontal planes shared fundamental design approaches with Mies van der Rohe. **FIG. 12**

In 1928 Cologne hosted Pressa, a large and much-noticed international exhibition for the printing and publishing industries, with a series of decidedly avant-garde buildings. Erich Mendelsohn designed a superbly elegant structure for the Mosse publishing house—all white stucco, steel, and glass, with a semicircular transparent observation deck on the second floor: according to contemporary critics, it was "a splendid demonstration of the modern spirit."[15] **FIG. 13** Cologne architect Hans Schumacher built a large exhibition hall for the Workers' Press (funded by the local trade unions and the Social Democratic Party), whose main facade bears an uncanny resemblance to Le Corbusier's Villa

8

10

7 TESMA Zigaretten Stand, Berlin, 1924
Designer: Wilhelm Deffke

8 Austrian Pavilion at the Paris Exposition des Arts Decoratifs, 1925
Architect: Josef Hoffmann

9 Russian Pavilion at the Paris Exposition des Arts Decoratifs, 1925
Architect: Konstantin Melnikov

10 Pavillon de l'Esprit Nouveau at the Paris Exposition des Arts Decoratifs, 1925
Architect: Le Corbusier
Photographer : H. Thibaud

9

13 Guillaume Jeanneau, *L'Art décoratif Moderne. Formes Nouvelles et Programmes Nouveaux* (Paris, 1925), n.p., quoted in Helen Searing, "International Exhibition of Decorative Arts, Paris (1925)," in *Encyclopedia of Twentieth-Century Architecture*, ed. Stephen Sennott (New York: Fitzroy Dearborn, 2003), 680–81.

14 El Lissitzky, "The Reconstruction of Architecture in the USSR (1929)" in *El Lissitzky, Russia: An Architecture for World Revolution*, ed. Eric Dluhosh (Cambridge, MA: MIT Press, 1970), 35–36.

15 Paul Fred Schmidt, "Die Kunst auf der Pressa," *Der Cicerone* 20 (1928): 589–92.

11

12

13

14

Savoye, which was not designed until two years later. **FIG. 14** Schumacher's remarkable exhibition pavilion was published extensively in *La Cité* and was probably known to Le Corbusier. Wilhelm Riphahn's house for the *Kölnische Zeitung*, with its imposing symmetrical facade and luminous tower, became the best-known building of the fair. **FIG. 15** The Pressa exhibition was extensively discussed in the Werkbund journal *Die Form* in the summer and autumn of 1928, just when Mies was beginning to think about the design for the Barcelona Pavilion. Editor Walter Riezler pointed out that previous temporary exhibition pavilions had not "warrant[ed] earnest consideration," but the "elegant and intelligent" solutions at the Pressa could now serve as models for permanent architecture and had to be taken seriously.[16]

Even Mies himself, in one of his typically vague but emphatic short essays, recognized the importance of exhibitions and their demand to address the "central problem of our time," namely, "the intensification of life." They had the potential, he said, to "revolutionize the way we think."[17] Mies had not been invited to design anything at the Pressa, and it is plausible to read his Barcelona Pavilion as a contribution to the emerging debate about the building type rather than, as Mies liked to claim, a building without precedent. After all, Lilly Reich and Mies themselves had recently added to the range of stylistic, structural, and material innovations in the field of exhibition design. Reich had long experience as an exhibition designer for the Messeamt in Frankfurt, and the Glasraum she designed jointly with Mies at the Stuttgart Werkbund Exhibition in 1927 had enjoyed considerable attention. Similarly, their Café Samt und Seide at a 1928 fashion fair in Berlin and the stand for the German Linoleum Works at Leipzig in 1929 had all presented inventive contributions to the evolving building type.

Back in Barcelona, what company did Mies find himself in? As to be expected, most national pavilions at the 1929 exposition

15

16

11 Danish Pavilion at the Paris Exposition des Arts Decoratifs, 1925
Architect: Kay Fisker

12 Raumstadt at the Paris Exposition des Arts Decoratifs, 1925
Architect: Friedrich Kiesler

13 Pavilion of the Mosse Publishing House at the Pressa exhibition, Cologne, 1928
Architect: Erich Mendelsohn

14 House of the Workers' Press, at the Pressa exhibition, Cologne, 1928
Architect: Hans Schumacher

15 Pavilion of the *Kölnische Zeitung* at the Pressa exhibition, Cologne, 1928
Architect: Wilhelm Riphahn
Photograph: Werner Manz

16 Belgian Pavilion, Barcelona International Exposition, 1929
Architect: Arthur Verhelle

followed long-established patterns and sought inspiration in celebrated historical monuments or vernacular architecture, while more adventurous and modern approaches were found among the commercial pavilions.[18] Mies's pavilion was clearly the most radical country pavilion at the fair, but it was not the only one designed in a contemporary idiom.[19] While its formal language positioned it closer to the many modern trade pavilions, his choice of semiprecious stone—marble and travertine as its dominant materials—set it apart from its peers in both categories, which were usually built of stucco over a light frame of metal or wood, in anticipation of their short lifespans.

All country pavilions (except those of France and Germany) were located in the international section on the hill, next to the National Palace and quite far away from the center of the exhibition. Belgium erected a large building **FIG. 16** in the style of a medieval town hall crowned by a tower (Arthur Verhelle), and Hungary was represented by a rather forbidding, vaguely pre-Columbian structure designed by Dénes Györgyi. The Danish (Tyge Hvass), Norwegian (Ole Lind Schistad) and Romanian (Duiliu Marcu) constructions were reminiscent of each country's vernacular traditions, whereas France, Italy, Yugoslavia, and Sweden commissioned their architects to work in a contemporary idiom. The French presence was bankrolled to a large extent by the industrialist André Gustave Citroën, who played a role similar to that of Georg von Schnitzler, and for his country's pavilion, Citroën had selected the little known Beaux-Arts architect Georges Wybo, who had designed a series of car showrooms and garages for him. The small, cubic pavilion was placed diagonally in the inside corner of the two-winged Alfonso XIII exhibition hall. **FIG. 17** Elsewhere, the mercurial Italian avant-gardist Piero Portaluppi reinterpreted a Palladian villa in an exuberant and fashionable Novecento style.[20] **FIG. 18** The building's pedimented center and two flanking wings were heavily ornamented. The most remarkably and determinedly modern pavilion after Mies's was the

16 Walter Riezler, "Die Sonderbauten der Pressa," *Die Form* 3, no. 9 (1928): 257–63.

17 Ludwig Mies van der Rohe, "Zum Thema: Ausstellungen," *Die Form* 3, no. 4 (1928): 121.

18 Laura Lizondo Sevilla recently made the same point. Laura Lizondo Sevilla, "Mies's Opaque Cube: The Electric Utilities Pavilion at the 1929 Barcelona International Exposition," *Journal of the Society of Architectural Historians* 76, no. 2 (June 2017): 197–217, here 205.

19 For an overview of the architecture, see Marius Gifreda, "L'arquitectura de l'Exposició," *D'Aci i d'Allà* (December 1929): 89–93.

20 On the Italian Pavilion and Fascist representation at the Barcelona Exposition, see Rubén Domínguez Méndez, "El fascismo italiano y la Exposición Internacional de Barcelona de 1929," *Diacronie: Studi di Storia Contemporanea*, no. 14 (2013), dialnet.unirioja.es/descarga/articulo/4495575.pdf.

17

Yugoslav pavilion by Zagreb modernist Dragiša Brašovan. The small two-story building had a planar facade with stark ribbon windows and a flat roof, but the little structure seemed to have undergone a process of violent folding, its walls zigzagging in and out in late-expressionist convulsions. **FIG. 19** German critic Walther Genzmer, however, stressed that the windowless, unornamented Swedish pavilion by Peder Clason was the only other modern structure worth mentioning, besides Mies's pavilion.[21] **FIG. 20**

Predictably, pavilions representing an industry or a company were architecturally more adventurous, and most of them modern in style. Good examples were the Hispano-Suiza pavilion by Eusebi Bona i Puig, the CSHE (Ebro Water Authority) pavilion by Regino Borobio, the Nestlé Kohler chocolate pavilion, or the towers for Asland Cement and Rocalla building materials. **FIGS. 21-23** The pavilion for the Danish shipbuilders Burmeister & Wain was also interesting, as it was placed in the inner corner of the Victoria Eugenie exhibition hall, the location originally selected for the Barcelona Pavilion. **FIG. 24** Together with the French pavilion, it faced a rather disjointed panoply of other small commercial pavilions on the plaza between them. **FIG. 25**

One structure escaped this busy melee, having been placed (probably at the last minute) right across from the southeastern corner of the German pavilion in the calm heart of the fairgrounds. It promoted the famous Swiss Maggi bouillon cubes,[22] and until late at night the stand offered free samples of hot soup. **FIG. 26** Perhaps buoyed by bouillon, several of the visitors to the fair remarked how the restrained formal language of the German pavilion, in particular, offered a welcome place of "sublime calm and uplifting silence," as a "refuge for anyone who feels burdened by the crazy commotion and loud noise of the buildings, towers and fountains."[23]

As we have seen, this formal language, together with the building's spatial sequences, evolved from Mies' earlier designs and would have been perfectly at home (and caused less of a sensation) at any of the exhibitions mentioned above, where modern design or the contemporary printing industry were the main themes. In contrast, national pavilions at world's fairs, burdened with the task of representing the country as a whole, had been slow to adopt the language of modern architecture and were averse to risk-taking. An important part of what made the German pavilion so remarkable, then, was its unexpectedness, its "out-of-place-ness" in representing an entire nation rather than a material and its trade, a company, or an organization. Of course,

17 French Pavilion, Barcelona International Exposition, 1929 Architect: Georges Wybo

18 Italian Pavilion, Barcelona International Exposition, 1929 Architect: Piero Portaluppi

19 Yugoslav Pavilion, Barcelona International Exposition, 1929 Architect: Dragiša Brašovan

20 Swedish Pavilion, Barcelona International Exposition, 1929 Architect: Peder Clason

18

20

19

21 Walther Genzmer, "Der Deutsche Reichspavillon auf der Internationalen Ausstellung in Barcelona," *Die Baugilde* 11, no. 20 (October 1929): 1654-55. This pavilion was sold to the city of Barcelona by the Swedish government, dismantled, and rebuilt as a school in the Catalan town of Berga. It was later used as a military barracks and fell into disrepair. It was rebuilt in somewhat altered form in 2001. Currently efforts are under way to reconstruct the triangular tower in front of it at its original location in Montjuïc Parc, near the Olympic Stadium. See Gerardo García Ventosa, "Ochenta años de historia del pabellón de Suecia en la Exposición Internacional de Barcelona de 1929," *Revista de Arquitectura*, no. 17 (2015): 7-18, http://dadun.unav.edu/bitstream/10171/42161/1/03.pdf.

22 The company was founded in Switzerland in 1872; since 1897 it also had a large representation in Singen, Germany. See their advertisement in the special Swiss issue of the *Diario Oficial de la Exposición Internacional Barcelona 1929* 1, no. 30 (October 1, 1929): 4.

23 Eduard Foertsch, "Die Weltausstellung in Barcelona," *Vossische Zeitung*, June 11, 1929, 4.

21 Nestlé Kohler Pavilion, Barcelona International Exposition, 1929. Note the horizontal roof line of the Barcelona Pavilion in the lower left corner.

22 Asland Pavilion, Barcelona International Exposition, 1929

23 Rocalla Pavilion, Barcelona International Exposition, 1929

22

23

21

a brazen, provocative "out-of-place-ness" had become an important tool in Mies's quest to find new architectural expression and public recognition. Be it the use of nickel and chrome in furniture (previously used only on bicycles and cars), reinforced concrete beams, large display windows, walls of opal glass or freestanding columns in a residential setting—in each case, a vocabulary from a different sphere, namely from commerce and industry, was put to work in an unsuspecting environment, producing a shock effect reminiscent of Bertold Brecht's much-discussed alienation effect (*Verfremdungseffekt*) in his theater productions of the same period.[24]

24

25

26

24 The pavilion of the Danish shipbuilder Burmeister & Wain at the inner corner of the Victoria Eugenie Palace, the alternative site for the German Pavilion

25 View from the roof of the Victoria Eugenie Palace onto exhibition kiosks, 1929
Photograph: Josep M. Sagarra

26 Maggi Pavilion

24 Walter Gropius had proclaimed in 1914 that "a new development of form" had to emerge from works of industry and technology. Walter Gropius, "Der stilbildende Wert industrieller Bauformen," *Jahrbuch des Deutschen Werkbunds 1914* (Jena: Eugen Diederichs, 1914): 29–32.

Design and Construction

Before Mies van der Rohe and Lilly Reich were officially named artistic directors, Mies had already been retained by the silk industry for its own section at the 1929 Barcelona International Exposition, probably thanks to his connections with Joseph Esters and Hermann Lange, the clients for the two houses he was designing in Krefeld. Indeed, discussions about Mies's working in Barcelona seem to have begun sometime in April 1928 and led to a fascinating and ambitious project which was presented to the Spanish organizers in late April and May 1928.[1] Mies had initially hoped to appropriate one of the planned towers in the exhibition grounds for a nocturnal light installation—a widely visible sign for the spirit of cooperation between the silk, glass, and electrical industries.[2] The tower, to be located between the textile and communication palaces and overlooking the small Plaza de la Luz, was to be covered entirely with "plate glass and multicolored silk, to be changed frequently, all illuminated in a fantastic way. Apparently it is something very original and surprising."[3] Enrique Domínguez Rodiño, cultural attaché at the Spanish Embassy in Berlin and Agent of the Barcelona Exposition in Germany, informed his counterpart in Barcelona, Santiago Trias, that Mies was poised to discuss the project on his first trip to Catalonia in early June: "The Germans would like to achieve with this tower a strong representative statement. [...] Mr. Mies van der Rohe will use the opportunity of his trip to talk to you about it and see how to reach an agreement so that when the tower is built it will be with the modifications they need, which would mean great savings."[4] Rodiño assured Trias that the Germans would absorb the costs of those modifications or, if that tower could not be used, they would build one themselves.[5]

There remains no archival evidence indicating why this project with Mies was not realized. However, the tower in question was built as planned, in a moderate neoclassical style with stone cladding, cornices, and a cupola. As part of the exhibition's lighting scheme, each night it was floodlit in changing colors. Late in the planning process it was joined by Mies's white cube for the German electrical industry, right next to it on the Plaza de la Luz. **FIG. 1** The intended glass cladding would have somewhat modernized its appearance. It is tempting to speculate how much the bold gesture of such a luminous tower colored by translucent silk would have changed our understanding of Mies.

Even before signing his contract in November 1928, Mies took on more staff and rented additional office space in the building next door to his apartment on Am Karlsbad in Berlin. According to pay slips and correspondence, eighteen people worked on the German participation in Barcelona.[6] Many letters show how much Lilly Reich was involved in all decisions regarding the

1 This information amends Christiane Lange's speculation about the start of the conversation between Mies and Hermann Lange regarding the participation in Barcelona. See Christiane Lange, *Ludwig Mies van der Rohe: Architektur für die Seidenindustrie* (Berlin: Nicolai, 2011), 84.

2 See Valentín Trillo Martinez, *Mies en Barcelona: Arquitectura, representación y memoria* (Seville: UEUS, Editorial Universidad de 2017).

3 Enrique Domínguez Rodiño to Santiago Trias, 5 May 1928, Arxiu Contemporani de Barcelona (hereafter ACB), Archivo de La Organización de la Exposición de Industrias Eléctricas en Barcelona, Barcelona, AOB 026. We would like to thank architect Valentín Trillo, who discovered this project, for sharing this information and the contents of the letters with us.

4 Enrique Domínguez Rodiño to Santiago Trias, 4 June 1928, ACB, Archivo de La Organización de la Exposición de Industrias Eléctricas en Barcelona, Barcelona, AOB 054.

5 Enrique Domínguez Rodiño to Santiago Trias, 29 April 1928, ACB, Archivo de La Organización de la Exposición de Industrias Eléctricas en Barcelona, Barcelona, AOBI 011.

6 See Wolf Tegethoff, *Mies van der Rohe: The Villas and Country Houses* (New York: Museum of Modern Art, 1981), 74. The following names appear on the bills for the Barcelona Pavilion: Mrs. Schluessler, Karl Strauss, Clauss, Ernst Otto, Pabst, Willi Kaiser, Eggerstedt, Förster, Gutte, Sergius Ruegenberg, Ulsamer, Ernst Walther, Gerhard Severain, Schmidt, Ms. Elisabeth Hahn, Grete Uhland, Else Lichtnau, and Gabriele Seeger. In addition to Mies's team, von Schnitzler recruited Arthur Meyer-Gasters, head of the IG Farben building office, who oversaw that company's installations, but also helped in the final phase of the pavilion. Another member of IG Farben was the local representative Erich von Kettler. Both continued to receive their salaries from IG Farben. Dr. Maiwald to Georg von Schnitzler, 26 June 1928, HoeA, WaB 1927–1928, H0090398. I am grateful to Mrs. Cornelia Vilzmann, Frankfurt, for information about Arthur Meyer-Gasters. See also Arthur Meyer-Gasters to Lilly Reich, 22 July 1930, MoMA, MvdR Papers, Barcelona Pavilion, Folder 11; Georg von Schnitzler to several IG Farben Departments, memo, 10 July 1929, HoeA, WaB 1927–1929; and Meyer-Gasters to Mr. Krause, IG Farben, 14 August 1929, HoeA, WaB, 1929–1930.

1 Tower at the World's Fair site, Barcelona 1929. Mies van der Rohe had anticipated a light installation with glass and colored silk for this tower.

1

German industry sections in the palaces,[7] and the prominent German paper *Vossische Zeitung* gave her exclusive credit for their artistic design.[8]

Preference was given first to the installations of the different sections, their layout, dividing walls, and display cases, while the design of the pavilion itself was probably not begun in earnest before the site was secured in late November, as it was heavily dependent on the conditions of its location. Mies had promised to present his sketches of the pavilion to the von Schnitzlers on December 22, but postponed the date to January 4, 1929.[9] The delay was probably caused by the fact that his design for the Tugendhat House was moving full speed ahead at exactly the same time, and he had agreed to meet Grete and Fritz Tugendhat at her parents' house in Brno on December 28, 1928, to discuss his plans.

Georg von Schnitzler had to report on his general progress at a meeting of the Reich's Exhibition and Trade Fair Office on January 18. Mies provided some plans of the industry sections, but shied away from presenting the pavilion, claiming that it was "not advisable."[10] Finally, on February 4, 1929, he presented a model to a small, select group of officials, among them Peter Mathies of the German exhibition office and the German Arts Councilor, Edwin Redslob.[11] Mies was still hedging his bets regarding potential costs and the attendees might not have been aware of the full extent of Mies's intended use of marble and travertine. Repeatedly pressed for an estimate, he declared that he needed more time for his calculations.[12]

The core of any creative process with its countless small and large decisions ordinarily remains a mystery, even if we can trace multiple stylistic references and potential influences. The push and pull between courage and caution, dare and acceptance, invention and memory is usually not readable from the outside, especially with an artist as taciturn as Mies. We simply have no idea if residual memories of Adolphe Appia's stage sets with their barren expanses of stairs and stone platforms guided him when conceiving the pavilion's podium, or if his encounter with van Doesburg's drawings left traces in the floor plans of the Brick Country House or the pavilion. Did Mies first compose a balanced line drawing or imagine a spatial sequence? To which degree would it matter if the onyx wall were a foot longer or shorter, at a different location or made from another precious stone? The few surviving documents about the design process pose as many new questions as they suggest answers.

Mies's collaborator Sergius Ruegenberg recalled later that the design had unfolded with the help of a 1:50 scale model. On a base of white plasticine 6 centimeters wide strips of glass and of cardboard covered with marbleized paper were moved about to try out spatial sequences. Then came the installation of the support columns and the luminous wall: "Once the room had been defined by the position of the walls, the ceiling was applied in the form of a piece of cardboard. [...] Mies made a couple of sketches, squatting in front of the model."[13] Three of those sketches

7 See, for example, Mr. Seebohm and Georg von Schnitzler to IG Farbenindustrie Aktiengesellschaft, 12 February 1929, HoeA, WaB, 1929–1930.

8 Eduard Foertsch, "Die Weltausstellung in Barcelona," *Vossische Zeitung*, June 11, 1929, 4.

9 Dr. Maiwald to Georg von Schnitzler, 21 December 1928, HoeA, WaB 1929–1930.

10 Erich von Kettler to Georg von Schnitzler, 14 January 1929, HoeA, WaB 1929–1930.

11 Georg von Schnitzler to Erich von Kettler, 30 January 1929, HoeA, WaB 1929–1930.

12 Von Kettler to von Schnitzler, 14 January 1929 (see note 10).

13 The recollections were recorded in 1970, more than forty years after the event. Quoted in Eva Maria Amberger, *Sergius Ruegenberg: Architekt zwischen Mies van der Rohe und Hans Scharoun* (Berlin: Berlinische Galerie, 2000), 78–81. In a 1972 interview, Ruegenberg mentioned a second version of the model with 6mm marble slabs and thin glass walls. See Interview, Ludwig Glaeser with Sergius Ruegenberg, Berlin, September 8, 1972, Canadian Centre for Architecture. Ruegenberg claimed that it was his idea to place black glass at the bottom of the small pool and that he designed the travertine bench in front of the long wall connecting the main building and the small office at the end. Sergius Ruegenberg, "Worte: Mies van der Rohe zum Barcelona Pavillon" undated manuscript (ca. 1969). Berlinische Galerie, Ruegenberg Papers.

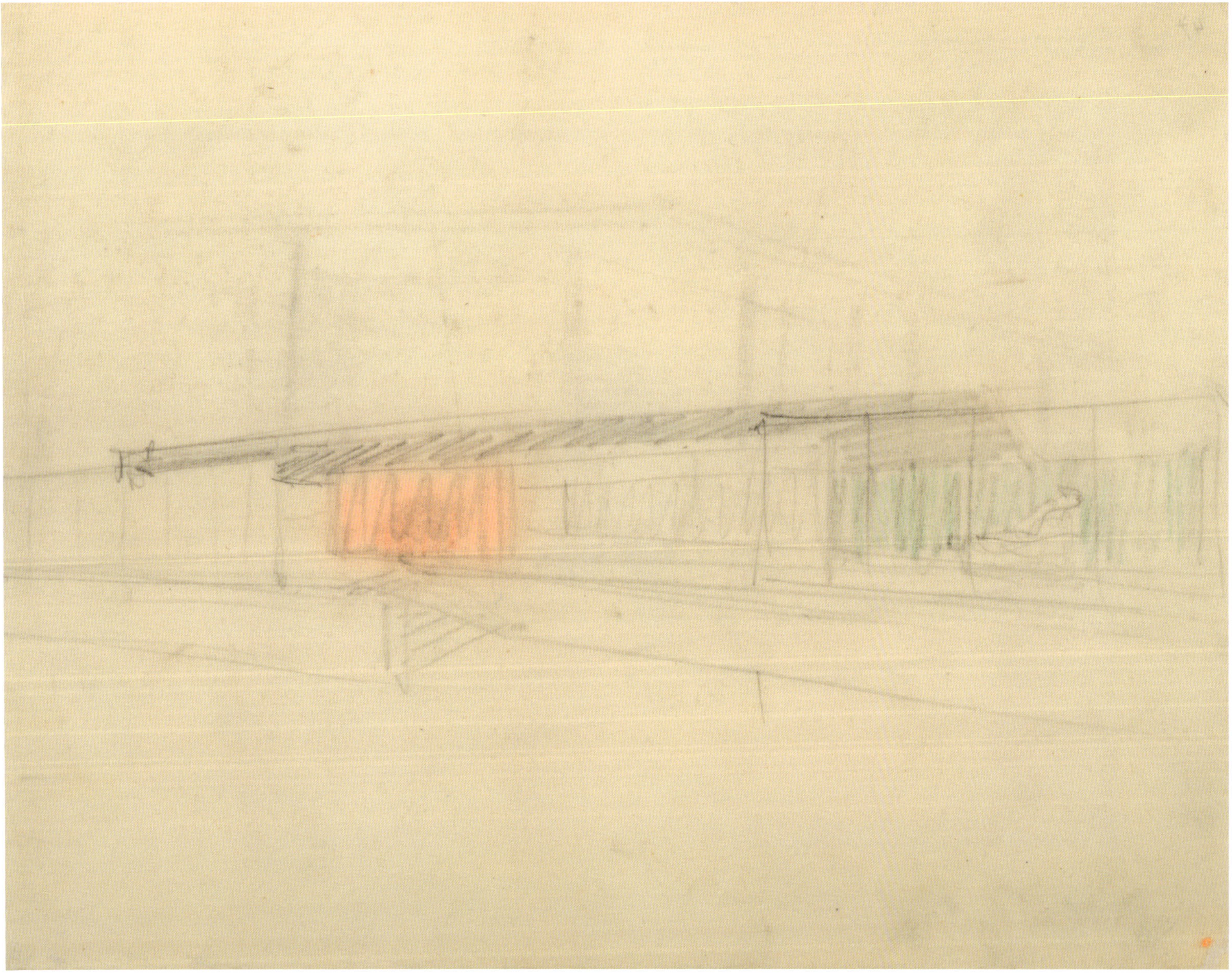

2

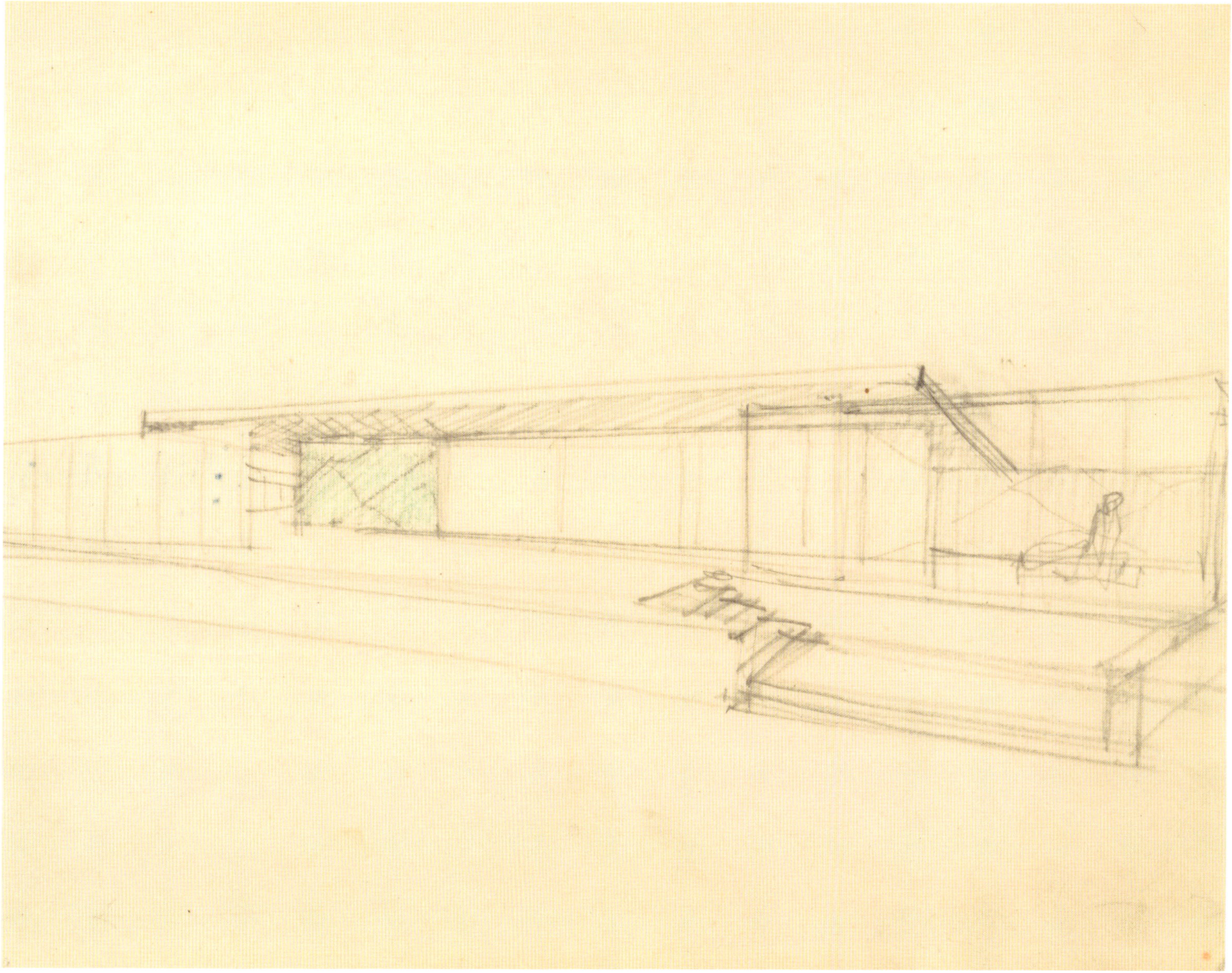

3

2, 3 Mies van der Rohe, early design sketches for the Barcelona Pavilion, late 1928. Note the absence of support columns.

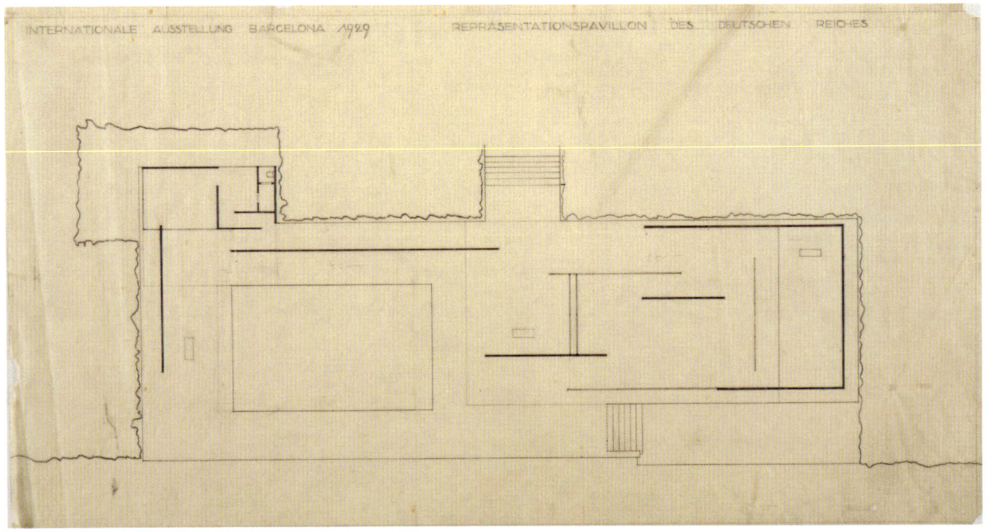

4

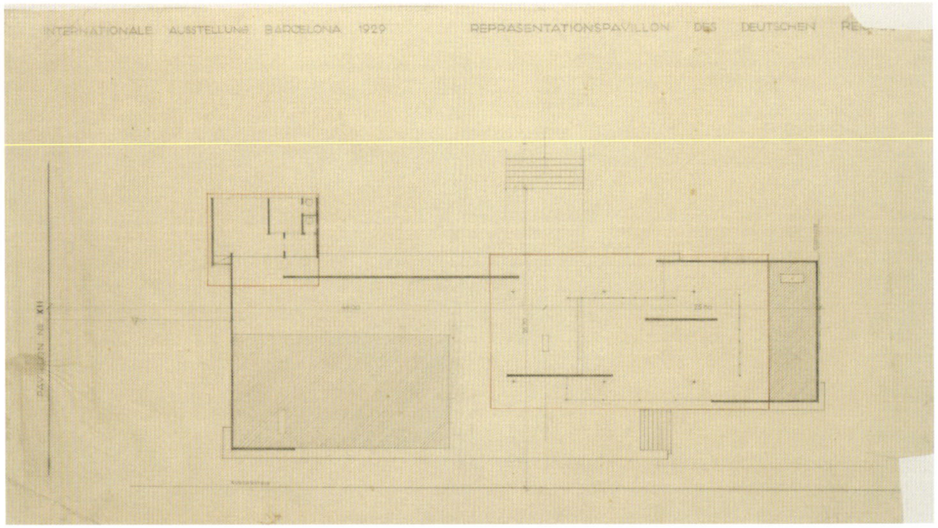

5

4 Ludwig Mies van der Rohe, German Pavilion, International Exposition, Barcelona, Spain. Floor plan, preliminary scheme without columns ca. late 1928

5 Ludwig Mies van der Rohe, German Pavilion, International Exposition, Barcelona, Spain. Floor plan, second preliminary scheme with six columns, 1928-29

6 Ludwig Mies van der Rohe, German Pavilion, International Exhibition, Barcelona, floor plan, final version, spring 1929

have survived.[14] **FIGS. 2, 3** In two of them the roof is not yet carried by metal columns and rests solely on the marble walls. A high enclosure on the left continues all the way toward the ascending stairs—blocking views not only onto the large pool and central open space but also onto the path in the back. This enclosing wall foreshadows the arrangement of Mies's court house designs, which he would frequently draw in the following decades and use as teaching exercises. While the arrangement of the frontal staircase differs in both sketches, the sculpture (and presumably the small pool) is visible to the approaching visitor through transparent glass. Successive changes (potentially initiated by the organizer's insistence on visible access to the path in the back) led to the executed sequence: the small pool with its sculpture is now invisible from the outside, and the staircase leads first to the podium with a view of the large pool ahead, before a 180-degree turn brings the visitor into the pavilion.

One of the five existing floor plans shows the general layout in place, still without columns, and with different dimensions for the larger pool, which is missing its eastern enclosing wall, and locations for three sculptures instead of just one.[15] **FIG. 4** Another plan documents an intermediary stage with six columns. **FIG. 5** Sergius Ruegenberg later recalled that there had also been a version with twelve columns which would ultimately be reduced to eight after consultations with the engineer Ernst Walther.[16] **FIG. 6** The other surviving drawings are two schematic pencil elevations and sections, a floor plan of the office, and four sketches of details.[17] The stone plan for the layout of the travertine floor slabs by marble supplier Köstner & Gottschalk also survived and played a major role in the reconstruction. **FIG. 7**

When the German delegation was granted the prominent site at the end of the central cross axis, it was most likely on the condition that they preserved access to the existing path in its center

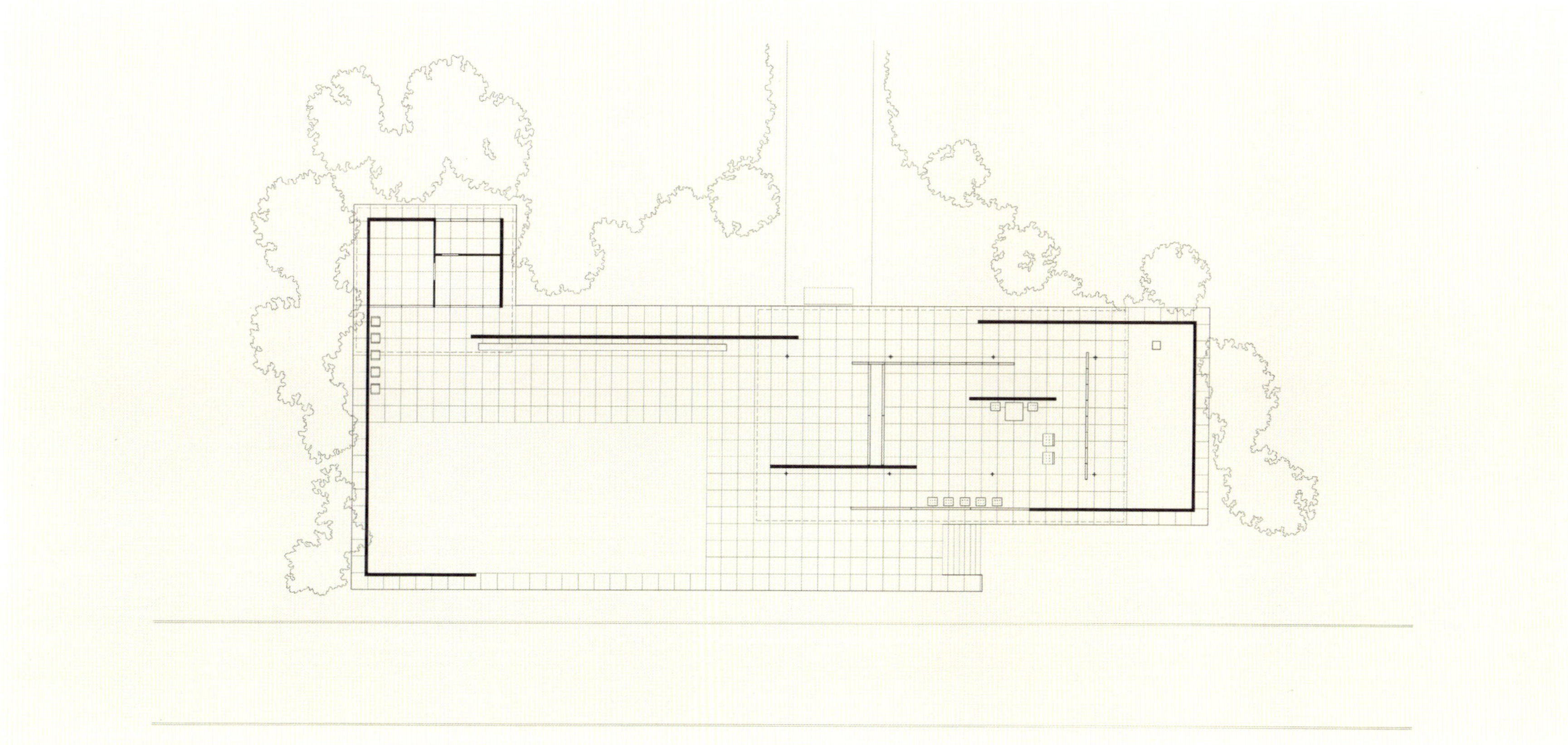

6

14 These sketches by Mies came from a sketchbook that Sergius Ruegenberg sold to the Berlin Kunstbibliothek in 1972. See Ekhart Berckenhagen, "Mies van der Rohe und Ruegenberg: Ein Skizzenbuch," *Jahrbuch Preussischer Kulturbesitz* 10 (1972), 274–80.

15 For a detailed analysis of the different versions of the floor plan, see Tegethoff, *Mies van der Rohe*, 71–83 (see note 6); and Pere Joan Ravetllat, "The Barcelona Pavilion: The Walls Came First," *Sites*, no. 15 (1988): 36–43.

16 Sergius Ruegenberg, Mies van der Rohe, *Einwirkungen auf Entwürfe und Bauten von 1908 bis 1939*, Berlinische Galerie, BG-AS 3.80 (ca. 1980), 3.

17 Arthur Drexler, ed. *The Mies van der Rohe Archive* (New York: Garland, 1986), 2:216–45.

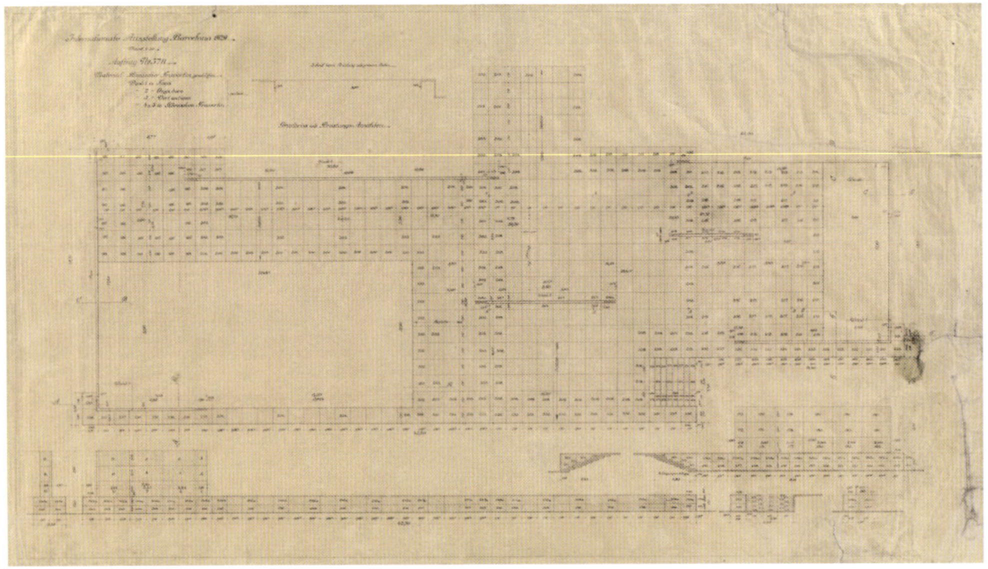

7

8

7 German Pavilion, International Exhibition, Barcelona, Köstner & Gottschalk Marble Suppliers Berlin, stone plan, spring 1929

8 Ludwig Mies van der Rohe, German Pavilion, International Exhibition, Barcelona, sketch from the back (with the columns in place) spring 1929

and the wide staircase behind. For any visitor, once inside the gated exhibition grounds, this was the most direct path to the Poble Espanyol (Spanish Village), one of the fair's most popular attractions. But if the organizers assumed that their largesse would inspire a cooperative attitude on Mies's part, they were mistaken. Mies seems to have been determined to render the path all but invisible. A slightly later sketch—now with the columns in place—shows the approach to the pavilion from the back as entirely closed. **FIG. 8** He clearly did not want his building to be experienced as a transitional space or, even worse, as some sort of entrance pavilion to the Poble Espanyol on the hill above. While that arrangement of copies of historic Spanish architecture was of great importance to the organizers, and became exactly the popular success they had hoped for, it probably had little significance for Mies—in fact many in Germany expected it to be "unbearable kitsch."[18] Although the executed version was slightly more accessible than in these early sketches, Mies still effectively blocked the view of the path in the back for visitors approaching from the plaza's central cross axis or the adjacent street to the north. The green marble wall near the entrance protruded far enough south to overlap with the travertine wall behind it. Visitors who walked up the off-center staircase to the podium would also have had to navigate around this protruding wall to glimpse the path in the back. The staircase leading up to the podium is exactly half the width of the staircase in the back leading to the Poble Espanyol, suggesting a bottleneck to slow down the throngs of visitors as they descended from the village. As historian Alan Colquhoun would later note, "the pavilion was not so much a dam as a filter."[19]

One of the most astonishing features of Mies's design was the enormous amount of carefully planned open space it included.

None of the other pavilions had claimed the outdoors to a similar degree, but Mies seems to have instinctively grasped the conditions of the local climate. He divided his plot into two parts; to the north was the building proper, and to the south, the enormous reflecting pool, with the adjacent long, freestanding wall and bench in front of it. At the very end of the plot we find the small auxiliary building, with an office and a bathroom. Once inside the pavilion, the visitor was confronted with the essential elements of architecture–floor, ceiling, walls, columns, and openings between them–pronounced starkly and separately, just as the influential publicist and critic Heinrich de Fries had suggested in 1924: "Building means leaving out everything that is not indispensable to the inner essence of a living structure."[20] "Now it becomes clear again," Mies himself noted a few years later, "what a wall is, what an opening, what is floor and what ceiling. Simplicity of construction, clarity of tectonic means, and purity of material reflect the luminosity of original beauty."[21]

The richness of the spatial, visual, and sensual experience of the pavilion interior stands in great contrast to Mies's laconic and pragmatic descriptions of his design process many years later. In 1956, long after the pavilion had been canonized as one of the masterpieces of modern architecture, he noted:

When I had the idea for this building I had to look around. There was not much time, very little time, in fact. It was deep in winter, and you cannot move marble in from the quarry in winter because it is still wet inside and it would easily freeze to pieces. So we had to find dry material. I looked around in huge marble depots, and in one I found an onyx block. This block had a certain size and, since I had only the possibility of taking this block, I made the pavilion twice that height.[22]

This matter-of-factness conceals the enormous significance of his decision to clad the entire 1,000 square meters of floor in travertine and all vertical walls in travertine or polished marble. It was a gesture of such unapologetic, provocative extravagance that one cannot help but salute Mies's courage and recklessness in engaging in this extraordinary gamble. Such a display of wealth and technological prowess could easily have backfired, appearing ostentatious at precisely the moment when the nations of Europe were looking to come together and recover some common ground, just eleven years after the end of the world war triggered by Germany's grandiloquent ambitions for dominance. Financially risky, politically risky, it was also a risk aesthetically–a slap in the face for Mies's fellow modernists, who were committed not to pathos and luxury but to the ethics of Neues Bauen, which emphasized simplicity, structural honesty, affordability, and matter-of-factness. In any event, Mies's gamble paid off: the response to his pavilion was almost unanimously enthusiastic, which suggested to later commentators that his pavilion represented "the ideological collapse of the modern project."[23]

Mies candidly acknowledged the impact of his design decisions in an interview at the opening:

18 Eduard Foertsch, "Die Weltausstellung in Barcelona: Die Spanische Stadt," *Vossische Zeitung*, June 11, 1929 (morning edition), 4.

19 Alan Colquhoun, *Modern Architecture* (Oxford: Oxford University Press, 2002), 176–77.

20 Heinrich de Fries, ed., *Moderne Villen und Landhäuser* (Berlin: Wasmuth Verlag, 1924), vi.

21 Ludwig Mies van der Rohe, "Was wäre Beton, was Stahl ohne Spiegelglas?" (1933), in Fritz Neumeyer, *Mies van der Rohe, Das kunstlose Wort: Gedanken zur Baukunst* (Berlin: Siedler Verlag 1986), 378. I am using–slightly adjusted–Mark Jarzombek's translation in Fritz Neumeyer, *The Artless Word: Mies van der Rohe on the Building Art* (Cambridge, MA: MIT Press, 1991), 314.

22 Interview with Mies, issued as a record, *Conversations Regarding the Future of Architecture*, Reynolds Metals Company, Kentucky, 1956; quoted in Tegethoff, *Mies van der Rohe*, 77n41 (see note 6).

23 Urtzi Grau, "Three Replications of the German Pavilion," *Quaderns* 263 (Fall 2011): 58–63.

Modern architecture, which has a lot of acceptance in Germany, tends to combine art and simplicity. There can and should be art in the new architecture. On the basis of correct and simple lines, smooth planes, one can solve the problem of architecture without compromising its aesthetic. For that we have to employ rich materials. Marble in different colors, bronze, and glass are obligatory elements of the modern style. When I constructed the German pavilion at the International Exhibition in Barcelona I was given complete freedom. Only then can an architect carry out his work. The furniture complements, in my opinion, the architecture. I have designed a new type of furniture made from materials not previously used. The results are very comfortable and resonate with the building.[24]

In claiming that "rich materials [...] marble in different colors, bronze, and glass are obligatory elements of the modern style" Mies was summarily dismissing notions of frugality, rationality, and efficiency—the justification for much of modern architecture. Instead, and for the first and only time, he suggested that "the problem of architecture" could be "solved" with formal means, rather than claiming the new architecture was an almost automatic response to the requirements of a "new age." While starkly different from his own previous proclamations, Mies's statement reveals how modern architecture was readying itself to move across class and economic divides. Its political affiliation with the left and the ethics and aesthetics of the working class was coming to an end.

When talking about the pavilion in later years, Mies often emphasized its spatial qualities. In 1952, for example, he recalled a key moment in the design process: "One evening, as I was working late on the building, I made a sketch of a freestanding wall and I gave myself a shock. I knew it was a new principle."[25] A few years later he claimed that the pavilion would have been just as good a building in brick, but added: "I am quite sure it would have been not as successful as marble, but that has nothing to do with the idea."[26] In the decades that had elapsed since his initial design process, countless critics had drawn attention to the flowing spaces of the pavilion and the need to experience them while moving. Mies's comments at the time suggest the exact opposite. In a little-known essay published in 1930 (and probably written in 1929), he described how modern architecture sought rest and stasis to counterbalance the dynamism and impermanence of contemporary life:

The Romans built for eternity: we build for a moment of rest. Our ancestors built firmly and enclosed, we prefer lightness and openness. We only build for a short time span—just like the Americans whose buildings are amortized in twenty-five years—we might demolish and rebuild a house tomorrow that we constructed only yesterday. We are constantly on the move. We do not build for eternity, but for today and tomorrow; but we build for quietude. Repose and tranquility are what our houses are supposed to give us. The eye wants to rest, it wants to calm down, it wants to compose itself: hence the new lines, the emphasized line, hence the new steel furniture, the steel houses, hence the new architecture.[27]

In the completed pavilion, of course, such modern quietude came hand in hand with a surprisingly sensual richness. Brightness and temperature varied considerably between the blindingly white travertine of the outer terrace and the darker interior. The depth of the roof overhang provided coolness and shade, and the resplendent play of light on the ceiling echoed the rippling of the water in the two pools, both open to the sky—one part of the outside terrace, the other part of the pavilion. Inside, the spatial continuum offered areas with different sensibilities—the light flooding in from the west contrasting sharply with darker areas toward the back—changing naturally with the time of day and intensity of light.[28]

Barely furnished, some parts of the pavilion came across as stark and unhomely, yet its center coalesced into an abstract intimation of domesticity, with a lush black wall-to-wall carpet in front of the onyx slab, a wall-high red curtain, and a few pieces of strangely unsubstantial and uninviting furniture. This space provided the quiet center of the spatial sequence, midway between the entrance and the small reflecting pool. An attentive observer might have noticed the acoustic changes that resulted from the soft surface underfoot and the muffled echoes from the curtain. The two overlapping corridor spaces behind the onyx wall are much darker and suggested movement rather than stasis. For most visitors, the exit would have intuitively happened at the western back door, where they were released onto a small plaza behind the luminous wall, shielded from the view toward the exhibition grounds, but right in front of the staircase to the Spanish Village.

Some of the pavilion's aesthetic stemmed from recent technological developments, in particular in the design of storefronts and display windows. The three glass panes at the front of the building, 3.5m (almost 12 feet) wide and wall-high, were so unusual in this setting that several visitors walked right into them, smacking their heads against the glass.[29] There were four kinds of glass: clear toward the plaza in front, green toward the small pool with Kolbe's statue; the darkest gray glass toward the back (once again, obscuring glimpses of the path toward the west); and a translucent and milky white opal glass for the luminous wall in the back. This rich palette was completed by three kinds of marble—onyx doré, timos, and verde antique—which gave the overall impression of a carefully calibrated composition.

And then there were the columns: never before had Mies used a series of freestanding, independent supports. His Esters and Lange Houses, then nearing completion in Krefeld, had only one single square metal support apiece for the flat roofs above the garden terraces. There were, however, precedents among Mies's peers: Le Corbusier had used freestanding columns in his sketch for the Domino system in 1914 and then again at his double house at the Weissenhof estate in Stuttgart in 1927 (which Mies had been very impressed with).[30] The Luckhardt brothers' houses at the Rupenhorn in Berlin (1928) had also employed freestanding metal columns inside the main living room. Sergius Ruegenberg even suggested that thin columns in African huts might have served as inspiration, just as the freestanding onyx wall might have been inspired in part by similarly freestanding walls for cult ceremonies in African architecture.[31]

It is tempting to speculate whether the eight Ionic columns **FIG. 9** across the street from the pavilion might have helped to inspire the eight cruciform columns in Mies's design—four of them visible from the front, four tucked away in the back. After all, Mies had been acutely aware of the political iconography of the demolished four

24 "El arquitecto Van der Roch [sic] creador del Pabellón de Alemania," *Diario Oficial de la Exposición Internacional Barcelona 1929* 1, no. 12 (June 2, 1929): 25.

25 Interview, February 13, 1952: "Six Students Talk with Mies," *Master Builder: Student Publication of the School of Design, North Carolina State College* 2, no. 3 (Spring 1952): 28.

26 "Conversations with Mies," in John Peter, *The Oral History of Modern Architecture: Interviews with the Greatest Architects of the Twentieth Century* (New York: Harry N. Abrams, 1994), reprinted in Moisés Puente, ed., *Conversations with Mies van der Rohe* (New York: Princeton Architectural Press, 2008), 59.

27 Ludwig Mies van der Rohe, "Vom Neuen Bauen," in *Deutsche Kunst und Dekoration* 66 (1930): 180.

28 Lance Hosey made this point particularly clear when he had the pavilion photographed at different times of day. See Lance Hosey, "The Ship of Theseus: Identity and the Barcelona Pavilion(s)," *Journal of Architectural Education* 72, no. 2 (October 2018): 230–47.

29 Mies had made precise suggestions regarding the position of the red curtain. It was only to be visible from the outside for a few feet, thus leaving much of the glass vulnerable to the impact of nearsighted visitors. Erich von Kettler to Lilly Reich, 19 September 1929, MoMA, MvdR Papers, Barcelona Pavilion, Folder 9.

30 Sergius Ruegenberg, Mies's assistant, claims in his recollections that Mies found the living room in Le Corbusier's house in Stuttgart "the only one worth visiting." Sergius Ruegenberg, "Mies und Zeichnung," undated manuscript (ca. 1969), Berlinische Galerie, Ruegenberg Papers.

31 Ibid.

9

9 German Pavilion, International Exhibition, Barcelona. Aerial view of German Pavilion with the eight ionic columns and the Maggi Pavilion visible across the street. Summer 1929

columns at the center of the exhibition site. His drawings of earlier versions without columns suggest that the supports may have been introduced as the design process unfolded in the winter of 1928, when Mies paid his third visit to Barcelona and witnessed the rise of the eight columns that replaced the original four. Could we imagine Mies, then, as a sly supporter of the besieged Catalan independence movement, adopting four columns visible to the street, but also immaterial, as the symbolic rendering of its cherished flag, the Senyera? An alternative, less farfetched explanation could be found in the immediate spatial context: the two southernmost cruciform columns are placed precisely at the center of the site (a distance of 25 square floor slabs to either side), on axis with the "magic fountain" and the central intercolumnar space of the colonnade. As a result, the spaces between the columns at the pavilion related to the Ionic columns across the street.

All speculation aside, the most likely reason for the introduction of columns was practical: compared to a system of irregularly placed and very slender supports inside the hollow marble walls, a rectangular steel frame made the roof construction much simpler to calculate and faster and cheaper to build. A simple grid of eight supports with individual foundations could be accommodated much more easily. It therefore seems likely that the columns entered the design when it became obvious that the pavilion had to be built in the shortest possible time span and would be mostly prefabricated in Germany.[32] Sergius Ruegenberg later gave credit to the engineer Ernst Walther, who "calculated the thinness and delicacy of the steel columns for the Barcelona Pavilion; Mies wanted them as thin as absolutely possible, he had actually only wanted a hovering plane as a roof. The columns could only be an intermediate element, almost invisible. That is why they were clad in reflective sheets of nickel."[33] The combination of four L-shaped, equilateral steel bands formed a strong column with the smallest possible footprint. **FIG. 10** [34] The reflective surface of their nickel-covered casings further helped to

10

12

11

10 German Pavilion, International Exposition, Barcelona, Spain, Horizontal column section, 1929.

11 Mies van der Rohe, Sergius Ruegenberg, unfinished interior perspective, ca. 1929

12 Mies van der Rohe's office, ca. 1932. Note the interior perspective on the wall.

32 Japanese architect and critic Hajime Yatsuka offers a similarly skeptical interpretation; see Hajime Yatsuka, "Mies and Japan," *Cornell Journal of Architecture* 7 (2003): 52-62.

33 "Der Skelettbau ist keine Teigware: Sergius Ruegenberg berichtet von Mies van der Rohes Berliner Zeit," *Bauwelt* (1986): 346-51, here 350. In his notes, Ruegenberg stressed the fact that these columns were nickel-plated. Ruegenberg, "Worte" (see note 13). See also Bruno Reichlin, "Conjectures à propos des colonnes réfléchissantes de Mies van der Rohe," in *La Colonne: Nouvelle histoire de la construction*, ed. Robert Gargiani (Lausanne: Presses polytechniques et universitaires romandes, 2008), 454-66.

34 Carl Kersten, *Der Eisenhochbau: Ein Leitfaden für Schule und Praxis* (Berlin: Wilhelm Ernst & Sohn, 1920), 108. Sergius Ruegenberg recalled that in Barcelona small wooden blocks were inserted between the L-beams to receive the screws holding the nickel casing. It bothered Mies so much that he later (in Chicago) altered the section drawing of the column to include small metal Ts. Ruegenberg, "Worte" (see note 13).

dematerialize them, in particular as the 90-degree angle in the center prevented frontal reflections.[35]

In the end, the final structure was something of a hybrid. Construction photographs show that the steel ceiling grid needed some additional support where it cantilevered out on the eastern and western sides beyond the central eight columns. During construction this was provided by six wooden A-frames; later on, the marble walls (or rather the invisible steel frame inside) would help. **FIG. 19** Once the decision for the slim columns had been made, Mies's office explored their visual and spatial impact against different marble surfaces and degrees of glass transparency, held together in a carefully calibrated balance. One particularly evocative unfinished drawing by Sergius Ruegenberg, which long adorned a wall in Mies's office, speaks to those efforts.[36] **FIGS. 11, 12**

Later critics have occasionally speculated that the interior color scheme referred to the pavilion's national affiliation.[37] It is true that when the bright red curtain finally arrived in early July, and was set alongside the black carpet and the golden onyx wall, the three colors of the national flag were all present. However, since the colors did not appear in their actual sequence, this reference would have been difficult to decipher, and they could equally well have referred to the Belgian flag. An important aspect complicates matters further: Germany's flag—the one the country still uses today—had been introduced only recently, in 1919, with the founding of the Weimar Republic. However, many conservatives, including members of the German Volkspartei (DVP), to which Stresemann, Curtius, and probably von Schnitzler belonged, still preferred the flag of the previous regime, with its black, white, and red stripes, which to them symbolized the strength, successes, and stability of the Kaiserreich that had come to an end in 1918. They associated the new flag with Germany's loss of sovereignty and with the Treaty of Versailles. The subject remained intensely emotive throughout the Weimar years—in May 1926 a "flag controversy" had even unraveled the government of Chancellor Hans Luther, when he had dared to voice his firm support for the new flag. In Barcelona both flags (apparently of enormous size) were flown in front of the German pavilion, to the confusion of many visitors, who wondered "which one was the real German flag."[38]

Other material finishes inside the pavilion include the translucent opal-glass screen that terminates the southern end of the main room. Made up of two 3-meter-wide panes of darkish gray glass, the screen is reflective during the day, but also emanates light thanks to the elongated skylight above it. The 1-meter-deep space between the two panes housed 16 suspended lightbulbs, which were not fully functional until mid-July, some months after the opening.[39]At night, this dull gray wall turned into a white luminous screen providing the pavilion's only source of light. Apart from offering respite from the kitschy symphony of colored illumination outside, the luminous wall integrated artificial light into the pavilion's architecture of essential planes. Correspondence in mid-July between Mies's Berlin office and the local administrator in Barcelona shows how important this function was for the architect. After two visitors had fallen into the small pool at night, Erich von Kettler asked if additional lights could be installed, since "after dusk it is difficult to see that there is water in the pool and the light from the luminous wall does not reach that far."[40] Ruegenberg later remembered that visitors also found the light from the wall "psychologically unpleasant," as it turned them into mere "silhouettes."[41] But Mies firmly rejected the idea of introducing more lights. (After another mishap in October, a temporary light was installed by the fair's administrators, but later switched off again by the architect's representative.) Clearly it was of crucial importance for Mies to limit the illumination of the pavilion to this one element, an integral part of its structure, and to keep the interior space as uncluttered as possible.

Among the many astonishing qualities of the pavilion is the fact that it was mostly prefabricated and shipped in parts from Germany. ("Only the water seems to be Spanish," joked a German reporter.[42]) This meant that it had to be planned with great precision and that its progress on the site was extraordinarily dependent on smooth transportation and working infrastructure. In terms of the marble, some of it may have been shipped directly from the quarry to Barcelona, but it seems more likely that all of it came from Köstner & Gottschalk's marble depot in Berlin Weissensee.[43] Mies later recalled how he had brought to bear his skills as a trained stonemason in order to see the color of the stone. He instructed the staff at the marble depot:

> *Give me a hammer and I will show you how we used to do this at home. They finally brought me a hammer and were very curious if I would really strike a corner off the block. I hit it very hard and off came a slice, the size of my hand, very thin, and I said go and quickly polish it, so I can see it. We then decided to use it, figured out the quantities, and then bought the material.*[44]

The marble was sent by train to Hamburg, from where it was then shipped to Barcelona. Thin marble slabs would be attached to both sides of a steel framework, with shorter solid pieces at the end. This clever arrangement lowered the weight and amount of material needed, while still providing the appearance of solidity throughout. The steel frame inside contained flat, lozenge-shaped pipes to drain water from the roof. Mies carefully arranged for the stone veneer's prominent grain to form symmetrical patterns. Two sequential cuts would be placed next to each other so that their patterns mirrored each other, the so-called book match, while four sequential cuts provided a quarter or diamond match. The diamond and book matches are clearly visible in the verde antique wall that provides part of the main facade and wraps around the small pool to the back. Here Mies managed to assemble double diamond matches, continuing over several fields horizontally. Adolf Loos was among the first to introduce such large-scale marble patterns into modern architecture, for example in his Café Capua of 1913 in Vienna. The onyx wall in the center consisted of larger pieces, 235 by 149 by 30 centimeters. Judging from the surviving photographs, Mies resorted to a random match here, probably due to the configuration of the slabs he could purchase.

It is no wonder that Köstner & Gottschalk's bill amounted to 187,580 Reichsmark—about 55 percent of the overall cost of the pavilion. To put the towering costs for the stone slabs into perspective, the next largest expenditure was the fee of 80,000

35 The nickel electro-plating applied at the columns, window frames, and structural parts of the furniture was a fairly recent innovation. It was mostly used in cars, bicycles, and storefront display cases.

36 The drawing appears in interior photographs of Mies's office when his team was working on the Verseidag commission in 1932; see Helmut Reuter and Birgit Schulte, eds., *Mies and Modern Living: Interiors, Furniture, Photography* (Berlin: Hatje Cantz, 2009). See also Desley Luscombe, "Drawing the Barcelona Pavilion: Mies van der Rohe and the Implications of Perspectival Space," *Journal of Architecture* 21, no. 2 (2016): 210–43.

37 Franz Schulze, "The Barcelona Pavilion Returns," *Art in America* 67, no. 7 (1979): 98–103. See also *Mies van der Rohe: The Barcelona Pavilion: 50th Anniversary*, text by Ludwig Glaeser (Friends of the Mies van der Rohe Archive in connection with the exhibition *Mies van der Rohe: The Barcelona Pavilion*, National Gallery of Art, Washington DC, October 14–December 2, 1979).

38 Wilhelm Hack, "Das Wunder der Ausstellung," *Deutsche Tageszeitung* (Berlin), June 11, 1929.

39 Erich von Kettler to Mies van der Rohe, 15 July 1929, MoMA, MvdR Papers, Barcelona Pavilion, Folder 2010 addition from Eduard Ludwig estate.

40 The luminous glass wall was finally functional six weeks after the opening. See Erich von Kettler to Lilly Reich, 10 September 1929, and Erich von Kettler to Lilly Reich, 29 October 1929, MoMA, MvdR Papers, Barcelona Pavilion, Folder 9.

41 Interview, Ludwig Glaeser with Sergius Ruegenberg (see note 13).

42 Eduard Förtsch, "Deutschland in Barcelona," *Tempo* (June 6, 1929).

43 A letter from Mies to Georg von Schnitzler in May 1929, two weeks before the opening, laments the fact that several shipments were held up at the harbor.

44 "Mies in Berlin," interview with Ulrich Conrads and Horst Eifler (record, 1964), http://www.bauwelt.de/cms/videos.html?s_text=mies#media=4440879.

13

14

13 German Pavilion, building site on March 29, 1929

14 German Pavilion, Mies van der Rohe at the building site, ca. March 30, 1929

15 German Pavilion, building site on April 14, 1929

16 German Pavilion, Sergius Ruegenberg on site, April 14, 1929

Reichsmark for Siemens Bauunion, which had supervised the entire construction: Berliner Metallgewerbe, who manufactured and supplied the nickel-covered supports, window frames, and Barcelona chairs, were paid 28,759 Reichsmark, while the total cost of the glass was about 16,000 Reichsmark, including transport and installation. At that time, small single-family houses could be had for between 10,000 and 30,000 Reichsmark.[45]

A few dated snapshots document the construction's late beginning and slow progress. The site had been dedicated on February 9, 1929, but by March 29, 1929 nothing had been built—while additional funds had been granted on March, precious days had been taken up with the re-hiring of workers and the ordering of material.[46] **FIG. 13** A day or two later we see Mies standing calmly amid mounds of dirt on the construction site as the foundations are staked out. **FIG. 14** On April 3, he went back to Berlin to take care of two pressing issues: finishing the design and submitting the building permit for the Berlin house of the painter Emil Nolde, due April 15, and supervising the production of the Barcelona chair at the metal shop. He returned to Barcelona on April 22.[47] By April 14, the foundations and the subfloor were nearing completion. **FIGS. 15, 16** Sergius Ruegenberg had arrived that day to supervise construction and proudly posed for photographs on the site. Simple brick foundation walls, steel beams, and special flat tiles for the "Catalan vault" construction of the substructure are visible between them, piled up in the foreground.[48] The marble and glass walls would later simply be placed on the subfloor without separate foundations, but the cruciform steel columns had their own supports underneath, independent of the vault structure.

The steel frame carrying the roof on its eight columns went up first. The cantilevers on the eastern and western side were temporarily supported by wooden A-frames, until the steel supports

15

16

45 Guido Harbers, *Das freistehende Einfamilienhaus von 10000–30000 und über 30000 Mark* (Munich: Callwey, 1932).

46 Mies had traveled to Barcelona at the end of March to supervise the beginning of construction and returned on April 3. See Georg von Schnitzler to the Marqués de Foronda, 6 April 1929, HoeA, WaB 1927–1929, H0090400.

47 Lilly Reich arrived on April 24, 1929. See requests for reimbursement from Lilly Reich and Mies van der Rohe, June 3 and June 10, 1929, MoMA, MvdR Papers, Barcelona Pavilion, Folder 6. See also Lilly Reich to Elisabeth Hahn and Grete Uhland, 26 June 1929, MoMA, MvdR Papers, Barcelona Pavilion, Folder 8.

48 This technique, which can be traced back in the region to the Middle Ages, had been revived since the 1880s as a particularly cost-effective vaulting method and also played a major role in the frequent curvilinear vault and roof structures in Catalonia's Modernisme architecture at the turn of the century. At the same time it was introduced by the Guastavino Company in the US. With the help of a very adhesive and fast-drying mortar, layers of flat bricks are assembled into vaults, domes, and curved ceilings without the need for formwork or scaffolding. The resulting structures are lightweight and fireproof. See John Ochsendorf, *Guastavino Vaulting: The Art of Structural Tile* (New York: Princeton Architectural Press, 2010), 18–39. Joan Bergós y Massó (1894–1974), the foreman of the local construction company, Sociedad Metropolitana de Construcciónes, had insisted on this construction technique as it saved time over the reinforced concrete foundation that Mies had originally suggested. Massó had been a pupil of Gaudí's and wrote a monograph on him which appeared posthumously in 1974. See Ignasi de Solà-Morales, Cristian Cirici, and Fernando Ramos, *Mies van der Rohe: El Pabellón de Barcelona* (Barcelona: Gustavo Gili, 1993), 15; and Juan Bassegoda Nonell, "El pabellón alemán de la exposición de 1929: Historia y anécdota de una obra de Mies van der Rohe," *La Vanguardia*, October 6, 1979, 6.

17

18

19

17-19 German Pavilion under construction, May 1929

of the marble walls were in place and took some of the load. **FIG. 17** A general shortage of construction equipment at the site meant the pavilion was assembled without the help of proper scaffolding. In another archival photograph, a mason is seen standing on a makeshift arrangement of boards and shipping crates. The steel frame of the ceiling slab was covered by wooden planks and tar paper; the underside had metal lath and was stuccoed over by specialist Spanish plasterers.[49]

The drama of the weeks leading up to the delayed opening becomes palpable in Mies's later report to von Schnitzler, in which he justified the increased costs—"I knew what was at stake and what a responsibility I had."[50] Mies explained that weekend and night shifts were common (several photographs show temporary lampposts), more workers had to be hired, and some material from Germany, alongside thousands of exhibits for other stands in the fair, had to be flown in by Lufthansa at the last minute.[51] Emotions also ran high. Mies fired both his longtime collaborator, engineer Ernst Walther, and his technical manager, Karl Strauss.[52]

Nevertheless, the pavilion was (mostly) ready for the opening ceremony on Monday morning, May 27, 1929. The still unfinished office building on the southern end had been hastily covered up with plasterboard. The back of the pavilion, missing its marble, was stuccoed and painted. The adjacent southern garden had not been planted, the luminous double screen did not yet work, and the red curtain had not been delivered.[53]

Mies and his team developed several pieces of furniture especially for the pavilion: a low cross-legged ottoman, a small square table, and a larger serving table, both with glass tops. Most importantly, the "Barcelona Chair"—meant ostensibly for the King and Queen of Spain to sit on during the opening ceremony. **FIG. 20** Although the royal couple did not avail themselves of this opportunity, the chair would later become one of the most iconic pieces of furniture of the twentieth century. Here, after experimenting with hollow tubular steel in previous years, Mies tried out a flat-spring steel of a higher, flexible strength and different carbon content, more commonly found in shock absorbers in trains and cars.[54] As with his use of large display windows, opal glass, or nickel-plated columns, Mies had begun to transfer

49 Ruegenberg, "Worte" (see note 13).
50 Mies van der Rohe to Georg von Schnitzler, 22 August 1929, MoMA, MvdR Papers, Barcelona Pavilion, Folder 2.
51 "Deutschland in Barcelona," *Dresdner Neueste Nachrichten*, June 22, 1929, 1, 2.
52 Ernst Walther to Mies van der Rohe, 20 August and 7 September 1929, MoMA, MvdR Papers, Barcelona Pavilion, Folder 2010 addition from Eduard Ludwig estate.
53 See Solà-Morales, Cirici, and Ramos, *Mies van der Rohe*, 14–15 (see note 48).
54 Robert Schwenke, "Die Verwendung besserer Stahlsorten im Automobilbau," *Zeitschrift des Mitteleuropäischen Motorwagen-Vereins*, no. 15 (1904): 306–8.

20

21

20-22 Chair, ottoman and table for the Barcelona Pavillon. Ludwig Mies van der Rohe

aesthetics or techniques from industrial or commercial applications into the home. His patent application for the Barcelona chair and ottoman was submitted on May 1, 1929, just weeks before the pavilion's opening. The support text for the application pointed out the crucial difference from a folding chair, which might look similar, but needed moveable joints instead of a fixed connection at the center. Mies wanted to "exploit the spring of metal bands from a flexible material in order to arrive at an elastic seat and elastic back rest [...] the arms of the cross of metal bands will be springy cantilevers and the result will be a soft, pliable seat, according to the flexibility of the material."[55] The resulting chair was a hybrid—lacking armrests, it was not an arm chair, but provided the depth, comfort, and inclination of an easy chair.[56]

The design of the Barcelona chair seems to have been a collaborative affair. Sergius Ruegenberg claimed in 1988 that he was asked to design the chair to go with the cross-legged ottoman, which had been designed first: "Three days before my departure as supervisor of the building site in Barcelona, Mies asked me to design a chair. The steel stool had already been realized. One of my designs was taken by Kaiser to be produced."[57] Willi Kaiser, also in Mies's office, later recalled that he too had worked on the chair with the same metalworker who was responsible for the cruciform columns at the pavilion.[58] Several drawings of the Barcelona chair have survived among Ruegenberg's papers in Berlin. Lilly Reich probably also had significant influence. The flat leather pillows with their square upholstery seams are strongly reminiscent of Josef Hoffmann's Kubus Fauteuil of 1910, developed during the period where she worked in his studio. Reich had already proposed comparable leather upholstery for furniture at the Wolf House in Guben. Mies continued to work on the central ideas behind the Barcelona chair in the following months and submitted a new, improved version to the patent office on November 18, 1930. The written documentation of this "seating furniture with a flexible frame" clarifies the intentions for the chair

22

and its unusual construction, highlighting the "leaf springs" and the flexibility of the frame for the way they "lessen the strain on the muscles" when getting up.[59] Such a lessening was especially useful for elderly users or the more heavyset (such as Mies himself), in particular since there was no armrest to offer support.

This argument would still apply to the low cross-legged ottoman, but to a lesser degree, since the leather bands underneath the pillow limited the legs' elasticity. Applying the same type of cross legs to a table was functionally nonsensical, as stability was needed here, rather than a springy response. Two tables were produced: a long one stood in front of the luminous glass wall—ostensibly to carry refreshments; and a square one in front of the onyx wall carried the leather-bound visitors' book. Miraculously, the small table has survived and is now at the Neue Galerie in New York. **FIG. 22**

Mies would use the same kind of springy metal bands for the easy chairs at the Tugendhat House in Brno, both for their supports and for a version with armrests, as well as for the Brno dining chairs. Countless drawings and a few more patents for further versions of chairs with curved metal bands followed in the next years, but none were successful.

55 Ludwig Mies van der Rohe, "Stuhl," Patentschrift no. 486722, Deutsches Reich, published November 7, 1929. On the Barcelona chair, see Wolf Tegethoff, "Der Pavillonsessel: Die Ausstattung des Deutschen Pavillons in Barcelona 1929 und ihre Bedeutung," in Reuter and Schulte, *Mies and Modern Living*, 144–73 (see note 36); see also Christiane Lange, "Barcelona Sessel," in Christiane Lange, *Ludwig Mies van der Rohe & Lilly Reich: Möbel und Räume* (Berlin: Hatje Cantz, 2007), 174–76.

56 Tegethoff, "Der Pavillonsessel," 154 (see note 55).

57 Sergius Ruegenberg to Tecta, 4 June 1988 (Tecta Archive), See also Eva-Maria Amberger, *Sergius Ruegenberg* (Berlin: Berlinische Galerie, 2000), 82–83.

58 Willi Kaiser, "Es war Mies, nicht Lilly," *Der Spiegel* 19 (1977), n.p.

59 Ludwig Mies van der Rohe in Berlin, "Sitzmöbel mit federndem Gestell," Österreichisches Patentamt, Patentschrift no. 128771, submitted November 18, 1930, published June 25, 1932.

Georg Kolbe's Sculpture

While it was fairly common for modern architects to introduce sculpture into their work, this was a practice that Mies, as the son of a stonemason, seems to have been especially drawn to. Sculptures were incorporated into a number of his unrealized early projects, such his design for a Bismarck Monument (1910), which centered around an enormous, heroic statue of the German chancellor, or the Kröller-Müller museum in the Netherlands (1912), which featured a sculpture next to an outdoor pool. In the *Glasraum* installation in Stuttgart, designed in collaboration with Lilly Reich two years before the Barcelona Pavilion, the centerpiece was a female torso by Wilhelm Lehmbruck. Visible upon entry behind veils of tinted glass, it dropped briefly out of sight before reemerging, beckoning visitors into the central space while remaining inaccessible in its own private courtyard.

The use of an equivalent element at the Barcelona Pavilion was similarly fundamental to its design, and three surviving early sketches show a reclining sculptural figure in an open space on the right, visible through glass to approaching visitors and vanishing briefly behind marble walls as one went inside—an arrangement very similar to that at the *Glasraum*. The two earliest floor plans suggest locations for as many as three of these sculptures, one inside each pool as focal points for viewing axes along the front and back perimeter, and a third facing visitors descending the steps from the Poble Espanyol.

The female figure at the Barcelona Pavilion was by Georg Kolbe, Germany's most prominent sculptor at the time, and probably better known to the public than Mies **FIG. 1**. Kolbe had a long history of collaboration with other modernists, such as Walter Gropius, Bruno Taut, and Hans Poelzig.[1] He had also become wealthy enough from a series of public commissions to build a new home and studio in Berlin's affluent Westend—a cubic brick construction completed in January 1929.[2] Fascinated with modern architecture, Kolbe took an intense interest in the design process and pushed his architects, Ernst Rensch and Paul Linder, toward starker and simpler forms **FIG. 2**. The result was something akin to Mies's Wolf House in Guben **FIG. 9, P. 42**. Mies had known Kolbe for a number of years—the two lived within walking distance of each other in the Tiergarten district, before Kolbe moved to the Westend.[3] In 1930 they both signed a plea to return the most famous piece in Berlin's Egyptian art collection, the head of Queen Nefertiti (which had been taken out of the country illegally), to Egypt.[4] Their common interests seem to have extended beyond the realm of art: in 1934 Kolbe and Mies were the two most prominent names among thirty-four artists who publicly pledged allegiance to Adolf Hitler in the National Socialist paper *Völkischer Beobachter* (see below).

Kolbe's important relationship with architecture had been displayed especially prominently in Munich a few years earlier, in 1927, when a special brick-lined room was designed exclusively for his work by Wilhelm Kreis, in the annual art exhibition held in the city's Glaspalast **FIG. 5**.[5] Around the perimeter of the room, Kolbe installed the two types of sculpture for which he was best known, alternating calm busts of well-known public figures with

1 Ursel Berger, "Georg Kolbe und die Architektur," in *Barcelona Pavilion*, ed. Ursel Berger and Thomas Pavel (Berlin: Jovis 2006), 126–31.

2 Among many others, Kolbe had created portrait busts of Ludwig von Beethoven, Max Slevogt, Paul Cassirer, and the recently deceased Reich president Friedrich Ebert (which induced a minor *cause célèbre*, when members of the Reichstag deemed it too modern to be installed there). See "Max Slevogt, Bronzebildnis von Georg Kolbe," *Vossische Zeitung*, October 24, 1926, 3; "Aus der Nationalgalerie," *Vossische Zeitung*, April 13, 1927 (morning edition), entertainment section, 2; "Die Ebert-Büste," *Vossische Zeitung*, July 23, 1925 (evening edition), 2; "Kolbes 'Beethoven,'" *Vossische Zeitung*, March 14, 1928 (morning edition), 1; "Totenmaske Friedrich Eberts, abgenommen von Prof. Georg Kolbe," *Vossische Zeitung*, March 8, 1925, 7.

3 Kolbe lived at Von der Heydt Strasse 7, Mies at Am Karlsbad 24. Kolbe kept his atelier at Von der Heydt Strasse mostly for the storage of plaster casts until 1932. See http://www.georg-kolbe-museum.de/museum-2/architektur.

4 "Berliner Künstler zum Nefretete Streit," *Vossische Zeitung*, May 25, 1930, section "Sport/Spiel und Turnen," 3, 4. Hitler ultimately prevented the return of the bust.

5 *Münchener Kunstausstellung 1927 im Glaspalast: 1 Juni bis 3 Oktober 1927: amtlicher Katalog*, ed. Münchener Künstler-Genossenschaft und Verein Bildender Künstler Münchens "Secession" (Munich: Knorr & Hirth, 1927). See also Claudia Beckmann, "The Statue *Morgen* in the Barcelona Pavilion," in *Barcelona Pavilion*, ed. Ursel Berger and Thomas Pavel (Berlin: Jovis 2006), 46; and "Die unbekannte Nationalgalerie," *Vossische Zeitung*, July 1, 1927 (evening edition), 3.

1

2

lively nudes. For the centerpiece, dramatically lit from above, Kolbe chose the sculpture of a young woman, standing approximately 2.5 meters tall on an inclined plinth. With her feet close together, and knees bent, her torso indicated a slight turn to the left, with both arms raised over her head, counterbalancing the precarious slope underfoot **FIG. 6**. The piece, painted to look like bronze, was actually a plaster cast version of one of a pair of earlier bronze female figures, created for the central green space of the Ceciliengärten housing estate in Berlin (1922–27) **FIGS. 3, 4**. When the exhibition closed on October 3, 1927, the plaster cast of "Cecilie," as Kolbe liked to call her, was returned to the sculptor's studio in Berlin.

It is impossible to know for sure how the sculpture for the Barcelona Pavilion was chosen, but much evidence points to a somewhat accidental selection at the last minute, determined by time pressure and circumstance rather than careful planning. What we do know is that as late as February 1929 Mies was talking about proposing works by either Lehmbruck[6] or Kolbe to the "people in charge."[7] With the uncertainty over the fate of the pavilion—canceled by order of the Reichstag for a sixteen-day period in March—the final decision on the sculpture appears only to have been made after work on the pavilion resumed, most likely during Mies's two-week stay in Berlin from April 3 on. Architect Peter Blake, who knew Mies well, recalled that Mies would have preferred a figure by Lehmbruck, but when that turned out to be impossible, he "grabbed a taxi on one of his last days in Berlin before leaving for Barcelona, drove out to Kolbe's studio and borrowed the best substitute he could find."[8] That "best substitute" turned out to be the plaster cast of "Cecilie." As a loan fee, Kolbe requested the manufacturing price of the cast, leading the general commissariat to believe that it was being custom-made for the international exposition. The sculpture was shipped immediately and arrived in time for the opening.

1 Georg Kolbe's female sculpture at the Barcelona Pavilion
Photograph: Cami Stone, 1929

2 Berlin, Georg Kolbe home and studio, 1929
Architect: Ernst Rensch and Paul Linder
Photograph: Margrit Schwartzkopff

6 Wilhelm Lehmbruck, an acquaintance of Mies, had taken his own life in 1919.

7 Mies van der Rohe to Lilly Reich, 22 February 1929, MoMA, MvdR Papers, Barcelona Pavilion, Folder 9.

8 Peter Blake, *The Master Builders* (New York: Alfred A. Knopf, 1960), 208–12.

3

4

3 Georg Kolbe, plaster models of two female figures for Ceciliengärten Housing Estate, Berlin, 1925

4 Georg Kolbe, female figure at Ceciliengärten Housing Estate Berlin, 1925

5 Georg Kolbe, female figure at the 1927 art exhibition at Munich's Kristallpalast in an installation by Wilhelm Kreis

5

6

While "Cecile" had traveled once before (to the 1927 exhibition in Munich and then back to Berlin), the longer and more complicated journey to Barcelona via rail and sea was not without risk. Sure enough, on the way back from Barcelona, the relatively fragile plaster figure was damaged "beyond repair"[9]–the right arm was completely shattered, the hip had a horizontal crack, and the base had several fissures up to the feet (the result, apparently, of "inadequate" packaging).[10] Kolbe, who had clearly anticipated using the figure on other occasions, was not amused–and was even less happy when he learned that the insurance company, under the impression that the cast had been entirely funded by the commissariat, argued that its destruction did not cause him a material loss.[11]

At the exposition, most critics responded positively to the "extraordinarily beautiful"[12] figure, assuming that it had been created for this specific location in the small pool at the back. Heinrich Simon, for instance, called her *Venus Anadyomene* (a Venus rising from the sea, reminiscent of the famous Titian painting of 1522).[13] Others referred to the figure as a *Badende* (bather),[14] or noted that her raised hand shielded her "against the flood of light entering the open court."[15] To a later critic she suggested the rise of a "new modern Germany."[16] Some described her as a *Tänzerin* (dancer),[17] but most critics just noted a "female figure" without giving her a name or association. Occasionally she was even mistaken for a young man.[18] Names such as "Morning" or "Dawn," which are frequently used today, came much later. As a modernist dedicated to the New Objectivity, Kolbe was interested in exploring the essence of human movements and gave his sculptures descriptive names, such as "walking woman," "squatting woman," "standing youth," "female dancer," etc. He rarely burdened his figures with the bathos of allegories. Later, however, when he was much celebrated by the National Socialist regime, he more frequently gave in to its culture of empty bombast and produced sculptures such as

6 Georg Kolbe, female figure at the 1927 art exhibition at Munich's Kristallpalast in an installation by Wilhelm Kreis

Great Rendition (1937) or *Great Guardian* (1937).[19] Strangely, Germany's postwar culture retained this knack for heavy symbolism, and it was possibly in this context that the two statues in the Ceciliengärten were retroactively given the titles *Morning* and *Evening* by Kolbe's former collaborator, Margrit Schwartzkopff, and his granddaughter Maria von Tiesenhausen. Both women were busy establishing a Kolbe Museum in his former home in West Berlin and eager to show Kolbe's contemporary relevance.[20] Wolf Tegethoff, in 1981, seems to have been the first to introduce the name *Morning* for Kolbe's sculpture in the pavilion (after more than fifty nameless years), perhaps inspired by a now common attribution of one of the two figures in the Ceciliengärten.[21] In 1985 the historian Franz Schulze also picked up on those names, referring, though, to the sculpture at the Barcelona Pavilion as *Evening* (the name now given to the second female sculpture there),[22] but since the large exhibition on Mies at MoMA in 2001 the title *Dawn* or *Morning* has found broad acceptance.[23] Given its placement, it is particularly convincing. The sculpture's position in the small reflecting pool in the northwestern corner secures her the first morning light, when the eastern sun makes her a luminous focal point for the entire structure.[24]

In the weeks immediately after the opening of the 1929 exposition, several writers used Kolbe's sculpture as a prompt to muse on the decoration of modern architecture. According to Swiss architect Hans Bernoulli, sculpture here adopted the "role hitherto played by leafy plants," and thus had to similarly "enrich and enliven" the "surrounding structure [...] and be understood as essential."[25] American critic Helen Appleton Read agreed that "the vitality it imparts to the austerity of the scheme" presented "a brief for the use of sculpture in modern arrangements."[26] Similarly, the architect Paul Bonatz saw at the pavilion "the most attractive example of a constellation of sculpture and architecture. It is inconceivable for a sculpture to have a better environment than the smooth walls, reflective marble surface, and the

9 W. Marziller & Co. to Mies van der Rohe, 30 April 1930, MoMA, MvdR Papers, Barcelona Pavilion, Folder 2010 addition from Eduard Ludwig estate. See also Helmut Reuter, "Georg Kolbe's Sculpture *Morning:* The Return from Barcelona," in Helmut Reuter and Birgit Schulte, *Mies and Modern Living* (Stuttgart: Hatje Cantz, 2008), 282, 283.

10 Jauch, Hübner & Co. to Georg von Schnitzler, 27 November 1930, MoMA, MvdR Papers, Barcelona Pavilion, Folder 2010 addition from Eduard Ludwig estate.

11 Erich Von Kettler to Mies van der Rohe, 5 February 1931, MoMA, MvdR Papers, Barcelona Pavilion, Folder 2010 addition from Eduard Ludwig estate.

12 Alfredo Baeschlin, "Barcelona und seine Weltausstellung," *Deutsche Bauzeitung*, no. 57 (1929): 497–504; and no. 77 (1929): 657–62.

13 Heinrich Simon, "Weltausstellung 1929: Deutsche Abteilung I," *Frankfurter Zeitung*, June 5, 1929, 1.

14 Eduard Foertsch, "Die Weltausstellung in Barcelona," *Vossische Zeitung*, June 11, 1929, 4.

15 Justus Bier, "Mies van der Rohes Reichspavillon in Barcelona," *Die Form* 16, no. 4 (August 15, 1929): 423–30.

16 Jan Maruhn, "Building for Art: Mies van der Rohe as the Architect for Art Collectors," in *Mies in Berlin*, ed. Terence Riley and Barry Bergdoll (New York: Museum of Modern Art, Harry N. Abrams, 2001), 318–23.

17 See Guido Harbers, "Deutscher Reichspavillon in Barcelona auf der Internationalen Ausstellung 1929," *Der Baumeister* 27, no. 11 (November 1929). 421–27; and Kenneth Frampton, *Modern Architecture: A Critical History* (London: Thames and Hudson, 1980), 164–65.

18 See Lenore Kühn, "Deutsche Arbeit auf der Internationalen Ausstellung in Barcelona," *Der Auslandsdeutsche* (June 1929): 400–402; and Vincent Scully Jr., *Modern Architecture: The Architecture of Democracy* (New York: George Braziller, 1961), 27.

19 Wilhelm Pinder, *Georg Kolbe: Werke der letzten Jahre* (Berlin: Rembrandt Verlag, 1937), 67, 75.

20 Claudia Beckmann, "The Statue *Morgen* in the Barcelona Pavilion," 34–51, here 40 (see note 5).

21 Wolf Tegethoff, *Mies van der Rohe: The Villas and Country Houses* (New York: Museum of Modern Art, 1981), 80.

22 Franz Schulze, *Mies van der Rohe* (Chicago: University of Chicago Press, 1985), 155–58. K. Michael Hays, who had in 1984 called Kolbe's statue *Dancer*, adopted Schulze's *Evening* in 1988. K. Michael Hays, "Reply to Jose Quetglas," in *Architectureproduction*, ed. Beatriz Colomina (New York: Princeton Architectural Press, 1988), 240–43, here 240.

23 Detlef Mertins, "Architectures of Becoming: Mies van der Rohe and the Avant-Garde," in *Mies in Berlin*, ed. Terence Riley and Barry Bergdoll (New York: Museum of Modern Art, 2001), 107–33. Robert McCarter and Juhani Pallasmaa instead introduced the name *Sunrise* in 2012. See Robert McCarter and Juhani Pallasmaa, *Understanding Architecture: A Primer on Architecture as Experience* (London: Phaidon, 2012), 103.

24 In great contrast, the central lawn in Berlin's Ceciliengärten runs strictly north-south, and thus both the *Morning* and *Evening* figures on either end receive the same amount of light at all times.

25 Hans Bernoulli, "Der Pavillon des Deutschen Reiches an der internationalen Ausstellung Barcelona 1929," *Das Werk* 16, no. 11 (1929): 350–51.

26 Helen Appleton Read, "Germany at the Barcelona World's Fair," *Arts* (October 1929): 112–13.

pool there."[27] Kolbe himself found his own sculptural style particularly compatible with modern architecture, as it offered him surrounding space rather than just a wall as a backdrop, and he recalled his collaboration with Mies as "mutually enriching."[28]

Among the few hesitant voices was that of Walter Riezler, editor of the Werkbund journal *Form*, who found the "otherwise very beautiful figure" not "truly fitting: it still stemmed from the world of the old space." Unable to square the realism of the sculpture with his own association of "space-time," Riezler argued that Kolbe's sculpture instead represented stasis and merely continued the spatial conditions of the Renaissance and Baroque. Other sculptors—be they Cubists like "Archipenko and his circle" or even naturalists such as "Lehmbruck or [Ernst] Barlach"—were in his view closer to the new "sculptural attitude," reflecting "the new sense of statics in architecture; these figures don't stand solidly on the ground anymore, even where their motive has nothing to do with weightlessness, they seem to be levitating."[29]

Many years later Reyner Banham would also note the striking difference in attitude between the sculpture and its abstract context—something he found so absurd as to be "faintly Dadaist." One would have expected, he explained, something entirely different among such "Mondriaanesque [*sic*] abstract logical consistency."[30] Vincent Scully, at the same time, was unbothered by the sculpture's naturalism, and found that it perfectly completed the pavilion, creating the Constructivist environment around itself and, once seen, controlling the building completely. All the planes seemed to be deriving from it, positioned by it, even as its lifted arm could still be faintly perceived from the far end of the platform. Consequently, the union was optimistic and exact: mobility and enclosure were reconciled; the architecture of a precise but fluid environment was shown as created by the human act. The Barcelona Pavilion was thus the temple, perhaps appropriately temporary, of the International Style, and it embodied the ideal symbols of the European and American components which had gone into its creation.[31]

Rudolf Arnheim, professor of the psychology of art at Harvard, argued similarly in 1975 that by placing the sculpture in "the far corner of the building, the architect stressed the strongly confined rectangularity of the whole design and underscored the diagonal correspondence between the large pool paralleling the longer side of the building near the open entrance and the small, hidden pool marking the building's shortest side at the remote end. As this example shows, not only does the setting determine the place of the object, but inversely the object also modifies the structure of the setting."[32]

In great contrast, Scully's friends Robert Venturi and Denise Scott Brown—who had uttered the battle cry for more "complexity and contradiction" in contemporary architecture—expanded on their argument in 1968 to deplore its lack of integration of art. Where modern architects did use art, they said, it was typically "used to reinforce architectural space at the expense of their own content." For them, a case in point was the Barcelona Pavilion, where the Kolbe statue was simply a "foil to the directed spaces: the message was mainly architectural."[33]

While Scully and Arnheim had arrived at their assessment of the sculpture's role via Stone's photographs, when the architect Paul Rudolph visited the rebuilt pavilion, he found "the dialogue between the sculpture and the building [...] unlike any other dialogue between a work of art and a building that I know of." Rudolph was convinced that Kolbe's sculpture held the key to a full understanding of the pavilion but that Mies had denied us access to this "profound mystery." He explained that "the whole Barcelona Pavilion becomes most clear" from a place inaccessible to us—"where not even fools can tread"—namely "the location of the sculpture": "If you stood where that sculpture stands [...] you would be seeing the layers of transparency and translucency, reflections of the unseen and seen and implied space presented in multiple ways. [...] You would have that multiple view of things all around you–the view the Cubists always talked about."[34]

When the pavilion was rebuilt in 1986, the German government contributed a new bronze cast of the sculpture. This led to a delightful paradox: at the original pavilion Kolbe's statue was the only element that was not truthful to its material appearance (a plaster cast painted to look like bronze), whereas in the rebuilt pavilion (a conjecture based mostly on Sasha Stone's photographs) the Kolbe statue was a bronze cast from the original, and thus closer than anything else to the building's 1929 state.

27 Paul Bonatz, "Ein Baumeister spricht über die Bauplastik," *Wasmuth's Monatshefte für Baukunst und Städtebau* 16, no. 8 (1932): 378.

28 Georg Kolbe, "Neues Bauen gegen Plastik: Ein Bildhauer spricht," *Wasmuth's Monatshefte für Baukunst und Städtebau* 16, no. 8 (1932): 381.

29 Walter Riezler, "Das neue Raumgefühl in bildender Kunst und Musik," in "Vierter Kongress für Ästhetik und allgemeine Kunstwissenschaft, Hamburg, October 7–9, 1930," *Zeitschrift für Ästhetik und allgemeine Kunstwissenschaft*, supplement no. 1 (1931), 179–216.

30 Reyner Banham, "On Trial 6: Mies van der Rohe: Almost Nothing Is Too Much," *The Architectural Review* 132 (1962): 125.

31 Vincent Scully Jr., *Modern Architecture: The Architecture of Democracy* (New York: George Braziller, 1961), 27.

32 Rudolf Arnheim, *The Dynamics of Architectural Form* (Berkeley: University of California Press, 1977), 22–24.

33 Robert Venturi and Denise Scott Brown, "A Significance for A&P Parking Lots or Learning from Las Vegas," *Architectural Forum* 128, no. 2 (March 1968): 36–43, 91.

34 Paul Rudolph and Peter Blake, "Conversation at 23 Beekman Place," (1986) in Roberto de Alba, *Paul Rudolph: the Late Work* (New York: Princeton Architectural Press, 2003), 203–17.

The German Sections

Covering more than 16,000 square meters and featuring 268 exhibiting firms, Germany had the second-largest presence (after France) among the foreign nations.[1] There were twenty-five industrial sections in eight exhibition palaces and a separate pavilion for Germany's electricity industry.[2]

Construction of the sections in the different exhibition halls had begun earlier, and continued, albeit at a slower pace, while construction of the pavilion was halted in March 1929, and both faced similarly dramatic final weeks. While photos show the king and von Schnitzler visiting several sections on opening day, there were conflicting accounts in the press regarding the state of completion of the other German exhibits. While Heinrich Simon, a close friend of Lilly and Georg von Schnitzler, reported in the *Frankfurter Zeitung* that they were "entirely finished, minus a few minor details,"[3] the *Rheinisch Westfälische Zeitung* found them "about to be finished,"[4] and the less reverential *Leipziger Neueste Nachrichten* considered them "far from ready,"[5] while another paper, finally, wrote that one could "only guess" where and what the German stands would be.[6]

Photographs of the German sections were frequently published in 1929, with the fair's *Diario Oficial* even dedicating a special issue to them.[7] Germany's own official catalogue, employing elegant sans serif typography (probably designed by Mies's old friend, Gerhard Severain) was printed in Berlin and appeared in early July.[8] **FIG. 1** Its map indicating the locations of the various sections was the only official publication that identified the site of the German Pavilion. **FIG. 2**

Many reviewers noted the continuity between the clarity of the pavilion and the unified appearance of the German sections.[9] Following a suggestion by Ernst Raemisch,[10] a high-ranking manager of the German silk industry, von Schnitzler and Mies had reserved the right to veto any individual exhibit, and to determine the look of each industry's section—its overall design, lettering, and signage (designed by Gerhard Severain).[11] This meant that every company had to forego its established corporate identity, and instead adopt the uniform appearance that signaled the common quality standards of a product "Made in Germany." In Barcelona, only the Swiss sections, designed by Hans Hoffman, displayed a similar degree of discipline and modernity.[12] As many reviewers noted, the tubular steel furniture designed by Mies and Reich—in particular the MR 10 and MR 20 chairs (and some of the MR 1 stools)—was another distinguishing common

1 France occupied 22,000 square meters. See Stéphane Lauzanne, "A l'Exposition de Barcelone," *Le Matin*, June 1, 1929, 1.

2 For a brief description of the section, see Dr. Maiwald, "Alemania en la Exposición Internacional de Barcelona," *Berliner Tageblatt* 7 (monthly Spanish edition, June 1929): 2; and "La aportación de Alemania a la Exposicion de Barcelona," *Diario Oficial de la Exposición Internacional de Barcelona 1929* 1, no. 34 (October 26, 1929).

3 Heinrich Simon, "Weltausstellung 1929: Deutsche Abteilung I," *Frankfurter Zeitung*, June 5, 1929, 1.

4 Dr. Paul Joseph Cremers, "Deutschland auf der Weltaustellung Barcelona," *Rheinisch Westfälische Zeitung*, May 28, 1929. See also Paul Joseph Cremers, "Deutschland auf der Weltausstellung Barcelona," *Essener Anzeiger*, May 29, 1929. Cremers pointed out that most other sections were still "almost uninhabited."

5 "Der deutsche Pavillon in Barcelona: Einweihung der deutschen Abteilung," *Leipziger Neueste Nachrichten*, June 1, 1929, 5.

6 Rudolf Friedmann, "Die Internationale Ausstellung in Barcelona," *Der Deutsche*, May 29, 1929; and "Die Deutsche Ausstellung," *Hannoversches Tageblatt*, May 28, 1929.

7 Maiwald, "La aportación de Alemania a la Exposición de Barcelona" (see note 2).

8 *Exposición Internacional de Barcelona 1929: Catalogo Oficial de la Sección Alemana* (Berlin: Reichsdruckerei, 1929). The guide was also published in German; see *Internationale Ausstellung: Barcelona 1929: Deutsche Abteilung* (Berlin: Reichsdruckerei, 1929). Since the catalogue contains one of the photographs taken for Berliner Bild-Bericht, we know that it could only have been produced after the last week of June, when those photographs were taken.

9 See Walther Genzmer, "Der Deutsche Reichspavillon auf der Internationalen Ausstellung Barcelona," *Zentralblatt der Bauverwaltung* 49, no. 34 (August 21, 1929): 541–46, here 542. See also the Catalan critic Rafael Benet: "Regarding the applied arts, none has seduced me more than the presentation of the sections of the German industries. A good example to avoid in the future is the more individualistic presentation, often wretched and senseless, which is typical of our own products." "El parer de la crítica contemporània: Rafael Benet," *D'Aci i d'Allà*, Special Edition Exposició Internacional Barcelona 1929 (December 1929): 105–6. One exception is the report by a local critic: "It should be emphasized that Germany has imposed a unity of style–exaggeratedly innovative–to all its installations and all its architectures. It is the most agonizing grief of the exhibition," P. Calzina, "Les arts decoratives a Montjuïc," *D'Aci i d'Allà* (December 1929): 80–83, 126, quote 81. See also the recent essay by Laura Martinez de Guerenu, "The Sequence of Mies van der Rohe in Barcelona: The German Pavilion as Part of a Much Larger Industrial Presence," *Docomomo* 56, no. 1 (2017): 57–63.

10 Ernst Raemisch to Mies van der Rohe, 21 June 1928, HoeA, WaB 1927–1928.

11 Regarding the collaboration between Mies and Severain, see Dietrich Neumann, "Haus Ryder in Wiesbaden und die Zusammenarbeit von Gerhard Severain und Ludwig Mies van der Rohe," *Architectura* 2 (2006): 199–219.

12 "Die Schweizer Abteilung der internationalen Ausstellung Barcelona 1929: Architekt Hans Hofmann," *Das Werk: Architektur und Kunst = L'oeuvre: architecture et art* 16, no. 11 (1929): 344–49.

1

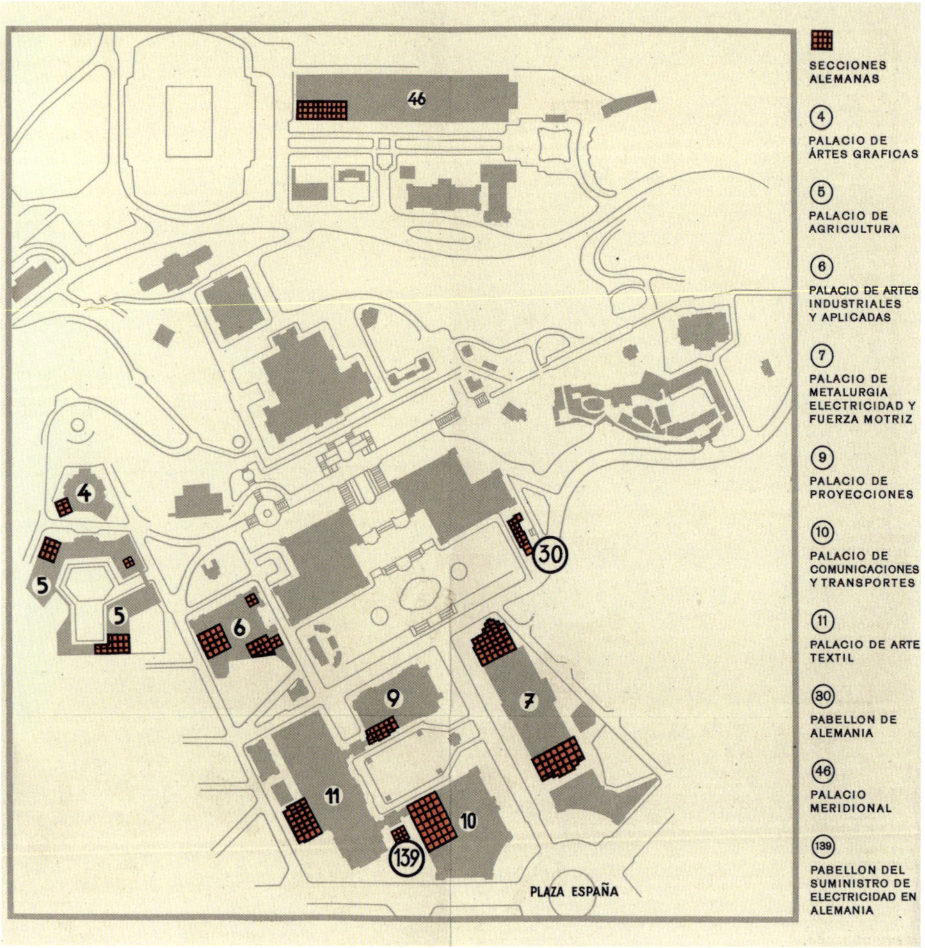

2

1 Catalogue of Germany's participation at the Barcelona International Exposition, 1929

2 Germany's representation in different exhibition palaces at the Barcelona International Exposition, 1929

3 Floor plan of the Palace of Electricity, Motors and Chemical Industries at the Barcelona International Exposition, 1929. German machinery was displayed on the right (northern) side; the information section was upstairs on a balcony.

4 IG Farben section at the Barcelona International Exposition, 1929

signifier of all the German sections. The straight and semicircular forms of the nickel-plated steel tubes, with leather or cloth for the seat and backrest, seemed to confirm an image of a Germany associated with hygiene, lightness, sobriety, and elegance.[13] These pieces were much commented on and praised by visitors, whose delighted surprise led to designations such as "steel snakes" or "reptilian chairs."[14]

In creating this unifying visual language, Reich and Mies applied many of the solutions they had developed for the 1927 Werkbund exhibition in Stuttgart or the Café Samt & Seide in Berlin,[15] such as white linoleum floors and backlit canvas ceilings, black letters and graphics on white backgrounds, and freestanding panels with large photographs. Glass and wall display cases, tables, panels, and structures for hanging fabrics were all designed by Lilly Reich.[16]

The Palace of Electricity, Motors and Chemical Industries, with its heavy concrete vaults and skylights, was located on the main axis of the exhibition grounds, the Avenida Maria Cristina, close to the German pavilion. At one end of the building was the chemistry section.[17] Unsurprisingly, the products of von Schnitzler's

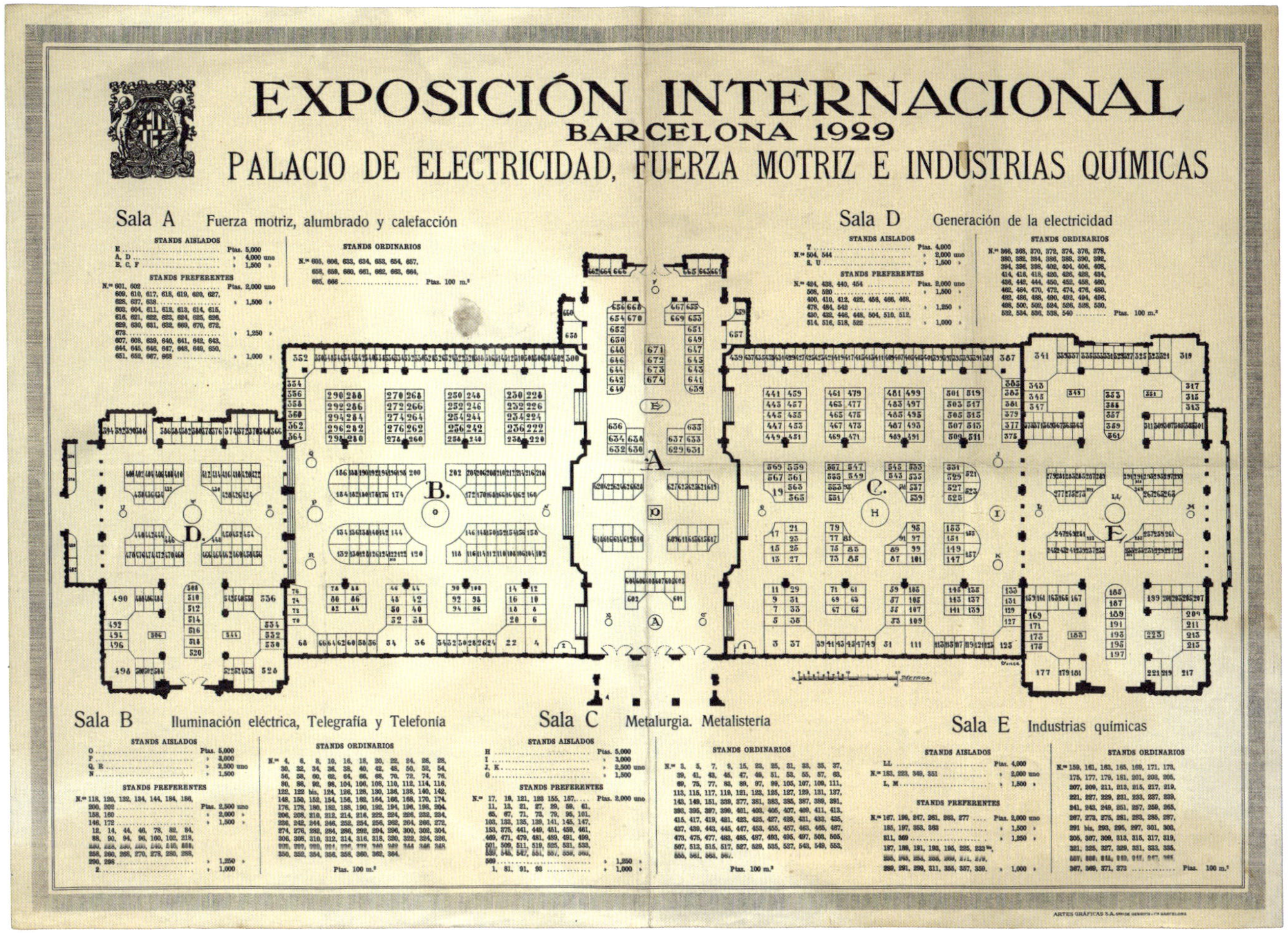

3

4

13 Raimond Vayreda, "Els moderns seients metàllics," *D'Ací i d'Allà* 19, no. 151 (July 1930): 226–27; Francisco Marroquín, "El Pabellón de Alemania en la exposición de Barcelona," *ABC*, January 25, 1930, 13–14.

14 Marta Romaní [Anna Murià], "Sillas Siglo XX," *Diario Oficial de la Exposición Internacional de Barcelona 1929* 1, no. 35 (November 2, 1929). See also Josep Mainar, "El mobiliari a l'Exposició (I)," *Mirador* 2, no. 61 (March 27, 1930): 8.

15 Wallis Miller, "Mies and Exhibitions," in *Mies in Berlin*, ed. Terence Riley and Barry Bergdoll (New York: Museum of Modern Art, 2001), 338–49.

16 See Genzmer, "Der Deutsche Reichspavillon," 545 (see note 9). See also Matilda McQuaid, *Lilly Reich, Designer and Architect* (New York: MoMA, Harry N. Abrams, 1996); and Miller, "Mies and Exhibitions" (see note 15).

17 For a description of the exhibitors, see S. de Llinas, "Apuntes para mi archivo (VI): El Palacio de Metalurgia, Electricidad y Fuerza Motriz," *La Vanguardia*, June 27, 1929, 8.

OFICINA DE INFORMACION
ALEMANIA
DEFRIES
BERLIN
ALFRED H SCHÜTTE
TOQUE EL BOTON
MAQUETA
DEMONSTRATIVA DE
EL SISTEMA Y TEORIA
DEL PROFESOR
JUNKERS

5

5 German machinery section at the Barcelona International Exposition, 1929. The German information section on the balcony is visible in the distance.

6 Information section about Germany on the second floor of the Palace of Electricity, Motors and Chemical Industries, Barcelona International Exposition, 1929

6

company, IG Farben, featured prominently and that section was ready to receive visitors on opening day. **FIG. 4** Black-and-white photographs don't do justice to what must have amounted to veritable symphonies of color, as Lilly Reich had arranged the company's pigments, lacquers, and paints in chromatically sequenced geometric fields. The effect was heightened by the evenly distributed light from the suspended canvas ceiling above.

At the opposite end of the palace were located the twenty-five exhibitors of the German machinery section. Heavy machines sat like sculptures on an improbably white linoleum floor, as if to illustrate AEG director Paul Jordan's famous advice to Peter Behrens: "An engine should look like a birthday present."[18] **FIG. 5** To place the company names near their exhibits, a barely perceptible system of suspended wires created the illusion of letters floating in space. The German information section was also

18 Henning Rogge, "Ein Motor muss aussehen wie ein Geburtstagsgeschenk," in *Industriekultur: Peter Behrens und die AEG 1907–1914*, ed. Tilmann Buddensieg (Berlin: Gebr. Mann, 1979), 91–126.

25 DAIMLER BENZ AG STUTTGART
ROBERT BOSCH AG STUTTGART
FAKRA
Kraftwagen

7

8

7 German cars in the Transportation section, International Exposition, Barcelona, 1929

8 German agricultural machinery in the Palace of Communications and Transportation at the Barcelona International Exposition, 1929

located in this northern section, upstairs on a balcony, to be reached via a narrow staircase on either end. It was made visible from below by a long row of monochrome photographs of German landscapes and tourist landmarks (among them, Trier's Roman city gate, Porta Nigra, and Neuschwanstein Castle). The space also featured MR chairs on a sisal carpet, an information desk, and two tables with German newspapers and information brochures. **FIG. 6**

The same suspended lettering technique spelled out "Daimler Benz" and "Adam Opel" above the displayed cars, airplanes, and boats in the Palace of Communications and Transportation across the street. Fittingly, this had a much lighter structure, with thin metal piers carrying several barrel-vaulted bays. Here, the German section was surrounded by enormous photographic murals up to 28 meters long showing all modes of transportation, by car, plane, train, suspended tram, zeppelin, and ocean liner.[19] **FIG. 7** German agricultural machinery was shown both in an indoors and outdoors section.

One of the most elaborate installations in the adjacent Palace of Textile Arts was the German silk[20] exhibit, which doubled as a reception area.[21] Here, the formal language of the Barcelona Pavilion was in full display, as Reich and Mies created a space within a space, composed of walls with built-in display cases that enclosed a central square, punctuated by four freestanding panels of clear or colored glass that appear to have had the same dimensions as those at the pavilion and might originally have been manufactured for it. **FIGS. 9, 10** A semicircle of black glass, reaching halfway to the ceiling, foreshadowed the wall of Makassar wood of the living room of the Villa Tugendhat, which Mies was designing at the same time. IG Farben also presented some of its products in this area.[22] The Bauhaus Dessau showed fabrics for curtains, wallpaper, and covers for divans.[23] German toys (in the section for industrial arts) were admired "for their

19 Maiwald, "Alemania en la Exposición Internacional de Barcelona" (see note 2).
20 On the relationship between Mies and the silk industry, see Christiane Lange, *Ludwig Mies van der Rohe: Architektur für die Seidenindustrie* (Berlin: Nicolai, 2011); on the Deutsche Seide (1929), see especially 83–98.
21 On the second day of German Week, a tea party was held in honor of the arrival of the battleship *Königsberg*, and on another occasion, there was a party with jazz music for industry representatives; See "Semana Alemana: Te en la 'Seda Alemana,'" *La Vanguardia*, October 22, 1929, 11.
22 *Exposición Internacional de Barcelona 1929*, 50, 55 (see note 8).
23 Ibid., 50, 55.

10

9

9, 10 German silk exhibit in the Palace of Textile Arts, Barcelona International Exposition, 1929

11 Hacker Pschorr Brewery section, Palace of Agriculture, Barcelona International Exposition, 1929

12 Display case of the German publishing industry, Graphic Arts Center, Barcelona International Exposition, 1929

pedagogical value and perfect production,"[24] particularly the metal constructor sets of the Märklin Company (represented by an elaborate ship model with a loading crane), Margarete Steiff's famous teddy bears,[25] Anchor building blocks, and Bauhaus toys.[26] These products were placed on white plinths or display cases attached to the freestanding walls. In the German section on farm products, machinery, and beer in the Palace of Agriculture,[27] Munich's Hacker Bräu showed hundreds of beer bottles on parallel shelves (also designed by Mies), as if on a conveyor belt in a modern bottling plant. **FIG. 11**

The German publishing industry was represented in the Graphic Arts Center, between freestanding metal panels, on exhibition tables, and in glass display cases.[28] **FIG. 12** It was this subject matter which made the journalist Anna Murià finally abandon the *Diario Oficial*'s usual line of supportive praise to express her displeasure with the uniform appearance of all German sections: "This polished and smooth room—like all the German rooms of our exposition—troubles us; the warmth of the letters and the art is not enough to stave off the coldness of the metals and glass and white walls; the poetry books inspire pity," she wrote. "They seem like prisoners inside those glass cases typically used to store scalpels. Only the machines seem satisfied [and] in their element."[29]

The second pavilion that Mies designed for the Barcelona fair—the Electric Utilities Pavilion, with an interior featuring large models, relief maps, photographs, and graphics—remains something of a mystery.[30] **FIG. 12** No drawings of it have survived and only two photographs of the exterior exist. The building is hardly mentioned in the voluminous correspondence. Initially, the German electrical industries were supposed to be represented in the Palace of Electricity, Motors and Chemical Industries on Avenida María Cristina.[31] The decision to create a separate building only came late in December 1928 as the result of a compli-

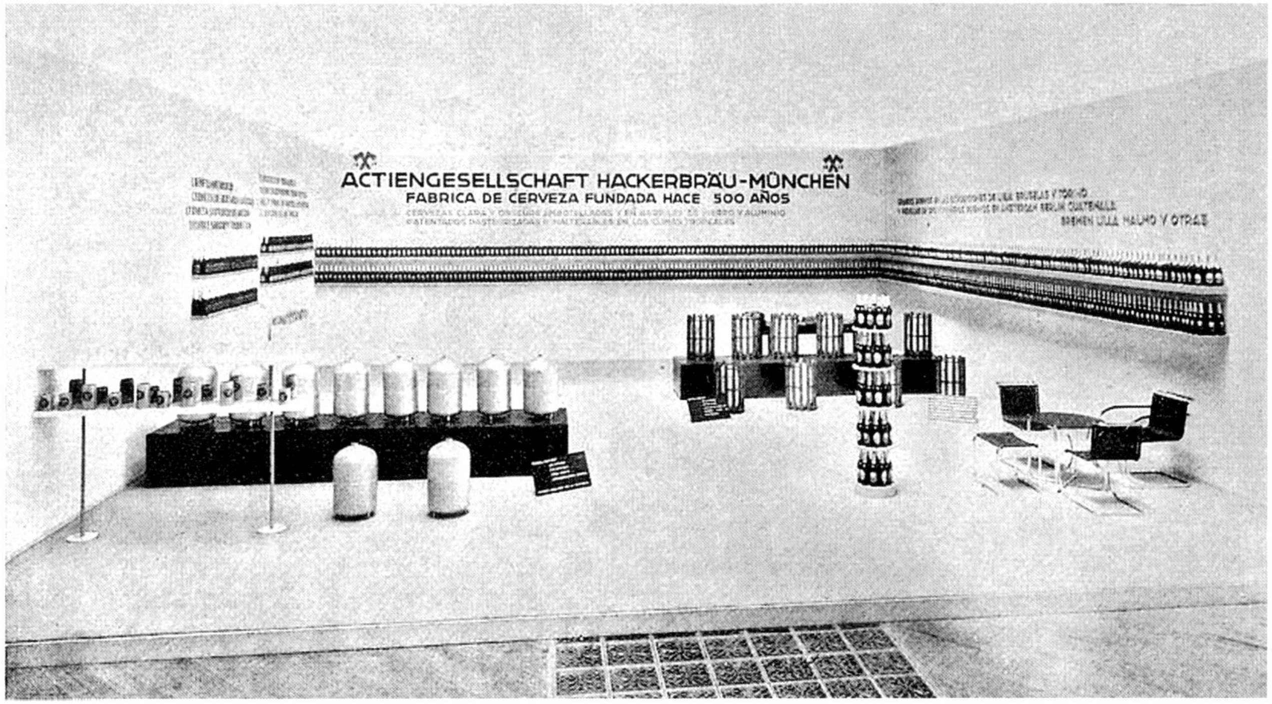

11

12

24 The official world's fair publication dedicated an article to the German toys, see: Marta Romaní [pseudonym of Anna Murià], "Los juguetes alemanes," *Diario Oficial de la Exposición Internacional de Barcelona 1929* 1, no. 36 (November 9, 1929).

25 Ibid.; see also S. de Llinas, "Apuntes para mi archivo (XVI): Palacio de las Artes Industriales," *La Vanguardia*, August 22, 1929, 4.

26 *Exposición Internacional de Barcelona 1929*, 65, 69 (see note 8).

27 Epifanio de Fortuny, "Alemania en el Palacio de Agricultura," *Diario Oficial de la Exposición Internacional de Barcelona 1929* 1, no. 34 (October 26, 1929).

28 For a view on the books, see "Libros alemanes sobre España," *Diario Oficial de la Exposición Internacional de Barcelona* 1, no. 34 (October 26, 1929).

29 Marta Romaní [Anna Murià], "Una muestra en un Palacio," *Diario Oficial de la Exposición Internacional de Barcelona 1929* 1, no. 23 (August 17, 1929). The connection between the materials used in the sections and the hygiene was also observed by the Catalan writer Josep Maria de Sagarra in his description of the pavilion.

30 Our account complements an essay by Laura Lizondo Sevilla. See Laura Lizondo Sevilla, "Mies's Opaque Cube: The Electric Utilities Pavilion at the 1929 Barcelona International Exposition," *Journal of the Society of Architectural Historians* 76, no. 2 (June 2017): 197–217. She provides excellent reconstruction drawings of the pavilion's interior layout. Independently, Valentín Trillo Martinez provided reconstruction drawings in his book, *Mies en Barcelona: Arquitectura, representación y memoria* (Seville: UEUS, Editorial Universidad de Sevilla, 2017). See also Matthias Horstmann, "Der elektrische Barcelona-Pavillon: Bildarchitekturen 1929–Berliner Riesenfotos in Barcelona," *Die Vierte Wand*, no. 7 (May 2017): 80–85.

31 Santiago Trias to Enrique Domínguez Rodiño, 6 December 1928, AMAB, Z102, Box 47132, Rodiño file, folder 1928.

14

13

13 Aerial view of the German Electric Utilities pavilion, Barcelona International Exposition, 1929

14 German Electric Utilities pavilion at the Barcelona International Exposition, 1929

cated trading of space with the Spanish, who needed more room in the exhibition hall for their own installation.[32] The building went up in Plaza de la Luz, a small space behind the Palace of Communications and Transportation, but clearly visible to anyone arriving from the city center by tram on the Gran Via. **FIG. 13** Above it rose the Torre de la Luz, mentioned before as the proposed site for a German light installation by the silk, glass, and electrical industries. The pavilion was constructed as a white cube, about 15 meters tall on a 20 by 20 meter footprint, and rose straight from the ground, without any base or plinth.[33] Its facade was similarly unadorned, and was interrupted only by the horizontal cutout of its entrance. **FIG. 14** Above this opening, black letters announced the Pabellon del Suministro de Electricidad en Alemania (Pavilion of the Electric Utilities of Germany), while its sides showed four protruding pilasters supporting the roof's steel structure, with twelve square ventilation openings at the upper edge.

Design and construction unfolded at the same hectic pace as the official pavilion, with numerous night and weekend shifts. Late in the process, Mies developed an ambitious new tectonic concept which required a tripling of the planned foundations. He changed the building's structural system from "a simple construction of brick walls and ordinary cement mixture" with a straightforward wooden roof (presumably carried by the outer brick walls) to a steel exoskeleton with U-section beams, brick, and Portland cement sheathing, and a "most complicated" steel roof structure, which was installed the night before the opening and sprang a leak as soon as the first drops of rain fell.[34] Mies had initially estimated the costs at 40–50,000 Reichsmark, while the Spanish builder Sociedad Metropolitana de Construcción was less optimistic, proposing 65,540 Reichsmark. Both estimates were way off, and final costs were closer to 140,000 Reichsmark.[35]

According to Mies, the Berlin architect Fritz Schüler was responsible for the interior design, and supervised the pavilion's execution.[36] But little is known about the role of the photographer Wilhelm Niemann (the owner of the Berliner Bild-Bericht agency), who later claimed that he was the author of the photographic murals inside and supervised the construction site from March 1929 onward.[37] The models and photomurals were fabricated in Germany and shipped to Spain just in time for the opening.[38] Two of the surviving photographs of the interior were taken by Sasha Stone for Berliner Bild-Bericht; the three others are by an unknown photographer for the journal *Iberica*.[39] **FIGS. 15, 16** The interior was illuminated with electric lights suspended above a canvas ceiling 10 meters above the floor. Thanks to a detailed description in *La Vanguardia*,[40] we know there was a large landscape model (8 by 6 meters) in the center, and additional models

32 See Dr. Maiwald to Georg von Schnitzler, 21 December 1928; and Erich von Kettler to Georg von Schnitzler, 9 January 1929, HoeA, WaB 1927–1928. Initially it was planned to also display models from the German aviation industry.

33 Two testimonies differ on this point: a journalist from *La Vanguardia* speaks of 13.3 meters, while a German reporter noted 15 meters. Both agree on the plan dimensions as 20 by 20 meters, or 400 square meters. See S. de Llinás, "Apuntes para mi archivo (XIX): Pabellón de Suministros Eléctricos de Alemania," *La Vanguardia*, September 1, 1929, 6; and Willy Lesser, "Der Deutsche Anteil an der Weltausstellung in Barcelona," *Technische Rundschau*, no. 30 (1929); quoted in Miller, "Mies and Exhibitions," 344 (see note 15).

34 Elektrowerke to Georg von Schnitzler, 10 July 1929, HoeA, WaB 1929–1930.

35 Erich von Kettler to Georg von Schnitzler, 9 January 1929, HoeA, WaB 1927–1928; Sociedad Metropolitana de Construcción Barcelona to Georg von Schnitzler, 2 April 1930, MoMA, MvdR Papers, Barcelona Pavilion, folder with newly purchased material (Reuters), no pagination.

36 See Fritz Schüler and Mies van der Rohe correspondence March 13 and 18, 1933. MoMA, MvdR Papers, Barcelona Pavilion, Folder 10. Schüler worked for the building department of the Berlin electricity company Elektrowerke AG. This information was kindly provided by Matthias Horstmann, doctoral student at Basel University.

37 Interview with Wilhelm Niemann, Werkbund Archiv Berlin, ca. 1979, 17–18. Thanks to Matthias Horstmann, who kindly provided the text. According to Horstmann, the murals were probably made by Niemann, based on photographs by Sasha Stone and produced by a Berlin company called Blum. E-mail from Horstmann to the author, January 7, 2017.

38 Dr. Maiwald to Santiago Trias, 29 December 1928, HoeA, WaB 1927–1928. Georg von Schnitzler's files contain an anonymous report about the opening with many candid observations ("Bericht über meinen Besuch der Internationalen Weltausstellung Barcelona 1929, May 19, 1929," HoeA, WaB 1929–1930; the author was probably a General Director Kauffmann); see correspondence Georg von Schnitzler and Elektrowerke 10 July and 22 August 1929. HoeA, WaB 1929

39 "Pabellones extranjeros en la Exposición de Barcelona" *Iberica*, no. 802 (November 1929): 290–93 (photographs 293).

40 Llinás, "Apuntes para mi archivo (XIX)," 6 (see note 33).

on each wall. The central display consisted of a contoured map of Germany, with small lightbulbs indicating different types of energy production. Another model showed a section of Berlin's urban space as it was served by the famous Klingenberg power station. Two additional models contrasted conventional and renewable energies, with a coal-fired plant (Golpa Zschornewitz) and a hydroelectric dam (Edertal near Kassel). Three walls were covered by large photo murals on square plywood panels, whose central motifs linked them to the model in front.[41] One showed an assemblage of Berlin buildings in the style of Paul Citroën's famous metropolis collages. On leaving, the visitor would face the entrance wall, with graphics and statistics about energy consumption by different user groups in Germany. The floor was again covered in white linoleum, and a few of Mies' tubular steel "MR" chairs, stools, and a table are visible in one of the photographs.

It is hard not to see this building as the deliberate opposite of the Barcelona Pavilion. There, Mies celebrated a complex spatial sequence, different qualities of natural light through the interplay of inner and outer spaces, and varied textures and colors of materials. The Electric Utilities Pavilion, on the other hand, was a building in black and white, with only one tall room, lit artificially from above, with a sequence of composite photo murals replacing any visible connection to the outside.[42] It is also Mies's first building in white stucco—which had become the lingua franca of the modern movement—as well as the first time that he had used an exoskeleton, something that would only reappear much later in the US at the Illinois Institute of Technology's Crown Hall and the Art Museum in Houston. The only common elements of the two pavilions are their two rows of four columns on each side. Somewhat strangely, given the building's daring appearance, it warrants barely a mention in all of the fair's assorted newspaper and journal articles, with the only recorded epithet being a Spanish critic's description of it as a "strange cubic pavilion" featuring an "excess of sobriety in the modern Teutonic style."[43]

Economically devastated after the First World War, Germany nonetheless had the most advanced network of urban and rural electrification in Europe. For visitors from Spain, where cities were still widely illuminated by gas lamps, Mies's mysterious white cube promised a veritable journey into the future. In this sense, a comparison with the Spanish Palace of Electricity and Light is instructive. There we see a playful Renaissance palace embellished with allegorical women clutching lightning bolts to represent electricity. Of course, the entire international exposition—or rather its European section in Barcelona—was a demonstration of the wonders of electricity, of sparkling color floodlights and luminous fountains. The contrast to Mies's mysterious white Kaaba could hardly have been more didactic. The joyous display of electricity's magic met the cool and controlled mastery of its power.[44]

15

16

15, 16 Pavillon of the German Electrical Industries at the Barcelona International Exposition 1929. Ludwig Mies van der Rohe. Design of displays inside: Fritz Schüler, photomontages on the walls: Wilhelm Niemann.
Photographs: Sasha Stone

41 Genzmer, "Der Deutsche Reichspavillon," 546 (see note 9).

42 Miller, "Mies and Exhibitions," 344 (see note 15). See also Dietrich Neumann, "'Wallpaper with Arctic Landscapes': Mies van der Rohe's Patents for Wallpaper Design and Printing Technology 1937–1950," in *Mies and Modern Living: Interiors, Furniture, Photography*, ed. Helmut Reuter and Birgit Schulte (Berlin: Hatje Cantz, 2008), 264–79.

43 Eliseo Sanz Balza, *Notas de un visitante* (Barcelona: Imp. Olympia-Pascual Yuste, 1930), 140.

44 It was reported several times that the Spanish delegation showed particular interest in this pavilion and its exhibits, and several papers noted a dismissive gesture by the king as he pointed at the "Polish corridor" on Germany's map—a result of the Treaty of Versailles. See "Bericht über meinen Besuch der Internationalen Weltausstellung Barcelona 1929" (see note 38) and Elektrowerke to von Schnitzler, 10 July 1929 (see note 34).

Events at the Pavilion

Thanks to extensive coverage in the contemporary press, newly discovered photographs, and film footage, we have a good idea who attended and what happened at the opening ceremony on Monday morning, May 27, 1929. At least five different Catalan photojournalists and two documentary filmmakers were on site, as well as several German journalists, but apparently no German photographers.[1]

The king, the queen, their three grown children, and many high-ranking politicians—such as the dictator Primo de Rivera and Barón de Viver, the mayor of Barcelona—arrived by car at 11 a.m. and were greeted at the steps of the pavilion by Lilly and Georg von Schnitzler and by the German ambassador in Madrid, Count Johannes von Welczeck. Onlookers crowded into the space between the cars and the Ionic columns across the street. **FIG. 1** In one photograph we can identify Ludwig Mies van der Rohe in the left foreground, clutching his top hat and gloves against his chest.[2] **FIG. 2** But perceptive visitors would have noticed a glaring absence: no high-ranking government representatives had made the trip from Berlin. "As to be expected, we have received almost nothing but rejections of our invitations," a resigned von Schnitzler noted three weeks before the opening.[3] Clearly, the financial complications and bitter discussions had taken their toll. The fact that the building was presented as if it were von Schnitzler's pavilion, rather than that of the German government, was not lost on the handful of lower-level officials who had come to Barcelona for the opening:[4] "Our role as representatives of the German government was not an easy one to play, as it was von Schnitzler, not us, who commanded all the funds,"[5] one of them grumbled.

The opening itself seems to have been a short and informal affair, certainly compared to the shows put on by other countries. The Italians, for example, mustered a guard of honor, a military band, and a chorus of schoolchildren,[6] while the French had "brought two ministers, one general and a hundred fashion models," and held a "glamorous party, where money and Champagne flowed freely," as a German critic noted, barely concealing his envy.[7] Georg von Schnitzler and the king delivered their remarks inside the pavilion to a small audience, all seated on Mies's MR chairs, installed specifically for the ceremony. The royal couple then signed a leather-bound book of honor, which probably rested on the square, black glass-topped table next to the onyx wall, and proceeded on a brief tour of the building.[8]

In his carefully worded remarks, von Schnitzler emphasized the general "modesty" of the displays, which he framed as a response to the "grave economic worries" and "hard times" at home. This tone was well received by reporters, who would present several of his statements as pledges of Germany's new mind-set:

1 Four of the Catalan photojournalists were Josep Branguli i Soler (1879-1945), Gabriel Casas i Galobardes (1892-1973), Carlos Pérez de Rozas Masdeu (1892-1954), and Josep Maria Sagarra i Plana (1885-1959); there was also one unidentified photographer who signed his name "Foto Maymó," and two documentary filmmakers with movie cameras. One of the images from the opening was published in the *World's Fair Journal*, but no details are known about the photographer, apart from the fact that he worked for the newspapers *ABC* and *La Vanguardia*.

2 The photographer was Josep Branguli (1879–1945). On the remarkable family of Catalan photographers, Branguli and his sons, Joaquim and Xavier, see *Branguli* (Madrid: Fundación Telefónica, 2010).

3 Georg von Schnitzler to Dr. Maiwald, 6 May 1929, HoeA, WaB 1929–1930.

4 The German delegation arrived on May 16 and consisted of Georg von Schnitzler and his wife, Dr. Posse of the Ministry of Economic Affairs, Dr. Mathies, Dr. Windel, and Dr. Wagemann of the Foreign Ministry. "La representación de Alemania," *La Vanguardia*, May 17, 1929, 8.

5 Legationsrat Windel to the Ministerial Council in Berlin, 28 May 1929, BArchL, Ausstellung Barcelona, AA, Abteilung II, R 9.01, 40029, 188. The *Deutsche Allgemeine Zeitung* reported similarly that von Schnitzler was invited to the opening banquet, but not Ambassador von Welczek; "Deutschland auf der Weltausstellung," *Deutsche Allgemeine Zeitung*, May 27, 1929, 2.

6 "L'Esposizione di Barcellona del 1929: l'inaugurazione del padiglione italiano," https://www.youtube.com/watch?v=OEbWEVuiguU

7 Eduard Foertsch, "Die Weltausstellung in Barcelona," *Vossische Zeitung*, June 11, 1929, 4.

8 "Der deutsche Pavillon in Barcelona. Die feierliche Eröffnung," *Münchner Neueste Nachrichten*, June 4, 1929, 15.

1

1 Opening of the German Pavilion, May 27, 1929: Georg von Schnitzler welcomes King Alfonso XIII and Queen Victoria Eugenie of Spain.

2 Opening of the German Pavilion, May 27, 1929: Mies van der Rohe on the left, top hat in hand

3 Opening of the German Pavilion, May 27, 1929: Georg von Schnitzler, King Alfonso XIII, Lilly von Schnitzler (in white)

In a country less favored by the sun than yours, where the winters are long and dark, and there are many rainy days, a new spirit of the age has emerged, which aims to collect and radiate as much light and clarity as the natural conditions permit. We reject anything that is labyrinthine, obscure, overwrought, and complicated, we want to act clearly, and we want to surround ourselves with things that are clear, straight, and pure. Utmost simplicity has to be accompanied by the deepest profundity. The hard times that we have gone through have led us to consider simplicity as essential and to reject anything that is unnecessary as superfluous. […] We do not want to summarize our program with a catchphrase, but please consider it the expression of our serious desire to be absolutely truthful, giving expression to the spirit of a new era, whose essence will be sincerity.[9]

Von Schnitzler called Mies "one of the most outstanding and original architects of the new generation," but referred to the pavilion only obliquely, sounding almost apologetic when he wondered if showing "such simple forms under your southern blue sky, amid your luscious vegetation, might have been risky. Perhaps everything we show here seems overly simple and inadvertently ascetic."

That latter point, in particular, must have struck some in the audience as rather perplexing, as they were surrounded by expansive walls of costly polished marble, shining nickel-plated metal columns and enormous glass walls. Schnitzler himself was not yet aware of the full cost of the pavilion. The last estimate provided by Mies had been around 150,000 Reichsmark.[10]

In his speech von Schnitzler avoided any specific references to Germany's role during the First World War, or its young and fragile democracy. He was mindful of his own political convictions and considerate of the host country, where the monarchy was tolerating Primo de Rivera's military dictatorship. King Alfonso XIII responded with a few brief remarks of his own. He thanked von Schnitzler and somewhat teasingly informed his audience that he "had driven by the pavilion every day for the past week, waiting for it to be finished." He finally realized, he said, "that the Germans had delayed the opening of the pavilion on purpose, in order to show off their uncanny technical and improvisational skills to a world audience."[11]

After the ceremony the visitors walked through the pavilion. A short newsreel clip shows the group moving eastward along the small pool and past the Kolbe statue. The king and von Schnitzler are seen in deep conversation, while Mies appears alongside the queen, Victoria Eugenie of Battenberg, a granddaughter of Queen Victoria and a German-speaker, just like her husband. A cluster of images shows the main group standing between the

2

3

9 "La sección alemana en la Exposición Internacional de Barcelona 1929," *Diario Oficial de la Exposición Internacional Barcelona 1929* 1, no. 10 (May 25, 1929): 18. A German version of the text is quoted: "Bericht über meinen Besuch der Internationalen Weltausstellung Barcelona 1929," anonymous typescript, HoeA, WaB 1929–1930 and can be found in the personal papers of Georg von Schnitzler at the family archive at Stiebar castle in Austria.

10 In July, some two months after the opening, von Schnitzler received an updated figure of 200,000 Reichsmark, but it was only at the end of September that he learned the true extent of the expenditure on the pavilion: 338,422.18 Reichsmark. Mies van der Rohe to Georg von Schnitzler, 28 September 1929, MoMA, MvdR Papers, Barcelona Pavilion, Folder 2010 addition from Eduard Ludwig estate.

11 Lilly von Schnitzler, "Weltausstellung Barcelona," *Der Querschnitt* 9, no. 8 (August 1929), 582–84. Lilly von Schnitzler's paraphrasing of the king's remarks differs slightly from the official transcript. As she was present at the ceremony, her account of the king's impromptu and somewhat mocking words seems credible, in particular as the king was known for spontaneous and unrehearsed remarks. See the official account in "Inauguración del Pabellón y Sección de Alemania," *Diario Oficial de la Exposición Internacional Barcelona 1929* 1, no. 12 (June 2, 1929).

4

5

large pool and the opal glass wall with a crowd of attentive spectators behind them. **FIGS. 3, 4** Here, Mies is seen in conversation with Alfonso XIII. After this tour, the visitors proceeded along the pool toward the space in front of the (as yet unfinished) small office building for a glass of Champagne and some canapés. **FIG. 5** The group then retreated back to their cars in order to tour the other German exhibits in the exhibition palaces. Their itinerary included visits to the Palace of Electricity, Motors and Chemical Industries, where the products of IG Farben were prominently displayed, as well as the Palace of Communications and Transportation, Mies's Electric Utilities pavilion, and the German products at the Palace of Textile Arts. **FIGS. 6, 7**

More speeches and toasts were delivered later that night at a lavish banquet in the ballroom of the city's Hotel Ritz. Count Welczeck read out a telegram from the German president, Paul von Hindenburg, to the Spanish king, which was met with enthusiastic applause.[12] Primo de Rivera then gave a short speech, and both national anthems were played. Georg von Schnitzler's remarks were next, followed by the Marqués de Foronda, director of the exhibition, and newfound friend and admirer of Lilly von Schnitzler—"whose blue eyes reflected the Spanish sky"—whom he thanked for constantly defending "our country in German periodicals when Spain was maligned as being riotous and disorderly."[13] Lilly was honored in the next issue of the *Diario*

6

7

4 Opening of the German Pavilion, May 27, 1929: Mies van der Rohe and King Alfonso XIII

5 Opening of the German Pavilion, May 27, 1929: Mies van der Rohe in the center

6 King Alfonso in the German Automobile exhibit

7 King Alfonso and Georg von Schnitzler touring the exhibition grounds. Mies van der Rohe is visible behind King Alfonso.

12 Johannes Bernhard Graf von Welczeck was the German ambassador in Madrid from 1925 to 1936. Together with German naval officer and spymaster Wilhelm Canaris, he brokered a secret agreement between Germany, Spain, and the Basque industrialist Horacio Echevarrieta over the production of German submarines in Cadiz, circumventing the Treaty of Versailles' ban on German rearmament. The first and only submarine built on the basis of this contract was produced at the time when the Barcelona Pavilion was built, 1929–30.

13 Losada, "De la Exposición de Barcelona: El banquete de los alemanes a la Comisión organizadora," *ABC*, May 28, 1929, 45. We have not been able to verify precisely which articles the marquis was referring to.

8

Oficial with a full-page portrait on the inside cover as "a distinguished and beautiful writer, whose work on behalf of Spain and our exhibition deserves enormous amounts of gratitude."[14] **FIG. 2, P. 26** Very few people (mostly high-ranking politicians) were similarly honored—her husband Georg received only half a page in a later issue—and we may speculate that her role was more prominent than the archival records indicate. **FIG. 1, P. 26** The official photograph of the banquet that evening shows Lilly Reich and Mies van der Rohe smiling proudly among a few hundred guests. **FIG. 8**

By all accounts the opening celebrations were a great success. It did not seem to matter much that the pavilion was not exactly finished (or that so few visitors were roaming the exhibition grounds).[15] The small kiosk at the northwestern end was still under construction, the luminous wall at the center did not yet function, the important red curtain in the interior was only delivered six weeks later, and the garden design in the back had not even started.[16]

Work at the pavilion and several German sections would continue for several weeks and many details were only ready just before German Week in October.[17] Overall Germany made a good impression,[18] helped, no doubt, by the fact that very few of the other national pavilions and exhibition areas were completed on

8 Festive banquet at the ballroom of the Hotel Ritz on May 27, 1929, on the occasion of the inauguration of the German Section. Note Mies van der Rohe and Lilly Reich third from the front on the left.

14 *Diario Oficial de la Exposición Internacional Barcelona 1929* 1, no. 12 (June 2, 1929): 2. Enrique Domínguez Rodiño, a cultural attaché at the Spanish Embassy in Berlin and Agent of the Barcelona Exposition in Germany, had requested photographs of both Lilly and Georg von Schnitzler for this publication in May. See Rodiño to Georg von Schnitzler, May 4, 1929, HoeA, WaB 1929–1930. During her visits to Barcelona, Lilly developed a personal friendship with the Marqués de Foronda, the director of the exhibition, which lasted beyond the war, when her husband was for many years the president of the Deutsch-Ibero-Amerikanische Gesellschaft. Lilly included him in a list of the most important persons in her life for her funerary chapel, which also included Mies van der Rohe, Karl Prinz Rohan, Leo Frobenius, and about seventy others. See Brigitte Salmen, ed., *Bereitschaft zum Risiko: Lilly von Schnitzler, 1889–1981: Sammlerin und Mäzenin* (Murnau: Schlossmuseums, 2011), 46–47.

15 Wilhelm Hack, "Das Wunder der Ausstellung," *Deutsche Tageszeitung* (Berlin), June 11, 1929.

16 Erich von Kettler to Mies van der Rohe, 15 July 1929, MoMA, MvdR Papers, Barcelona, Folder 1.

17 This becomes obvious from the final accounting of Mies's engineer Ernst Walther, who listed working hours up to June 19. Apparently, he and Mies had a disagreement on the site, and he was fired. The architect and technical director Karl Strauss submitted his resignation the day before the opening, but resumed working for Mies in the month of July in order to help with the final accounting. See: letters from Ernst Walther to Mies van der Rohe, 23 May 1929 and 20 August 1929; and Mies van der Rohe to Erich von Kettler, 22 August 1929, MoMA, MvdR Papers, Barcelona Pavilion, Folder 9 and Folder 2010 addition from Eduard Ludwig estate.

18 Several German industries, however, had still not sent all their exhibits in early July. See Erich von Kettler to Georg von Schnitzler, 5 July 1929, HoeA, WaB 1927–1928.

19 Heinrich Simon, "Barcelona Weltausstellung 1929" (offprint from *Frankfurter Zeitung*, 1929), 5.

20 "Bericht über meinen Besuch der Internationalen Weltausstellung Barcelona 1929, May 19, 1929." Anonymous typescript, HoeA, WaB 1929–1930. Also compare the report on the opening of the 1925 Paris Exposition Internationale des Arts Décoratifs: "It is the traditional privilege of exhibitions of all kind, not to be finished on time. [...] The journalists were peeved that at the opening they had to climb through mud and structural posts and did not get to see much beyond fences and scaffolding." R.I., "Die Pariser Kunstgewerbe-Ausstellung: Das Gelände und die Bauten," *Vossische Zeitung*, May 6, 1925, *Das Unterhaltungsblatt*, 1.

21 See "El Infante Don Fernando Inauguro El Pabellon de Hungria," *Diario Oficial de la Exposición Internacional Barcelona 1929* 1, no. 17 (July 7, 1929): n.p; Fernando Barango-Solis, "Lo que sera el Pabellón de Rumanía," *Diario Oficial de la Exposición Internacional Barcelona 1929* 1, no. 24 (August 24, 1929): 20; and "La Inauguración del pabellón de Rumania," *Diario Oficial de la Exposición Internacional Barcelona 1929* 1, no. 27 (September 14, 1929): 30.

22 See Lenore Kühn, "Auftakt in Barcelona," *Kissinger Saale Zeitung*, May 27, 1929; and Rudolf Friedmann, "Die Weltausstellung in Barcelona: noch unfertig, aber imposant," *Danziger Neueste Nachrichten*, May 28, 1929. The *Frankfurter Zeitung* reported in early November that "until very recently" individual pavilions were finally opened. See S., "Die Weltausstellung in Barcelona: Eine Nachlese," *Frankfurter Zeitung*, November 5, 1929 (evening edition).

23 "Visita a la Secció Alemanya," *La Veu de Catalunya*, May 29, 1929, 1.

24 "Stressemann [sic] en Barcelona," *La Vanguardia*, June 14, 1929, 6.

time—"exhibition islands in an ocean of boxes," was how the *Frankfurter Zeitung* characterized the fair.[19] Another highly critical report went into more detail: "In general [...] one is used to the fact that world fairs are not finished when they are opened, but I had not expected that this world's fair could be *so* unfinished at its opening [...] the poor pedestrians walked on gravel [...] many buildings were barely more than shells, while the foundations of others were only just being laid."[20] As cases in point, the Hungarian pavilion opened at the end of June and the Romanian pavilion at the beginning of September.[21] On the other hand, the National Palace and the Poble Espanyol were fully equipped to receive visitors from the day of the opening. Emphasizing a common Spanish culture and heritage, they broadcast an important propaganda message for the restive Catalans, who made up the majority of visitors in those first weeks.[22]

During its eight months of existence, the German pavilion hosted relatively few functions. On the day after the opening ceremony there was a morning reception for the press. Mies said a few words about the pavilion and then he and von Schnitzler took the assembled journalists on a tour through the German sections.[23] In the afternoon, tea was served to a group of expatriate Germans in Barcelona. Occasional gatherings for high-ranking visitors followed. Most important, the German foreign minister, Gustav Stresemann, who had been instrumental in securing funds to help finish the pavilion, came for a brief visit on June 18, 1929, on his way back from a diplomatic mission in Madrid. He was a member of the German Werkbund, and familiar with questions of contemporary architecture and design. A grand reception and festive dinner at the pavilion was planned for him, but time constraints led to a more modest affair.[24] Stresemann arrived in the morning and was given a quick tour of the city by car, taking in the medieval cathedral and the empty shell of Gaudí's Sagrada Familia. After a brief rest at the Hotel Ritz he arrived at the Barcelona Pavilion, where he spent a considerable amount of

9

time and signed the guestbook before embarking on a dutiful tour of all the German exhibits. After lunch at the Miramar restaurant, he headed back to the railway station for the evening train to Paris and sent a congratulatory telegram to Georg von Schnitzler in Frankfurt.[25] By the time he arrived back in Germany, however, he was feeling increasingly unwell. The arteries in his left leg were badly inflamed, and the German press was quick to blame this on his attendance at the exhibition in Barcelona, where he had stood and walked for many hours. Gustav Stresemann would die three months later, aged fifty-one.[26] The untimely death of this seminal and unifying figure (who had been Chancellor in 1923, Foreign Minister for six years, and a recipient of the Nobel Peace Prize, with Aristide Briand, in 1926), darkly foreshadowed the disintegration of the political culture of the Weimar Republic.

In a letter of July 15, 1929, Erich von Kettler, von Schnitzler's assistant and representative in Barcelona, reported that he was asked "several dozen times every day" about "the idea of the pavilion," and requested some words of explanation from Mies. No response has been found.[27] Other visitors, it seems, did not even realize they had just seen the German pavilion. One of them, a writer for the American magazine *Architectural Forum*, appeared completely unaware of its existence: "Only Italy, Belgium, and France have erected distinctive and consequential pavilions," he stated, confidently, in his otherwise extensive review of the Barcelona fair.[28] But his ignorance can partly be explained by the fact that the delays in assigning the site and starting construction work meant that none of the official maps in the exhibition brochures showed the location of the pavilion (with the exception of the German catalogue, which only appeared in July). Since the site was far from the international section on Montjuïc, visitors would not necessarily have expected to find a representative country pavilion in this spot. Other visitors mistook the structure for an exhibit of the marble industry—a forgivable mistake, since up until October its only inscription named the marble supplier Köstner & Gottschalk in Berlin.[29] This placed the pavilion in a well-established lineage of structures made from the material they advertised, such as Bruno Taut's pavilions for the steel industry in Leipzig 1913, his Glass House at the 1914 Werkbund exhibition, or Mies's own Glasraum in Stuttgart in 1927.

But perhaps the main reason for this overlooking of the pavilion was the astonishing fact that for four and a half months after the opening it had no identifying sign on its front.[30] All the iconic photographs, taken at the end of June, show the pavilion unadorned by the inscription "Alemania" (an omission repeated in

10

9, 10 Concert at the German Pavilion during German Week, October 23, 1929

25 See "Politicos ilustres: El ministro de Negocios Extranjeros de Alemania, señor Stressemann, [sic] llega a Barcelona dispensándosele un cariñoso recibimiento," *La Vanguardia*, June 19, 1929, 6; Erich von Kettler to Georg von Schnitzler, 17 June 1929; and Dr. Maiwald to Georg von Schnitzler, 19 June 1929. HoeA, WaB 1929–1930, H0090400.

26 See "Stresemann über seine Erkrankung," *Vossische Zeitung*, June 23, 1929, 1; and "Ha muerto el Dr. Stressemann!" *Diario Oficial Exposición Internacional de Barcelona 1929* 1, no. 31 (October 5, 1929): 3.

27 Erich von Kettler to Mies van der Rohe, 15 July 1929, MoMA, MvdR Papers, Barcelona Pavilion, Folder 1.

28 William Francklyn Paris, "The Barcelona Exposition: A Splendid but Costly Effort of the Catalan People," *Architectural Forum* (November 1929): 481–96.

29 In one of the exhibition brochures, the pavilion was simply identified as "marble visit." See Paolo Amaldi and Annelle Curulla, "Chairs, Posture, and Points of View: For an Exact Restitution of the Barcelona Pavilion," *Future Anterior: Journal of Historic Preservation, History, Theory, and Criticism* 2, no. 2 (Winter 2005): 18. We can assume that the above-mentioned letters with the name of marble suppliers Köstner & Gottschalk next to the entrance stairs were part of a deal with the company. They seem to have been retouched out of Sasha Stone's main view, but can be seen in other snapshots taken at the opening.

30 Two photographs of the inscription were discovered by David Caralt, and the inscription is mentioned in the correspondence between Gerhard Severain, the designer of the inscriptions, and Mies's office. Gerhard Severain and Mies, November 22, 1929, MoMA, MvdR Papers, Barcelona Pavilion, Folder 8. A British observer remarked that "Otherwise its only decorations are the black-lettered word 'Alemania' upon its front, and the four German flags at the borders of its domain." "A Visit to the Barcelona Exhibition," *The Spectator*, no. 5299 (January 18, 1930): 84–85. Gerhard Severain to Lilly Reich, Mies van der Rohe, and Piet van Aken, 26 November 1929; Lilly Reich to Gerhard Severain, 22 November 1929; Reich to Severain, 5 July 1929; and Reich to Severain, 4 November 1929; all in MoMA, MvdR Papers, Barcelona Pavilion, Folder 8.

11

11 A view of the German Pavilion from the back, fall 1929. Note the inscription Alemania on the right (half obscured by the shade from the roof overhang).

the reconstruction of the pavilion in 1986).[31] The letters were only finally applied in the second week of October 1929, just in time for German Week, bringing the pavilion into alignment with the other German sections and the Electric Utilities pavilion, where the identifying signage (in a special font that Gerhard Severain had developed for the occasion) naturally played a prominent role. **FIGS. 9, 10** In a report on a concert in front of the pavilion during German Week, the newspaper *La Vanguardia* published a photograph that shows the newly installed black lettering ALEMANIA next to the steps leading up to the podium.[32] Another photograph, in the collection of the Fundació Mies van der Rohe, shows that the back entrance for visitors descending from the Poble Espanyol received an inscription at the same time. **FIG. 11** Mies never saw either one.

We can only speculate why it took so long to give the German pavilion its name. It was probably the only one in the exhibition grounds that did not broadcast its provenance. Was this a simple oversight, a lack of funds, or a lack of confidence because the pavilion was not entirely finished? Mies himself might have actually preferred the building's clean lines without any inscriptions, and he had earlier famously rejected the government's request to have a sculpted eagle applied to the onyx wall inside.[33]

But Georg von Schnitzler had the most compelling motives for withholding the label. As long as the German government refused to pay for the pavilion, he was still its legal owner. After all, he had been the one who had personally authorized and financed the building, contravening clear government directives. While that issue was still far from being resolved, perhaps von Schnitzler relented in time for German Week, when many visitors were expected from Germany and from the German community in Spain.

A further reason for the difficulties in identifying the pavilion was the fact that there were no exhibits inside. While all other national pavilions offered an array of travel brochures and information about the country's beauty, its industry, art, and heritage, Mies had moved the entire information section about Germany to the second floor of the Machinery Hall, where it was probably only seen by those who came looking for it. While the pavilion's emptiness has generally been seen as a deliberate choice by Mies—a means to present a pure rendering of space—there is so far no evidence to back up this assumption. It seems perfectly possible that a lack of time or money ruled out the planning of such an exhibition. And, in fact, in planning for events during German Week in October, Mies, Lilly von Schnitzler, and the Frankfurt newspaperman Heinrich Simon discussed several ideas for staging an exhibition inside the pavilion without Mies's objecting that this would violate his concept.

Numerous cultural events were scheduled for German Week itself.[34] While the budget was not quite as small as it had been when Georg von Schnitzler left the Reichstag's finance meeting on March 2, the extra funds had all been swallowed up by the exorbitant costs of the pavilion. As a result, von Schnitzler ended up paying for much of the entertainment himself. The contribution of the German state—or more specifically, the defense minister, Wilhelm Groener—was to send the brand-new battleship *Königsberg* to Barcelona and to organize for a military band to play the Spanish March and the German national anthem at the opening of German Week on October 19.[35] By this point, all the remaining work on the pavilion had been finished, it was properly identified, the office on the southern end with a bathroom and small kitchen was open, the luminous glass wall functioned, and the garden in the back had grown. A few weeks earlier, von Schnitzler had even asked for a specialist from Köstner & Gottschalk to come to Barcelona to refinish the reflective stone surfaces of the pavilion.[36]

In an obvious nod to the many business representatives in front of him (and clearly influenced by some of the critical writing that had appeared in the meantime) von Schnitzler referred to the pavilion in his opening remarks as "a spiritual demonstration of our serious effort of collaboration in the world economy." But rather than seeing the pavilion first, he suggested that his guests should "contemplate it at the end of a visit to the different German sections in order to find again, in an abstract form, the qualities that each of the exhibits exemplifies."[37] His wife, Lilly, meanwhile, had been planning quite a different demonstration of the pavilion's "essential purpose," as part and expression of a larger modern project extending beyond architecture to art, dance, music, and technology. For one night, on October 23, the pavilion was to become the centerpiece of German Week.[38] Lilly von Schnitzler had discussed the details of this event with Mies and Heinrich Simon. Their conversation about a bibliographic exhibition of book art or a "tasteful show of modern graphic arts" reveals how the emptiness of the pavilion was not necessarily programmatic. They also discussed commissioning a documentary film about Germany to be shown in the pavilion, or staging a classical concert by the Busch, Guarneri, or the modern Hindemith Quartet, or a dance performance of the Laban school.[39] Rudolf Laban (1879–1958) would have been a particularly apt choice as he was not only the prominent leader of the German *Ausdruckstanz* (Expression Dance) movement, but also trained as an architect at the École des Beaux-Arts in Paris and was deeply interested in human motion in response to built space.[40] Mies was also a close friend of Laban's student Mary Wigman. When Laban proved to be unavailable, two other modern dancers were hired for an evening performance at the pavilion—Ernst Matray and his wife, Katta Sterna, who had been part of Max Reinhardt's ensemble, among the most prominent progressive dancers in the Weimar

31 At a conference in Barcelona on the occasion of the rebuilt pavilion's thirtieth birthday, Dietrich Neumann asked the Fondació Mies van der Rohe and its director Anna Ramos to reinstall the inscription.

32 "Notas Gráficas," in *La Vanguardia*, October 24, 1929, 3. David Caralt deserves credit for discovering this image.

33 Note Edwin Redslob, 4. Februar 1929. Reichskunstwart, Weltausstellung Barcelona, BArchL R 32 1929.

34 "Hablando con el Dr. Von Schnitzler: La participación de Alemania en nuestro certamen," *Diario Oficial de la Exposición Internacional Barcelona 1929* 1, no. 13 (June 9, 1929).

35 "La Semana Alemana," *La Vanguardia*, October 20, 1929, 11.

36 Köstner & Gottschalk to Mies van der Rohe, 26 September 1929, MoMA, MvdR Papers, Barcelona Pavilion, Folder 2010 addition from Eduard Ludwig estate.

37 "Inauguració Oficial de la Setmana al Pavelló Alemany," *La Publicitat*, October 20, 1929, 5.

38 Georg von Schnitzler to Ministerialdirektor Ritter (?), 23 June 1929, BArchL, Ausstellung Barcelona, AA, Abteilung II, R 901, 40029, 169.

39 Paul Hindemith (1895–1963) was a much-celebrated contemporary composer and professor at the Berlin Music Academy. Internal memorandum, Foreign Ministry, 25 June 1929, BArchL, Ausstellung Barcelona, AA, Abteilung II, R 9.01, 40029, 179.

40 See in particular Rudolf Laban, *Choreographie: Erstes Heft* (Jena: Diederichs, 1926); Vera Maletic, *Body, Space, Expression: The Development of Rudolf Laban's Movement and Dance Concepts* (New York: Mouton de Gruyter, 1987); Holger Otten, "Architecture, Painting, and Sculpture as a Creative Unity: About Mies van der Rohe's Vision on Art and Architecture," in *Mies van der Rohe Montage = Collage*, ed. Andreas Beitin, Wolf Eiermann and Brigitte Franzen (Aachen: Ludwig Forum, Koenig Books, 2017), 188–208. Unfortunately, no traces of any choreography of Rudolf Laban for the Barcelona Pavilion have survived in the archives of the Laban Institute in London.

12

Republic.[41] A famous publicity shot by Trude Fleischman of their silhouettes in front of a luminous glass wall gives us an approximate idea of their appearance in the pavilion. **FIG. 12** Georg von Schnitzler paid their fee and travel expenses and invited Mies to attend: "I am giving a little party on Wednesday October 23 in the German pavilion as part of German Week, where Mr. Matray and Mrs. Kattasterna [sic] will dance. It would be truly a great pity if you, the creator of this pavilion, were absent on this day, and I am asking you kindly to be there for at least a few days, and in particular on that Wednesday." At the same time von Schnitzler allowed himself to remind Mies of the exorbitant costs of the pavilion, and slyly suggested that Mies should cover his own travel expenses, for which he would be reimbursed from the proceeds from the sale of the pavilion.[42] Mies politely declined.[43]

The modern dance performance at the pavilion was the only nighttime activity ever scheduled. Kolbe's statue was temporarily lit for the occasion—its raised arms and slightly bent knees making it a still echo, perhaps, of the dancer's movements. The day of the performance was carefully selected to coincide with what the public would later remember as "the moment of greatest brilliance" of the German celebrations of 1929: the arrival in the city of the famous Zeppelin LZ 127, cruising above Barcelona for more than an hour in the afternoon.[44] After a much publicized world tour earlier that year, the Zeppelin made a special trip to the Mediterranean, in particular the International Exposition sites in Seville and Barcelona. The humming of its engines overhead brought Barcelonans out onto their balconies and rooftops. They waved at it with their handkerchiefs and took countless photographs. As a kind of encore, it reappeared at night and made three further loops above the exhibition grounds. The powerful searchlights behind the National Palace focused on it, integrating it into its luminous spectacle. "Above the fires of the exposition, the Zeppelin, touched by the beams of the searchlights, resembled an enormous fish swimming above in the bluish sea of the

12 The dancers Ernst Matray and his wife, Katta Sterna Photographer: Trude Fleischmann

sky," gushed one journalist.[45] The invited guests at the dance performance at the pavilion stepped outside to see the stunning play of lights above, reflected in the large pool. As the Zeppelin finally returned to the Prat airfield and slowly faded into the distance, it suddenly lit up again—picked up this time by the searchlights of the battleship *Königsberg* in the harbor nearby. **FIG. 13** It was a quintessential modern moment.[46]

The appearance of the Zeppelin and the battleship were the anomalies in an otherwise rather conventional German Week. Four Wagner operas—*Rheingold*, *Tannhäuser*, *Siegfried*, and *Götterdämmerung*—were performed in the Liceu theater. And there were lectures on the wonders of the German electrical and chemical industries and another on modern architecture.[47] Invited by Georg von Schnitzler, the speaker was not Mies but Martin Elsaesser (1884–1957), director of Frankfurt's municipal construction department and a successful modern architect who had remodeled the von Schnitzler's new home on Frankfurt's Westendplatz in 1928. Lilly von Schnitzler may have been pondering the difference between Mies and Elsaesser when she commented in a book on Elsaesser's work (which included her own home): "The great teachers of architecture, who appear when times are changing, are above all theoreticians and fanatics, as they develop a new style from its elements. Only their followers become the type of practical architects that a client needs, only they truly realize the great thoughts of their teachers."[48]

Initially planned to be held at the pavilion, Elsaesser's illustrated lecture on "The Problems of Modern Architecture" was relocated to the German Cinema Room at the Projection Center. He was careful to point out that modern architecture—still widely unknown in Spain—was not a German invention, but rather "supranational," originating in several nations at the same time. It searched for "unity, essence, and purity," he said, in a "close relationship with the spiritual life of our age."[49] Mies would certainly have agreed.

41 See Georg von Schnitzler to Mies van der Rohe, 10 October 1929; and Mies to von Schnitzler, 16 October 1929, both MoMA, MvdR Papers, Barcelona Pavilion, Folder 2010 addition Eduard Ludwig estate. See also a letter from Heinrich Simon to Georg von Schnitzler, in which he reports that Lilly von Schnitzler, Mies, and himself had discussed the program, and suggested commissioning a film about German culture, to be shown during German Week, and the dance performance by Matray and Sterna; Heinrich Simon to Georg von Schnitzler, 8 July 1929, HoeA, WaB 1929–1930.

42 Georg von Schnitzler to Ernst Matray, 10 October 1929, HoeA, WaB 1929–1930.

43 Mies van der Rohe to Georg von Schnitzler, 16 October 1929, MoMA, MvdR Papers, Barcelona Pavilion, Folder 2010 addition from Eduard Ludwig estate.

44 "El Presidente del Club Germania, de Barcelona, Señor Rüggeberg," in *Diario Oficial de la Exposición Internacional Barcelona 1929* 1, no. 35 (November 2, 1929). "El majestuoso vuelo del Conde Zeppelin," in *La Vanguardia*, December 28, 1991, 10.

45 "El Conde Zeppelin en Barcelona," in *La Vanguardia*, October 24, 1929, 6.

46 This moment was also captured by a draftsman inside the Zeppelin, Ludwig Dettmann: "Barcelona! I never saw the city from above that beautiful; as if borne from the sea." Ludwig Dettmann, *Mit dem Zeppelin nach Amerika* (Berlin: Verlag von Reimar Hobbing, 1929).

47 "Programa de la Semana Alemana," *Diario Oficial de la Exposición Internacional Barcelona 1929* 1, no. 32 (October 12, 1929). Privy Counselor Dr. Wilhelm Lenzmann (1885–1935) spoke about "The German Electricity Industry" and IG Farben manager Franz Ahlgrimm reported about "Nitrogen, its Fertilizing Qualities and Importance for Spanish Agriculture," in the Palace of Agriculture. Dr. Ahlgrimm, "El nitrógeno, sus cualidades fertilizantes y su importancia para la agricultura española," *Boletín Agrario* 5, no. 48 (October/November 1929): 4–5.

48 Martin Elsaesser had been one of the finalists for the IG Farben Haus (eventually designed by Hans Poelzig), which Georg von Schnitzler had also supervised. Barbara C. Buenger, "Some Portraits from Weimar-Era Frankfurt," in *Of "Truths Impossible to Put in Words": Max Beckmann Contextualized*, ed. Rose-Carol Washton Long and Maria Makela (Bern: Peter Lang, 2009), 165–98, here 167. See also Lilly von Schnitzler, "Was erwarte ich von meinem Architekten?" in Martin Elsaesser, *Bauten und Entwürfe aus den Jahren 1924–1932* (Berlin: Bauwelt Verlag, 1933), 6.

49 "Setmana Alemanya: Conferència del Doctor Martin Elsaesser," *La Veu de Catalunya*, October 22, 1929, 7. Elizabeth Elsaesser, private correspondence, October 22, 1929 (Martin Elsaesser Stiftung, Frankfurt). I would like to thank Professor Thomas Elsaesser, Amsterdam, for sharing this text with me. For the original program, see Georg von Schnitzler to industry representatives with preliminary program for German Week, 7 October 1929, HoeA, WaB 1929–1930.

A. GIL
LA EXPOSICION MILAGROSA
THE MARVELLOUS EXHIBITION – L'EXPOSITION MIRACULEUSE

13

13 The Zeppelin LZ 127 above the exhibition grounds in the evening of October 23, 1929

Elsaesser then went on to show some of his recent school buildings in Frankfurt, embodying new ideas about reforming education: mobile furniture and bright classrooms with views onto the surrounding nature.

The months passed, but some things remained unchanged. The pavilion continued to sit rarely used in the exhibition grounds, while still attracting wide notice in the press. And the drama of its financing continued unabated. "Very worried about incomprehensibly high bills. Please call immediately tomorrow morning 9 a.m."[50] Georg von Schnitzler's anxious telegram to Mies in mid-July 1929, more than six weeks after the opening, was typical of their correspondence as von Schnitzler attempted to reckon the final costs for the German participation and recoup some of his personal investment.[51] The documents leave no doubt about the agony and complications caused by Mies's unreliable accounting and his slack arrangements with the participating industries, which led to numerous disagreements about payable costs.[52] Mies also had a fluid notion of budgetary boundaries and responsibilities, generously providing, for example, "tips, beer, cigarettes, and food" to the workers—which he then charged to von Schnitzler's budget. By July 5—work was still continuing despite the official opening more than a month before—additional travel bills, materials for the pavilion, and other organizational expenses for both Mies and his team had pushed the pavilion's estimated total cost up to 277,000 Reichsmark, already an overrun of some 100,000 Reichsmark. And more expenses were on the horizon.

According to the final count, the German participation in the exhibition ended up costing 1,414,801 Reichsmark (including the pavilion), of which von Schnitzler himself, most likely with some help from IG Farben, prepaid 740,000 Reichsmark to suppliers and builders (considerably more than the 150,000 Reichsmark he had initially pledged).[53] The pavilion alone cost 338,422.18 Reichsmark (equivalent to around $1.5 million today). In comparison, the Frankfurt house designed for Georg and Lilly von Schnitzler the previous year had cost approximately 250,000 Reichsmark,[54] and Mies's House Esters in Krefeld around 150,000 Reichsmark.[55] Both of those houses had considerably more floor space, a large kitchen, several bathrooms, and large retractable windows. Even the Tugendhat House (whose famous, solid onyx wall in the living room came with a price tag of 60,000 Reichsmark) cost 300,000 Reichsmark – still less than the much smaller German pavilion. Similarly, the cost of the Electric Utilities pavilion ballooned from Mies's initial estimate of 40,000 Reichsmark to some 140,000 Reichsmark. Mies blamed these exorbitant cost overruns on local inflation, the interruption of work during the budget dispute in March, which required much overtime and night shifts afterward, and organizational issues with Spanish bureaucracy. While these issues certainly contributed to the financial disaster, they were clearly not the only reasons. Astonishingly, Mies's claims were never challenged in the correspondence between the somewhat reserved von Schnitzler and the bullish Mies. Never one to shy away from confrontation, Mies knew that he could hold his ground.

50 See, for example, Georg von Schnitzler to Mies van der Rohe, 14 July 1929, MoMA, MvdR Papers, Barcelona Folder 2010 addition from Eduard Ludwig estate.

51 See, for example, his requests in late summer and fall of 1929: Georg von Schnitzler to Ministerialdirektor Ritter at the Foreign Office, 25 July 1929, BArchL, Ausstellung Barcelona, AA, Abteilung II, R 9.01, 40029, 204–07; Georg von Schnitzler to Gustav Stresemann and Julius Curtius, 29 September 1929, BArchL, Ausstellung Barcelona, AA, Abteilung II, R 9.01, 40029, 105–07; copies in HoeA, WaB 1929–1930.

52 A good example of the complexities of the financial situation is the six-page letter by Erich von Kettler to Georg von Schnitzler, 5 July 1929, HoeA, WaB 1929–1930.

53 See lists with costs spent, attached to a report by Mies, 3 October 1929, BArchL, Ausstellung Barcelona, AA, Abteilung II, R 9.01, 40029, 110–13.

54 Georg von Schnitzler's annual income was around 300,000 Reichsmark. Georg von Schnitzler Denazification File 1946 HHSA (Abt. 520, FZ Nr. 6728).

55 Letter from Hermann John to Mies van der Rohe, private collection. Quoted in Christiane Lange, *Ludwig Mies van der Rohe: Architektur für die Seidenindustrie* (Berlin: Nikolaische Verlagsbuchhandlung, 2011), 110.

Despite the obvious public success of the pavilion, Schnitzler's appeals for reimbursement were repeatedly denied by the Reichstag's finance committee through the fall of 1929.[56] Internal correspondence between various government agencies reveals the Minister of Economic Affairs' unhappiness with "von Schnitzler's incompetence" and grumblings about the generous terms of Mies's contract and the extravagant and wasteful ways of the "young architects" who had traveled on the "Train Bleu" and had massively overcalculated the required materials. One official demanded a parliamentary commission to examine the mismanagement at the Barcelona building office.[57] Rumors about the enormous cost overruns also reached the Werkbund secretary Ernst Jäckh, who noted in private that Mies could not be entrusted with a leading role at the next Werkbund exhibition, planned for Cologne in 1932.[58] When Mies got wind of Jäckh's remark he angrily confronted him and asked for clarification. He even requested letters from his current clients Esters and Lange in Krefeld confirming that their buildings had been built strictly within the budget.[59] For someone who nonchalantly disregarded deadlines, budgets, and agreements in pursuit of his vision, he was astonishingly thin-skinned. When confronted with questions about his vague budgeting methods and massive miscalculations when ordering materials, Mies typically either haughtily dismissed them or responded with farfetched counteraccusations or conspiracy theories.[60]

Mies was generally of little help with von Schnitzler's increasingly urgent appeals, refusing, for instance, to show up at a crucial meeting at the Ministry of Economic Affairs in September because he did not want to lose three days of his vacation on the island of Sylt.[61] On December 15, an exasperated von Schnitzler threatened to close the German section prematurely and advise all the suppliers to sue the German government. This desperate tactic worked. Shortly afterward, a check arrived for a loan of more than 550,000 Reichsmark from the Minister of Economic Affairs.[62] The exhibition stayed open for another month and closed as originally planned on January 15, 1930, after which the pavilion was dismantled.[63]

In order to recover costs, attempts were made at selling the pavilion's materials, the Mies-designed furniture, and many of the goods and exhibits that German firms had left in Barcelona, often in lieu of the extra payment that had been requested from them. Selling the goods in Spain, however, turned out to be difficult and unprofitable, since they incurred high customs duties. Von Schnitzler found himself in the curious situation of suddenly owning a considerable number of toy cars and several large stuffed teddy bears and elephants made by the famous German manufacturer Steiff, who had been among the exhibitors. A large coffee house in Madrid and a collector in Toulouse expressed interest in Mies's chairs, but nothing came of these offers. Their final destiny is still a mystery.[64]

Efforts to recuperate some of the costs were also complicated by the onset of the world economic crisis and renewed political unrest in Spain. Primo de Rivera resigned on January 30, 1930, and died a few weeks later. After an initial proposal to rebuild the pavilion in Biarritz came to nothing, its marble and travertine slabs were shipped to Hamburg in March to be sold.[65] When this proved impossible they were taken into the possession of the Ministries of Finance and Economic Affairs, who had given von Schnitzler a debt guarantee for this instance. The marble and travertine was apparently reused in government building projects in Hamburg.[66] It was not until July 1932 that all outstanding financial issues were finally resolved.[67]

56 Memorandum about a meeting of November 14, 1929, between the Reichschancellor and all party leaders, rejecting additional funds for Barcelona, as well as Georg von Schnitzler to representatives of the Foreign Office and Ministry of Economics, 11 December, 1929 BArchL R 240.031, AA, Abteilung II, R 901, 40031, "Einzelausstellungen Spanien: Internationale Ausstellung Barcelona 1929," vol. 5, 248, 264.

57 See internal memorandum, 25 September 1929, BArchL, Ausstellung Barcelona, AA, Abteilung II, R 9.01, 40030, 11; von Kettler to Mies, 15 July 1929 (see note 27), and memorandum about a meeting regarding the financing of the exhibition, 22 August 1929, both in MoMA, MvdR Papers, Barcelona Pavilion, Folder 1.

58 The ambitious Werkbund exhibition in Cologne that Ernst Jäckh planned for 1932 had to be cancelled due to the world economic crisis. While Jäckh responded to Mies with great diplomacy (without denying his remarks), he must have been particularly disappointed that this exhibit was one of those sections lost in the cost-cutting measures in March and not resurrected when funds emerged later. Georg von Schnitzler to the Marqués de Foronda, 6 April 1929, HoeA, WaB 1929–1930.

59 Mies van der Rohe to Ernst von Jäckh, 22 August 1929 (copy to von Schnitzler), MoMA, MvdR Papers, Barcelona Pavilion, Folder 2010 addition from Eduard Ludwig estate.

60 When confronted with 70,000 Reichsmark cost overruns each at both the silk industry section and the electricity pavilion, Mies, without addressing specifics, claimed that his "negotiations had not been conducted as naively as the documents might suggest" and that in any event, the fault for any additional costs lay with the general commissioner and his organization. Mies van der Rohe to Erich von Kettler, 25 July 1929, MoMA, MvdR Papers, Barcelona Pavilion, Folder 1; and von Kettler to Mies, 15 July 1929 (see note 27).

61 Georg von Schnitzler to Mies van der Rohe, 19 September 1929, and Mies to von Schnitzler, 21 September 1929, MoMA, MvdR Papers, Barcelona Pavilion, Folder 2. Disagreements between von Schnitzler and Mies delayed the payment of the final segment of his honorarium until December, see Erich von Kettler to Lilly Reich, 16 December 1929, MoMA, MvdR Papers, Barcelona Pavilion, Folder 7.

62 Minister of Economic Affairs to Georg von Schnitzler, 15 December 1929, MoMA, MvdR Papers, Barcelona Pavilion, Folder 3.

63 A smaller "National Exhibition Barcelona 1930" continued for another six months, emphasizing exhibits from Spain's different regions, the Poble Espanyol, and the water and lighting displays. The numbers of visitors dwindled and the exhibitions ended with a considerable deficit of 250 million pesetas. See General Consulate Spain to Foreign Office Berlin, 24 July 1930; Augustin Calvet Pascual Gaziel, "Pequeña elegía: Adiós, Exposición!" *La Vanguardia*, July 18, 1930, 3 (BArchL, Bestand R 240.031, AA, Abteilung II, R 901, 40031, "Einzelausstellungen Spanien. Internationale Ausstellung Barcelona 1929," vol. 5, 69–72, 73–74).

64 Dr. Maiwald to Georg von Schnitzler, 3 January, 1930, HoeA, WaB 1929–1930. A set of two early Barcelona chairs from the pavilion seems to have ended up in the house of Gerhard Severain in Wiesbaden, an old friend of Mies's in charge of the design and application of the lettering. They are still in the possession of the family.

65 See Mies van der Rohe to Count Johannes von Welzceck, German ambassador in Madrid, 18 March 1930, MoMA, MvdR Papers, Barcelona Pavilion; Folder 2010 addition from Eduard Ludwig estate; and G. Mainrath to Mies van der Rohe, 5 March 1930, MoMA, MvdR Papers, Folder 9.

66 See Reichs-Kredit-Gesellschaft to Ministerialdirektor Ritter, AA (Foreign Office), 24 February 1930; Georg von Schnitzler to Reichs-Kredit-Gesellschaft, 10 February 1930; and Georg von Schnitzler to Ministerialdirektor Ritter at the Foreign Office, 15 February 1931, BArchL R 240.031, AA, Abteilung II, R 901, 40031, "Einzelausstellungen Spanien: Internationale Ausstellung Barcelona 1929," vol. 5, 25, 27, 113–18.

67 In February of 1931, von Schnitzler was still dealing with a deficit of 550,000 Reichsmark. See Georg von Schnitzler to Ministerialdirektor Ritter at the Foreign Office, 15 February 1931, BArchL R 240.031, AA, Abteilung II, R 901, 40031, "Einzelausstellungen Spanien: Internationale Ausstellung Barcelona 1929," vol. 5, 25, 27, 113–18.

The Photographs

Has any set of photographs ever played a more central role in a building's history than the thirteen famous images of the Barcelona Pavilion taken by Sasha Stone in late June 1929? In the absence of the building itself and of any other readily available images, it was the strikingly stark vision of these prints that shaped both the critical perception and the historiography of the pavilion for the ensuing five decades. And when the moment came to rebuild, again the photographs served as prime evidence and guide for the reconstruction, since almost no architectural drawings had survived.

Breaking with his usual practice, Mies had failed to arrange for a photographer to document his work in the days and weeks after the completion of the pavilion. Perhaps this had something to do with the hectic pace leading up to the opening, or his own departure shortly afterward, or, indeed, the certainty that the building would not be completely finished for quite some time. While the pavilion was his costliest building to date, it was also a temporary structure that would be dismantled just eight months later, and Mies was clearly not aware of the prominent role it was going to play. At the same time he was preoccupied with a number of other projects: the Esters and Lange Houses in Krefeld were under construction; plans for the Tugendhat House in Brno and the house for Emil Nolde in Berlin were being finalized; the second Friedrichstrasse skyscraper competition was under way; and he was also developing the patents for the Barcelona chair. Another reason for the scarcity of photographs, however, was the high cost of the permit required for official photography at the exposition. In order to buy himself political support, Primo de Rivera had apparently awarded certain privileges—for example, charging for vehicular access to the exhibition grounds, or the exclusive rights to photography there—to sway influential Catalan businessmen who had been opposed to his regime.[1]

As a result, the first published photographs of the German pavilion were snapshots by an amateur—a bit out of kilter and out of focus, the lighting uneven.[2] They appeared in the weekly exhibition journal *Diario Oficial de la Exposicion Internacional Barcelona 1929*, and it seems safe to assume they were taken by a member of Mies's staff and that Mies authorized their release.[3] **FIG. 1** They seem to show the building on May 26, on the eve of the opening and stand in great contrast to the official photographs taken by Stone later that summer.[4] The outside view is taken from one of the vantage points that became popular in the following months: from the southeast corner of the large water basin looking back at the pavilion, reflected in the water in front. A group of workers on the left is busy arranging a set of MR chairs. Others move up or down the stairs; the flowerpots for the opening are in place. Two men in hats, one noticeably taller than the other, observe the moving of the chairs. They are identified on the back as Mies and the local German representative Erich von Kettler.[5] The two interior views thematize the reflections in the pavilion. In one of them a woman (probably Lilly Reich) surveys the interior; a blinding light is coming from the right—the

1 "Der Deutsche Pavillon in Barcelona: Einweihung der deutschen Abteilung," *Leipziger Neueste Nachrichten* no. 152 (June 1, 1929): 5.

2 On the amateur snapshots see: David Caralt, "Pabellón cotidiano vs Pabellón mítico: Notas sobre las fotografías casuales del Pabellón de Alemania en la Exposición Internacional de Barcelona 1929," in *Congreso internacional: Inter photo arch "Interferencias,"* ed. R. Alcolea and J. Tárrago (Pamplona: Universidad de Navarra, 2016), 26-37, http://dadun.unav.edu/handle/10171/42439. See also Dietrich Neumann, "Architektur der Reflexionen: Zur kritischen Rezeption des Barcelona Pavillons," in *Spiegel: Mies van der Rohe und die Geschichte von Glanz und Abglanz*, ed. Jan Maruhn and Wita Noack (Berlin: form + zweck, 2015), 97–117.

3 See *Diario Oficial de la Exposicion Internacional Barcelona 1929* 1, no. 12 (June 2, 1929), n.p.

4 They survived in the papers of Mies's collaborator Eduard Ludwig and were first published in Helmut Reuter and Birgit Schulte, eds., *Mies and Modern Living: Interiors, Furniture, Photography* (Ostfildern: Hatje Cantz, 2008), 54-55, 84-85, and 280-81. Ludwig himself could not be the photographer, as he had not yet joined Mies's office, and he did not travel to Barcelona in 1929.

5 Ibid., 53. Dr. Erich von Kettler was the Representative of the Commissar General. The inscription on the back of the photograph reads "Mies u Kettler vor der Eröffnung" (Mies and von Kettler before the opening).

1

2

1 Three snapshots of the Barcelona Pavilion taken on the evening before the opening
Photographer unknown

protective red curtain would not be delivered for another few weeks. The woman is facing a glass screen in which we can make out the mirror image of several visitors and the photographer with his tripod in front of the light wall.[6] Thanks to the dark marble behind the glass, the reflections are particularly efficient, and we can see the depth of the pavilion on its western side, the sunny terrace behind the photographer, the bright wall of travertine at its end, and above it the adjacent Victoria Eugenie palace. The photographer rendered the reflections complicit in the building's spatial complexities. The second interior view, even more out of kilter and also overexposed, similarly demonstrates the interplay of reflections: the black pool of water fuses with the dark interior carpet, and the glass wall shows the colonnade outside, punctuated by the same group of visitors on the podium, gleaming in the western light of the setting sun.[7]

As the photographs reveal, Mies was present when the pictures were taken and most likely approved their publication in the *Diario Oficial*. The play of reflections was undoubtedly a quality that he and his staff were aware of, particularly after Siegfried Kracauer's reference to the reflections and kaleidoscopic effects in his negative review of the Glasraum in Stuttgart. But we do not know if this effect was simply tolerated or the result of deliberate planning. Catalan photographer Carmelo Vives also took a few photographs around the day of the opening, and while his were more professional in their setup and lighting, he, too, captured reflections much more than Stone would do in his later photographs.

Canonical views emerged early on—testifying to the pavilion's inherent visual and spatial order—strongly suggesting certain views while discouraging others. Several versions of the view from the southeast corner across the pool toward the main building, the outside view from the north, the main room toward the small pool, and a view of the Kolbe statue appeared in the local press, in a picture book, and on postcards by Spanish photographers.[8] **FIG. 2**

The fact that there were a number of often repeated views also had to do with constraints from the building and site. The building's reflective surfaces made many other views difficult, certainly if one wanted to avoid shadowy images of oneself taking the photograph. The colonnade across the street also stood in the way of frontal views from outside, and discouraged photographs back toward that direction. The large openings, the reflective gleam of the travertine floor outside, and the brightness of the Mediterranean sun made for particularly strong contrasts, which eliminated shots from the inside out. All the early photographers avoided areas that were still unfinished, such as the office pavilion on the southern end, the outside walls, or the garden toward the back.

A few weeks after the opening (Mies and Reich had long left), a manager in the German silk industry commissioned Sasha Stone to photograph the silk section and the rest of the German

6 These three images, however, are taken with a small-format camera, not with the plate camera visible in the picture. They are also taken without a tripod. This leaves us with the question of what might have happened to any photos taken with the plate camera that evening. I would like to thank Helmut Reuter, Berlin for this suggestion.

7 On May 26, 1929, the sun set in Barcelona at 9:13 p.m. The location of the shadows suggests a low western sun at around 7 p.m.

8 Commercial Spanish photographers included the Barcelona Pavilion in series of photographic postcards in October and September. Erich Von Kettler to Lilly Reich, 10 September 1929, MoMA, MvdR Papers, Barcelona Pavilion, Folder 9. See also the photograph of the pool and Kolbe statue in an official publication with illustrations by unknown photographers of most pavilions: *Catalogo con 56 Huecograbados, Exposición Internacional de Barcelona 1929* (Barcelona: Concesiones Graficas, 1929). The representative of Georg von Schnitzler's commissariat, Erich von Kettler, wrote to Lilly Reich on October 29 that the postcards of the Barcelona Pavilion by a Spanish photographer were enjoying brisk sales; von Kettler to Reich, 29 October 1929, MoMA, MvdR Papers, Barcelona Pavilion, Folder 9.

3-5 German Pavilion, late June 1929. Photograph: Sasha Stone

3

4

5

exhibits, which he did during the last week of June.[9] Stone, born in St. Petersburg as Alexander Sergeyevich Steinsapir, had been a commercial photographer in Berlin for five years. He had worked for all the leading magazines, photographing fashion, science, and theater sets, often with a sense of visual humor. Up to then, his best-known study of a single building was a series of photographs of Erich Mendelsohn's Einstein Tower, made the previous year for the *Berliner Illustrirte Zeitung*.[10] Again, these photographs are characterized by visual originality and wit. The tower was shown spookily lit at night, for example, or from a "worm's-eye view" peeking up between the blades of grass in the surrounding lawn. Stone had also received commissions from Bruno Taut, and had photographed the Weissenhofsiedlung in Stuttgart in 1927.[11] Perhaps it was Stone's recent picture book about Berlin[12] that inspired Erich Raemisch to hire him, rather than an established architectural photographer such as Arthur Koester, Lux Feininger, or Lucia Moholy. The urban scenes in *Berlin in Bildern* are inhabited by ordinary Berliners, whom Stone portrays with tenderness and sympathy as they sweep the streets, crowd around a vendor, or negotiate traffic in the rain. If Raemisch

8-10 German Pavilion, late June 1929.
Photograph: Sasha Stone

10

12

11

11-12 German Pavilion, late June 1929. Photograph: Sasha Stone

the point that Robin Evans would make ten years later, namely that floor and ceiling created something akin to a mirror image, "smuggling" symmetry into an otherwise carefully asymmetrical building and by extension into a style that had largely abandoned it.[13]

Twice, however, Stone could not help himself and allowed samples of his native wit and visual ingenuity to surface: a view west toward Kolbe's statue in the small basin—canonized by other photographers and even available as postcards—reflects just enough of the sculpture in the glass wall to the left that a disembodied hand is seen reaching ghostlike into the picture. **FIG. 14** Sadly, his sense of humor was not shared by the editors at Berliner Bild-Bericht, which sent out retouched versions. **FIG. 15** Similarly, in a view from the inside toward the same glass wall, the reflected image of Kolbe's figure appears fractured on the onyx wall. To the right we can decipher some letters, their mirror-image spelling out the enticement "MAG"[GI] and [DE]"GUSTACIONES GRATUITAS," offered by the Swiss manufacturer of bouillon cubes across the street. **FIG. 16** This image, not published widely at the time, was also censored and retouched, but much later. When Hans Maria Wingler, then director of the Bauhaus Museum, included it in a major publication in 1962, he had it carefully manipulated to remove all reflections.[14] **FIG. 17**

Recognizing the pavilion's inherent visual order, Claire Zimmerman, in 2014, imagined it as a kind of "photographic architecture," its "spatial proposition" designed for an existence in photographs. Stone, she assumed, had simply responded to the "obvious" spell of the spatial composition and delivered the "visual tableaux" Mies had in mind when designing his "spatial choreographies."[15] Given the building's anticipated short lifespan, it is plausible to assume that Mies was eager to create something photogenic for black-and-white reproductions. Judging from his early sketches however, he might have imagined

13

14

15

13 Mies van der Rohe, 1934. Portrait photograph by Werner Rohde. Note Sasha Stone's photo of the Barcelona Pavilion (see no. 12 on the previous page) in the background.

14-15 German Pavilion, late June 1929. Photograph: Sasha Stone. Notice the small reflection of the hand reaching into the picture on the left. Retouched and cropped version below.

13 Franz Schulze, "The Barcelona Pavilion Returns," *Art in America* 67, no. 7 (1979): 98–103. See also Ludwig Glaeser, *Mies van der Rohe: The Barcelona Pavilion: 50th Anniversary* (Friends of the Mies van der Rohe Archive in connection with the exhibition, *Mies van der Rohe: The Barcelona Pavilion*, National Gallery of Art, Washington DC, October 14 – December 2, 1979); and Robin Evans, "Mies van der Rohe's Paradoxical Symmetries," *AA Files* 19 (1990): 56–68.

14 Hans Maria Wingler, *The Bauhaus: Weimar, Dessau, Berlin, Chicago* (Cambridge, MA: MIT Press, 1969), 536.

15 Claire Zimmerman, *Photographic Architecture* (Minneapolis: University of Minnesota Press, 2014), 53, 56, 70.

16

17

18

16 Interior view late June 1929, photograph: Sasha Stone

17 Retouched version of 1961

18 Night view from the back: Wilhelm Niemann, October 1929

ended up taking. And, of course, the chaos of the building's genesis ultimately prevented him from commissioning photography at all.

A second professional photographer came from Germany in late October—Wilhelm Niemann (1891–1980), the owner of the Berliner Bild-Bericht agency, to which Stone had sold his images. As mentioned above, he would later claim to have been in Barcelona in March and April 1929 already to supervise the execution of the Electric Utilities Pavilion. Attribution is complicated by the fact that the agency habitually put only its own stamp on the back of prints, without crediting the photographer. Given the known dates of their visits, though, those distributed by the Berliner Bild-Bericht and used widely before late October can be assigned to Stone,[16] and the nocturnal image from the back **FIG. 18** to Niemann, since the luminous wall was not yet functional when Stone was in Barcelona.

The surviving correspondence makes it clear that the visual documentation of the pavilion was hardly felt to be an urgent matter. In early November 1929 Reich noted that "Mies and I had thought about having a little picture book put together, but then we lost the desire again to do so." At yet at the same time she was curious to see whether Niemann's visit to Barcelona in late October would yield "more good pictures."[17] Toward the end of November, Erich von Kettler urged Reich (apparently in vain) to "preserve the pavilion for posterity," for example in the form of a series of postcards, like those of the Romanian pavilion (which he enclosed).[18] But while Mies did not commission his own photography, he seems to have been happy to embrace Stone's, which he sent out to participants at the exhibition as well as to magazines, sometimes with the request to reproduce them in a suitably large format, or put them on prominent display.[19] A large print of the straight view on the longitudinal axis toward the Kolbe figure in the back **FIG. 12** adorned a wall in Mies's own office, and in 1934 Werner Rhode positioned Mies in front of it when he took his portrait. **FIG. 13** This was also the only image of the pavilion Mies chose to include (in a wall-high enlargement) in his 1947 exhibition at the Museum of Modern Art.

Undoubtedly, Sasha Stone turned out to be one of Mies's most important allies. He sold his images to Wilhelm Niemann's Berliner Bild-Bericht agency, which distributed them widely to print publications.[20] If it were not for the visual coherence of these thirteen photographs, the short-lived pavilion might not have attained its almost mythical status.[21] The power and single-mindedness of Stone's particular vision becomes clear when compared to the three amateur shots discussed earlier, and to a few photographs taken at the same time.

16 Dr. Erich Raemisch to Lilly Reich, 2 July 1929, MoMA, MvdR Papers, Barcelona Pavilion, Folder 11. See Birgit Hammers, "Vom Dokument zur Legende: Zur Autorschaft der Fotografien des Barcelona Pavillons," *Zeitschrift für Kunstgeschichte*, 72 (2009): 545–56. I would like to thank Birgit Hammers for additional information via e-mail on November 12, 2013. Niemann is mentioned in letters from Lilly Reich to von Kettler, 4 November and 8 November 1929, MoMA, MvdR Papers, Barcelona Pavilion, Folders 3 and 9. The Stone photographs were probably the ones that Mies's office sent out to some participants in Barcelona at the end of July. See Mies van der Rohe's office to Georg Kolbe, 24 July 1929, and A. Meyer-Gasters to Lilly Reich, 22 July 1929, MoMA, MvdR Papers, Barcelona Pavilion, Folder 9. The Berliner Bild-Bericht sent twenty-five photographs of the Barcelona exhibition to Georg von Schnitzler on August 25 and an additional twelve prints on December 28, 1929; see HoeA, WaB 1929–1930 H0090400.

17 Reich to von Kettler, 4 November and 8 November 1929 (see note 16).

18 Erich von Kettler to Lilly Reich, 26 November 1929, MoMA, MvdR Papers, Barcelona Pavilion, Folder 4. Von Kettler had asked Lilly Reich 2 months earlier on behalf of a Spanish photographer already who had purchasesd a licence and wanted to produce postcards, but Lilly Reich and Mies did not respond. Von Kettler an Lilly Reich, 10. September 1929, MoMA, MvdR Papers, Barcelona-Pavillon, Folder 9.

19 "The exceptional art and beauty of the building compelled us to follow the architect's wishes regarding the large size of the reproductions and their careful placement." "Der Pavillon des Deutschen Reiches auf der Ausstellung in Barcelona: Architekt Ludwig Mies van der Rohe," *Stein Holz Eisen*, no. 39 (September 26, 1929): 609–13.

20 A close reading of Stone's canonical images suggests that they were taken at different times and perhaps on different days. In some, not all, of them, flowerpots line the pavilion's periphery, as they did on opening day. The placement of the furniture varies. For the interior shots, the outside brightness was hard to balance with the darkness indoors.

21 Partial sets of Stone's photographs exist at the Bauhaus Dessau Foundation, the Museum of Modern Art in New York, and the Fundacío Mies van der Rohe in Barcelona. The importance of Stone's photographs for the pavilion's success has been discussed by Birgit Hammers, George Dodds, and Wolf Tegethoff. See also Ursula Berger and Thomas Pavel, eds., *Barcelona Pavillon: Mies van der Rohe, Architektur und Plastik* (Berlin: Jovis, 2006).

19

Sasha Stone's wife, Cami, had come along on the trip to Barcelona, and two of her own photographs have survived, providing a refreshing counterpart to her husband's earnest work. One shot picks up on the play of reflections that her husband (or later editors) had studiously tried to avoid. **FIG. 20** Slightly tilted and clearly taken without a tripod, her photograph looks from the main space toward Kolbe's figure under the bright noontime sun. There is no water in the basin. The glass that separates her from the figure overlays reflections from the back of the pavilion with what we see in front of us. Two nickel-clad posts stand in front, probably used to cordon off sections, and likely designed by Mies and his team. **FIG. 20**

Gabriel Casas y Galobardes (1892–1973), one of the official photographers at the fair and one of the most significant Spanish photographers of his time, was fascinated with the dynamic photographic conventions in the work of the avant-garde (high and low angles, prominent diagonals, off-center framings, elongated shadows, stark contrasts, etc.)—all things Stone had studiously avoided.[22] He took only one photograph of the pavilion (unpublished at the time) from a low vantage point at the edge of the plinth, looking toward the main stairs and the blank wall of the Victoria Eugenie exhibition hall. **FIG. 19** While Casas also carefully avoided the Ionic columns and the Maggi building across the street, he emphasized the dynamic interaction of the pavilion's horizontal planes, marble wall, and glass enclosures. He seems also to have delighted in the slight absurdity of the oversized pot of Black-eyed Susans in the immediate foreground. (These flowerpots, by the way, were not intended to soften the starkness of Mies's building in particular, but rather were dispersed for festive effect at the opening ceremonies of many pavilions.)

A few other snapshots have surfaced over time, such as a stereoview by an anonymous photographer, meant to be seen through a stereoscope for an immersive, three-dimensional impression. Taken near the small office building, it shows the pavilion's terrace after a rain shower, with visitors hastily crossing its platform on their way back from the Poble Espanyol, apparently unimpressed by the pavilion itself.[23] **FIG. 19** But another amateur image, taken later that summer, is far more instructive. It shows how the pavilion might have looked on any given day without being spruced up for a photoshoot. Five Barcelona chairs (two black, three white) and a white ottoman sit in a somewhat irregular circle in the foreground. There are five ottomans to the left and a small glass table in front of the onyx wall, while two white Barcelona chairs and another ottoman flank the large glass table and the opal glass wall in the back, where a pile of pillows has been dumped in the far corner. The black carpet is missing, but the red curtain has been drawn toward the front, darkening the entrance passage—perhaps by the photographer in order to dampen a blinding flood of light from the left. The space seems uninviting, uncared for, and badly lit. The Swiss architect Alfredo Baeschlin lived in Spain since 1928 and probably took the photograph himself to accompany an essay on the building commissioned by the *Deutsche Bauzeitung*. He provided one of the few critical voices at the time, with his photograph appearing to underline his observations that this "perplexing" pavilion looked unfinished, was missing a central "idea," and was "not entirely convincing" as a representation of Germany.[24] It seems fair to assume that the Barcelona Pavilion would never have enjoyed the same measure of success had Baeschlin been its official photographer. **FIG. 22**

20

21

22

22 Casas had recorded historical buildings all over Spain for the design of the Poble Espanyol. For Casas's biography, see Gabriel Casas, *Fotomuntatges* (Barcelona: Generalitat de Catalunya, 2002). His work frequently appeared in the daily paper *La Vanguardia*, as well as in magazines such as *Mirador*, *D'Ací i d'Allà*, or *Barcelona Gráfica*.

23 This image is in the collection of Juanjo Lahuerta in Barcelona. See Juan José Lahuerta, *Photography or Life & Popular Mies*, Columns of Smoke 1 (Barcelona: Tenov, 2015).

24 Alfredo Baeschlin, "Barcelona und seine Weltausstellung," *Deutsche Bauzeitung*, 63, no. 57 (1929): 497–504; and no. 77 (1929), 657–62, here 658.

19 The Barcelona Pavilion on the evening before the opening, May 26, 1929. Note the old German flag in black, white and red in the background. Photograph: Gabriel Casas

20 Barcelona Pavilion late June 1929. Photographer Cammie Stone

21 Anonymous stereoview, 1929

22 Interior View. Photographer: Alfredo Baeschlin

Clients and Architects

Since the Barcelona Pavilion would not have existed without the singlemindedness, courage, and considerable financial sacrifice of Lilly and Georg von Schnitzler, let us look for a moment at these two patrons and their political leanings. **FIGS. 1, 2, P. 26** Georg von Schnitzler was probably close to the Deutsche Volkspartei (DVP), or German People's Party, to which the Foreign Minister, Gustav Stresemann, and the Minister of Economic Affairs, Julius Curtius, belonged. Industrialists typically aligned themselves with this right-of-center party, which had originally opposed the new political system of the Weimar Republic, calling for the restoration of the monarchy. Curtius and Stresemann had helped broker the financial compromise to save the pavilion in March of 1929, and Curtius provided another substantial sum to offset von Schnitzler's expenses in December 1929.

On February 20, 1933, just six weeks after Adolf Hitler became Chancellor of the German Reich, von Schnitzler was one of several industrialists (among them Friedrich Flick and Gustav Krupp von Bohlen und Halbach) who attended a secret conference at Hermann Göring's office in Berlin, at which Hitler presented his party's goals and asked for financial support for the parliamentary elections on March 5. The group of industrialists obliged, pledging three million Reichsmark.[1] In September 1933—three and a half years after the Barcelona Pavilion was dismantled—von Schnitzler became a member of the National Socialist SA (Sturmabteilung), a voluntary paramilitary organization;[2] his records indicate that he rose swiftly through its ranks, attaining the position of Hauptsturmführer in 1941.[3] In November 1933 he also became a member of the government's Außenhandelsrats, or Foreign Trade Commission, organized jointly by the foreign and economic ministers.[4] His membership of the National Socialist Party followed three and a half years later, on May 1, 1937, in response to a campaign to recruit prominent industrialists to the cause.

Despite his rapid rise up the National Socialist hierarchy, it is difficult to judge the strength of von Schnitzler's loyalty to the regime. In classified Party documents he was considered "politically reliable," despite an incident in 1939 when the Gestapo reprimanded him for not paying due attention to a speech by Göring.[5] In 1940 he also published an essay in the American journal *Atlantic Monthly* in which he emphasized a German desire for peace and economic prosperity after the end of the war, and advocated a strong role for industry in that process.[6]

We know more about Lilly von Schnitzler's cultural and political interests, thanks to her publications, letters, and social activities. Among these were the many evening salons she hosted in her Frankfurt apartment, not least the occasion in 1925 when she first met Mies van der Rohe. Other prominent guests in the same

1 Wolfgang Klötzer, ed., *Frankfurter Biographie*, vol. 2, *M–Z*, Veröffentlichungen der Frankfurter Historischen Kommission 19/2 (Frankfurt: Kramer, 1996), 320. See also James Pool, *Hitler and His Secret Partners: Contributions, Loot, and Rewards, 1933–45* (New York: Pocket Books, 1997), 31.
The previous two sources allege that von Schnitzler produced a check for more than 400,000 Reichsmark from IG Farben for the NSDAP at this occasion, but the transcripts of his statement in front of the Nuremberg War Tribunal do not confirm this. See *Trials of War Criminals Before the Nuremberg Military Tribunals* (Washington, DC: US Government Printing Office, 1953), 7:555.

2 See the personnel files in the Wiesbaden Document section of the US Military Government in Hessen (Dept. 649), HHSA. Occasional reports that von Schnitzler had already been a high-ranking member of the SA in 1930 are not confirmed by the source material in the HHSA. The wrong date is quoted in, for example, Klötzer, *Frankfurter Biographie*, 320 (see note 1), and in Jens Ulrich Heine, *Verstand und Schicksal: Die Männer der I.G. Farbenindustrie A.G. (1925–1945) in 161 Kurzbiographien* (Weinheim: VCH Verlagsgesellschaft, 1990), 133–36.

3 This was the equivalent of a captain in the US Army or a flight lieutenant in the Royal Air Force. Within the SA it was eleven ranks above the entry-level SA Sturmmann and eight ranks beneath National Leader.

4 "Die Mitglieder des Außenhandelsrats," *Vossische Zeitung*, November 24, 1933, 13.

5 See the file of the NSDAP district commission (Kreisleitung) of Greater Frankfurt from 1941 (Abt. 483, no. 10572) in the HHSA.

6 Georg von Schnitzler, "Germany and World Trade after the War," *The Atlantic* 165 (June 1940): 817–21.

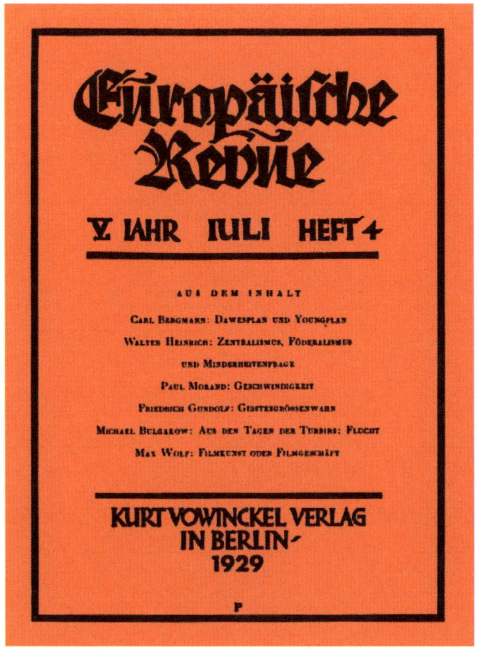

1

1 Europäische Revue, 1929

2 Karl Anton Prinz Rohan, ca. 1936
Photograph: Lichtbild Fayer, Vienna

3 The gathering of the European Cultural Association in Barcelona, October 16-19, 1929. Prince Karl Rohan is in front at the center, the architect Martin Elsaesser three figures behind him. Photograph: Josep Branguli

period included the writers Rudolf Binding and Hermann Graf Keyserling, Africa researcher Leo Frobenius, actor Heinrich George, and journalist Heinrich Simon, editor-in-chief of the liberal daily *Frankfurter Zeitung*. From 1924 on she was also the most important supporter of the painter Max Beckmann, assembling a substantial collection of his work.[7] It was in light of this cultural patronage, as Lilly von Schnitzler herself suggested in a 1974 interview, that her husband was chosen for the role of German commissioner for the Barcelona International Exposition. What is also clear is that she played a crucial role in Mies's appointment as artistic director of the German section, but in his subsequent commission to design Germany's national pavilion.

Lilly von Schnitzler would go on to publish two essays about Mies's pavilion and the German participation in Barcelona that helped lay the foundations for the interpretation of the building that has prevailed to this day. One of them appeared in the conservative literary and political magazine *Europäische Revue*, which she had founded in 1924 together with her close friend, the Austrian writer and aristocrat Karl Anton Prinz Rohan (1898–1975). **FIGS. 1, 2** Thanks to her husband, the publication was initially financed by the cultural funds of IG Farben.[8] It had an impressive list of contributors, among them Theodor Heuss, Thomas Mann, Paul Valéry, Winston Churchill, Max Beckmann, and Le Corbusier. For Rohan, the journal was merely one part of a vision for a pan-European intellectual elite—of successful writers, artists, businessmen, and politicians—who would transcend national, class, and religious differences, and form a bulwark against both the advances of Soviet Communism and America's unbridled capitalism. Inspiration came from figures such as the Austrian writer Hugo von Hofmannsthal, who had popularized the notion of a "conservative revolution," as well as from the Spanish philosopher Ortega y Gasset, author of *The Revolt of the Masses* (1930), in which he wrote of his fear that the "mediocrity" of the masses made them dangerously susceptible to totalitarian influences. Rohan's vision (also shared by his friend and fervent supporter Lilly von Schnitzler) was decidedly antidemocratic. The "ideas of 1789"—parliamentary democracy, equality, and liberty—were rejected as "untenable."[9] He joined the National Socialist Party as soon as it assumed power in Germany, but became disillusioned in 1938, following the annexation of his homeland, Austria.

The wider organization behind the *Europäische Revue*—the Europäischer Kulturbund (European Cultural Association)—held annual conferences in Paris, Milan, Vienna, Heidelberg, Frankfurt, and Prague from 1924 on. Le Corbusier gave a speech at the 1928 Prague conference on the theme of the "Neue Gesinnung in der Baukunst" (New Attitude in Architecture), which was published in the magazine a few months later. In one of his most ambitious and far-reaching essays, he allied himself with Rohan's vision, singling out the "seeing man" as a new "elite," separate from the "man in the street." This new elite, he suggested, was redefining the art of architecture, moving toward a comprehensive notion of design that encompassed all spheres of life and brought about a new order.[10] After the war Rohan reciprocated this support and published a surprisingly perceptive book on Le Corbusier's chapel at Ronchamp.[11]

The 1929 conference of the Kulturbund was held at the city center university campus in Barcelona between October 16 and 19, on the eve of "German Week" at the exposition. **FIG. 3** Among the speakers were Carl Schmitt (the influential German jurist, philosopher, political theorist, and soon a major voice in National Socialist ideology) and the Italian Fascist Giuseppe Bottai (later responsible for the planning of the envisioned 1942 World's Fair in Rome), alongside many other intellectuals, most—though not all—of them of a conservative bent.[12] The writers Aldous Huxley from England, Jean Guéhenno from France, and Rudolf Binding from Germany also took part in the proceedings, as did the architect Martin Elsaesser. The theme of the conference, "Le problème

2

3

sociale de la vulgarisation de la culture" (translated by the reporter of the *Vossische Zeitung* somewhat less offensively as "Culture as Social Problem"), hinted at the organizers' vision of a conservative aristocracy of intellectuals as an alternative to a culture and government ruled by a democracy of the masses. As Rohan pointed out in his concluding remarks at the conference, what was at stake was the survival of a "European will to culture," threatened by the infiltration of simplistic formulas emerging from the US and USSR. Also in attendance were Georg and Lilly von Schnitzler, who presented "their" pavilion to the delegates on the first evening.[13] With its marble from Greece, Italy, and Morocco, and a formal language that seemed to marry ancient and modern materials, asceticism, and luxurious exuberance, the pavilion might have seemed emblematic for their shared goal of a conservative pan-European union. One also cannot avoid thinking of the many critics who found the pavilion only accessible to an educated elite, to "visitors open to contemporary tendencies."[14] It would be "completely incomprehensible to an innocuous visitor, but a true experience for someone sensitive to modern artistic manifestations"[15] wrote one critic, while another added "the poor couldn't have built it nor a fool imagined it; it is the manifestation of a higher spirit."[16]

Lilly von Schnitzler's own 1929 article about the Barcelona Pavilion in the *Europäische Revue* conjured up some of the most lyrical formulations celebrating Mies's achievement: "as if from a fairy tale, not from the *Arabian Nights*, but from an almost supernaturally inspired music of eternal space, not as a house, but as a drawing of lines in such a space by a hand that defines the human reach toward infinity." Mies had, she claimed, cast "our spiritual existence into form."[17] She closed with a remark that can be read as a thinly veiled reference to the military dictatorship of Primo de Rivera, and her own willingness to tolerate a similar turn of events in Germany:[18]

7 Klötzer, *Frankfurter Biographie*, 321–22 (see note 1).

8 D. Duisberg to G. von Schnitzler, Ringbinder „Spenden & Beiträge E-Gem" H0090098. 10 January 1925, HoeA, Ringbinder H0090098. According to this letter, IG Farben commissioned advertisements in the amount of 3,000 Reichsmark in order to pave the way for the magazine in Germany. Its first print run was intended to be 10,000 copies.

9 For more about Rohan and the European Cultural Association, see Guido Müller, *Europäische Gesellschaftsbeziehungen nach dem Ersten Weltkrieg* (Munich: R. Oldenbourg, 2005), 309ff, here 331 and 351.

10 Le Corbusier, "Neue Gesinnung in der Baukunst," *Europäische Revue* 4, no. 9 (December 1928): 689–700.

11 Karl Anton Prinz Rohan, *Besuch in Ronchamp* (Nuremberg: Glock and Lutz, 1958).

12 Max Clauss, "Kultur als soziales Problem: Europäische Revue in Barcelona," *Vossische Zeitung*, November 5, 1929. Max Clauss was a journalist and translator of Malraux's work into German. With Rohan he edited the *Europäische Revue* until 1932, when disagreements with Rohan about the political direction of the magazine led to his dismissal. He joined the NSDAP in 1933.

13 After the pavilion, they presented the rest of the German sections. See "Avui comença el VI Congrés de la Federació Internacional d'Unions Intellectuals," *La Publicitat*, October 16, 1929, 4; and "VI Congrés de la Federació Internacional d'Unions Intellectuals," *La Veu de Catalunya*, October 16, 1929, 1. See also Federico Enriques, "La síntesis intelectual de Europa," *Diario Oficial Exposición Internacional de Barcelona 1929* 1, no. 31 (October 5, 1929): 15. Rohan's magazine, *Europäische Revue*, printed several of the lectures and a summary of the proceedings in the three following numbers: Carl Schmitt, "Die europäische Kultur in Zwischenstadien der Neutralisierung" *Europäische Revue* 5, no. 8 (November 1929): 517–30; Giuseppe Bottai, "Kultur und Masse," *Europäische Revue* 5, no. 9 (December 1929), 585–99; and Prinz Karl Rohan, "Kultur als Soziales Problem, (VI. Jahrestagung des Internationalen Verbandes für kulturelle Zusammenarbeit in Barcelona vom 16.–20. Oktober 1929. Diskussion von Jean Guéhenno, Emil Wolff, Albert Gleizes, Luigi Valli, Pierre de Lanux, Richard von Kühlmann)," *Europäische Revue* 6, no. 1 (January 1930): 51–62.

14 See Heinrich Simon, "Präludium," *Frankfurter Zeitung*, June 2, 1929, 1; and Heinrich Simon, "Weltausstellung 1929: Deutsche Abteilung I," *Frankfurter Zeitung*, June 5, 1929, 1. As a Jew, Simon had to leave the newspaper in 1934; he emigrated via Paris and Tel Aviv to Washington, DC, where he was tragically murdered in an attempted robbery a few years later.

15 Eduard Foertsch, "Die Weltausstellung in Barcelona," *Vossische Zeitung*, June 11, 1929, 4.

16 Francisco Marroquin, "Hacia una nueva arquitectura: El Pabellón de Alemania en la Exposición de Barcelona," *ABC*, January 26, 1930, 13–14.

17 L.S.M. (Lilly von Schnitzler), "Weltausstellung Barcelona," *Europäische Revue* 5, no. 4 (July 1929), 286–88, here p. 287.

18 Guido Müller, "Von Hugo von Hofmannsthals Traum des Reiches zum Europa unter nationalsozialistischer Herrschaft: Die 'Europäische Revue' 1925–1936/44," in *Konservative Zeitschriften zwischen Kaiserreich und Diktatur*, ed. Hans-Christof Kraus (Berlin: Duncker & Humbolt, 2003), 155–86.

4

4 Max Beckmann, Paris Society, 1931

Spain seems to be Europe's last haven for conviction, attitude, character, metaphysics—the sole values through which Europe can recover and resist the impending Americanism. [...] Spain's experiment in Barcelona, which is symptomatic for all of Spain to drive out the devil with the help of Lucifer, is for all of us a most enthralling adventure, whose result can become authoritative for us as well.[19]

Less than two years later, when the European Cultural Association had drifted further to the right and lost some of its prominent participants, Lilly von Schnitzler's friend and protégé Max Beckmann painted a number of members of her conservative circle at a seemingly disjointed and joyless musical soirée—perhaps at the opening of an art exhibition in Paris. The canvas itself overpainted an earlier, unfinished group portrait of 1925 that was set among Frankfurt's society—in all likelihood already including the von Schnitzlers. In the painting Georg von Schnitzler seems to be the only one enjoying himself, flirting with a woman in a red dress in the foreground on the left. His blonde wife, Lilly, is depicted sternly ignoring the scene, which is, however, carefully and critically observed by Karl Anton Rohan in the center. The French politician Anatole de Monzie, the Frankfurt banker Albert Hahn, and the German ambassador Leopold von Hoesch (bottom right, with his head in his hands) are also present.[20] **FIG. 4**

The *Europäische Revue* continued to appear until 1944, secretly funded by Joseph Goebbels's Ministry of Propaganda. In 1937 Rohan published *Schicksalsstunde Europas* (Europe's fateful hour), a vast philosophical survey ranging from human relationships to politics to interior decoration. Regarding modern architecture and design, Rohan's remarks—"the new style creates an atmosphere of unconditional spirituality and mental freedom"—seem to echo the critical reception of the Barcelona Pavilion. Despite his aversion to mass culture, he championed Italian Fascism as "a rebirth of the European heritage" and a "revolution of the spirit." With similar exuberance he welcomed National Socialism and defended anti-Semitism and the Nuremberg racial laws. Lilly von Schnitzler loved this book, and repeatedly recommended it to her friends, among them the influential Jewish industrialist Richard Merton, who responded somewhat wearily to her recommendations by quoting back to her some of its more offensive anti-Semitic passages.[21]

Close friendship with a number of Jewish intellectuals, including Merton and Heinrich Simon, prevented the von Schnitzlers from becoming either fervent Nazis or radical anti-Semites. On the other hand, they had little difficulty coming to terms with the new regime. Lilly von Schnitzler, in particular, adapted her Frankfurt salon to the changing times: "it seemed to me that the important task was to try and establish a mediating role between the emerging political forces, which were not to be ignored, and the carriers of tradition, the previous creative forces in the city."[22]

The National Socialists also established their own mediating practices, integrating the European Cultural Association—now renamed the Deutsch-Europäischer Kulturbund—the cultural wing of its party in the summer of 1933. Lilly von Schnitzler became vice president. She also joined the NS Frauenschaft[23] (the National Socialist Women's League) and a number of other state-controlled groups. Eager to demonstrate her helpfulness to the Führer, in 1942 she even proposed that her local Red Cross support group should jointly knit a large rug with a red cross in the center as a present for Hitler. When informed about their intentions, however, the Führer let it be known that "he had enough rugs already."[24]

But what do we know about Mies van der Rohe's political leanings? "Politically, Mies was the Talleyrand of modern architecture,"[25] the historian Richard Pommer sarcastically declared, referring to the famously opportunistic French diplomat Charles Maurice de Talleyrand-Périgord (1754–1838), active under different masters before, during, and after the revolution. And indeed, a series of projects by Mies seem to suggest his indifference to political persuasions, be they the Bismarck Memorial, the Liebknecht-Luxemburg Monument, the Barcelona Pavilion, or the design of the National Socialist regime's pavilion for the Brussels Universal Exhibition. In late 1928 Mies appears to have belonged to a group of artists in Barcelona who protested against the move by Primo de Rivera's proto-Fascist and centralist government to dismantle the four columns—a symbol of Catalan independence—at the center of the fairground. Little more than a year later, in 1930, he decidedly depoliticized the Bauhaus when he became its director. In 1933, after the secret police had shut down the Berlin Bauhaus, he agreed to sacrifice his colleagues Ludwig Hilberseimer and Wassily Kandinsky, whose presence on the faculty the Nazis found particularly objectionable, so the school could reopen—an unnecessary gesture, it turned out, as soon afterwards the funding dried up, and the school could not be saved after all.[26] A group of Bauhaus students, probably mobilized by Mies, wrote an open letter to Alfred Rosenberg, head of the Militant League for German Culture (Kampfbund für Deutsche Kultur), to whom Mies had turned for support. They pledged their allegiance to the new regime and asked for a reopening of the school.[27] Mies might have also solicited the support of the architect Ernst Neufert, who enjoyed the National Socialists' trust, and published an article in April 1933, immediately after the Bauhaus's closing, arguing that the Barcelona Pavilion—and by extension,

19 L.S.M., "Weltausstellung Barcelona," (see note 18).

20 I would like to thank Prof. Barbara "Suzy" Buenger for many discussions about this painting and Lilly von Schnitzler's circle. Guido Müller deserves credit for having been the first to convincingly identify Lilly and Georg von Schnitzler in this group portrait. Neither Beckmann nor his wife Quappi ever provided any hints for an identification of the protagonists. Guido Müller, *Europäische Gesellschaftsbeziehungen*, 309ff (see note 9). An examination of the painting in June 2018 by the Guggenheim Museum's conservation department, using X-ray, ultraviolet, and infrared light, revealed an even greater likeness to Lilly von Schnitzler than in the later version. Many thanks, in particular, to Senior Painting Conservator Julie Barten.

21 Richard Merton to Lilly von Schnitzler, 31 December 1936, Richard Merton Papers, Hessisches Wirtschaftsarchiv, Abt. 2000. I would like to thank Professor Suzy Buenger, University of Wisconsin, Madison, for this reference.

22 Lilly von Schnitzler, "Frankfurt zwischen den beiden Weltkriegen [...] Erinnerungen von Lilly von Schnitzler Mallinckrodt," recorded on tape for the Municipal Archive Frankfurt, March 5, 1962, Stadtarchiv Frankfurt. Again, thanks to Prof. Buenger for giving me access to a transcript of this tape.

23 Personnel files in the collection of the Wiesbaden Document Section of the US Military Government in Hesse (Division 649).

24 Bernd Biege, *Helfer unter Hitler* (Hamburg: Kindler Verlag, 2000), 47–48.

25 Richard Pommer, "Mies van der Rohe and the Political Ideology of the Modern Movement in Architecture," in *Mies van der Rohe: Critical Essays*, ed. Franz Schulze (New York: Museum of Modern Art 1989), 96–145, here 96.

26 This little-known fact becomes obvious from the exchange of letters in July and August 1933 between Mies, the students of the Bauhaus, and the secret police. See Peter Hahn, ed., *Bauhaus Berlin* (Berlin: Kunstverlag Weingarten, 1985), 142–44.

27 They wrote that the "de-politicization of the Bauhaus (through Mies) has created the basis for a positive collaboration in the new Germany. [...] The Bauhaus [...] wants to put all of its powers in the service of this cause." "Bauhaus und Kampfbund: Ein Brief der Bauhausschüler," *Deutsche Allgemeine Zeitung*, April 15, 1933, quoted in Hahn, *Bauhaus Berlin*, 131 (see note 27).

5

5 Georg von Schnitzler at the Nuremberg Trial, 1947

modern architecture—was as much "a German expression" as the traditional pitched-roofed houses by Paul Schmitthenner.[28] One year later, Mies was one of thirty-seven mostly conservative writers, artists, and architects who signed a public pledge of allegiance to Adolf Hitler in the National Socialist paper *Völkischer Beobachter*: "We believe in this leader who has fulfilled our burning desire for unity. We trust his work, which requires commitment beyond critical rationalism, we place our hopes in this man, who is, beyond human and material things, faithful in God's providence."[29] That signature is perhaps the most unforgivable of Mies's few political gestures, because it seems so gratuitous—Mies's hope of getting a government commission had just been dashed when his design for the German pavilion at the 1935 Brussels Universal Exhibition had not been selected. It appears that Josef Goebbels, the Reich's Minister of Propaganda, who had written the text, pressured a number of progressive artists to sign the letter, as it was meant to gather broad support for a national referendum in favor of strengthening Hitler's position on the next day, August 19, 1934 (Hitler won 89.9 percent of the vote). Mies agreed to sign, but immediately apologized to his friends.[30] Only four architects in total signed the declaration. One of them was the fervent National Socialist Paul Schultze Naumburg, who had been instrumental in closing the Bauhaus under Mies's directorship. Georg Kolbe, the sculptor of the figure at the pavilion, also signed.

Two years later, Sergius Ruegenberg, who had been Mies's closest collaborator, published a piece (no doubt coordinated with Mies), which, in the guise of a birthday greeting, tried rather hard to make Mies's work palpable to the regime and to position him for major commissions. While cautiously critiquing the recent return to neoclassicism, Ruegenberg pointed out that Mies was embracing that same style, and had been inspired by Karl Friedrich Schinkel's Charlottenhof in Potsdam—not its "classical forms, profiles, capitals," but its true essence, realized with his own means. This led straight to the Barcelona Pavilion, as "Mies's first work in this spirit"—a "northern approach" under "the southern sun, [...] driven by the desire to lend form to the German spirit. A strong sense of beauty does not need to overemphasize functionality. Careful execution goes hand in hand with progressive building methods."[31] This attempt to appeal to the new regime's sensibilities was the first time that Mies was presented as a closeted neoclassicist, a claim that would be repeated many times in the following decades.

Late in her life, Lilly von Schnitzler recalled how in 1937 Mies had asked her to use her political connections to help him find work. Soon after, she found herself at a dinner seated next to Joseph Goebbels. She asked him if he knew Mies and if he could do something for him. Goebbels answered: "Well, yes, he is our most outstanding architect, next to Troost."[32] Despite this hymn of praise, he was unable to give him a commission, as he explained: "Mrs. von Schnitzler, you don't seem to realize that we are a totalitarian regime. We depend on the support of the masses. We dance, precariously, on a wave. If that wave ceases to carry us, we vanish overnight. I cannot do anything for Mies, as the masses behind me have entirely different ideas, and if I propose Mies, it won't be accepted."[33] When Mies finally realized that he would have to give up his hard-won position as a respected avant-gardist in order to be considered for an official commission, he promptly took up an offer to teach in Chicago. Up until his departure to the US, Lilly von Schnitzler remained a close friend, and would visit him occasionally in Berlin. After the war she saw him again during a visit to Chicago in 1954 and on one of his later trips to Germany. Her subsequent recollections hint that there may have been romantic aspects to their relationship.[34]

Because of his role as a high-ranking IG Farben manager in several occupied countries during the war, Georg von Schnitzler was tried as a war criminal at the Nuremberg Military Tribunals in

1947. He was given a five-year sentence. However, the new High Commissioner for Germany (the immensely influential American lawyer, banker, and political advisor, John J. McCloy), proceeded to commute von Schnitzler's sentence to just five days per month, before dismissing it entirely.[35] McCloy knew von Schnitzler personally, as he had been IG Farben's international legal advisor during the National Socialist years. Married to a woman of German heritage, he had developed a great interest in German design and architecture, and no doubt appreciated von Schnitzler's fundamental role in Barcelona.[36] McCloy became a central figure in the founding and initial funding of the Hochschule für Gestaltung in Ulm, the successor to the Bauhaus in West Germany. Mies was invited to join the school's advisory board.[37]

After the war, both von Schnitzlers continued to play important roles in Frankfurt's society. Georg von Schnitzler, who converted to Catholicism in 1950, became president of the German Ibero-American Society. He died in 1962. Lilly von Schnitzler founded the Max Beckmann Society in 1951 and donated a large part of her collection to Cologne's Wallraf Richard Museum in 1957 (today Museum Ludwig). She died in 1981, having lived out most of her last thirty years in Murnau, south of Munich.[38]

28 Ernst Neufert, "Das Deutsche Wohnhaus," *Zentralblatt der Bauverwaltung* 53, no. 17 (April 19, 1933): 200–201. In 1936 Neufert's enormously popular *Bauentwurfslehre* appeared for the first time. It contained sample solutions and detailed measurements for all fields of building (the American equivalent and immediate predecessor was Charles Ramsey's *Architectural Graphic Standards* of 1932). Neufert showed a floor plan and perspective of Mies's House for a Childless Couple at the Berlin building exhibition (the most immediate successor to the Barcelona Pavilion) as the "House in the Year 2000," and emphasized its spatial openness, thanks to the separation of supports and walls. Ernst Neufert, *Bauentwurfslehre* (Berlin: Bauwelt Verlag, 1936), 33.

29 "Aufruf der Kulturschaffenden," *Völkischer Beobachter*, August 18, 1934, quoted in Hahn, *Bauhaus Berlin*, 148 (see note 27). The architects on the list, besides Mies and Paul Schultze Naumburg, were Emil Fahrenkamp, who considered himself apolitical but received important commissions in the Third Reich, and Walter March, the brother of Werner March, the architect of the 1936 Olympic Stadium.

30 Ibid. See also Alfred Rosenberg to Joseph Goebbels, 20 October 1934, in Ernst Piper, *Nationalsozialistische Kunstpolitik* (Frankfurt: Suhrkamp, 1987), 116–18. Rosenberg was less inclined than Goebbels to work with progressive artists, whom he called "Kulturbolschewisten" (cultural bolshevists). He mentioned the sculptor Ernst Barlach, Emil Nolde, and Mies van der Rohe, who had all signed the letter.

31 Sergius Ruegenberg, "Ein Fünfzigjähriger," *Bauwelt* 14 (1936): 346. Fifteen years later, in 1951, Ruegenberg repeated his birthday wishes, proudly referring to his earlier "courageous" piece: "Dear esteemed master: We all congratulate you cordially on your birthday. Often I have tried, just like the others, to reach you, and an answer came—but only through the newspapers. We could thus see that you were overwhelmed with work." Ruegenberg published a sketch of the Barcelona Pavilion, two interior photographs, and repeated the reference to Schinkel's Schloss Charlottenhof. Sergius Ruegenberg, "Mies van der Rohe 65 Jahre," *Neue Bauwelt* 19 (1951): 80.

32 If this conversation happened as Lilly von Schnitzler remembered it, Goebbels was likely referring to Albert Speer, as Paul Ludwig Troost had died in January 1934.

33 Interview, Ludwig Glaeser with Lilly von Schnitzler, September 6, 1974, transcript, 11. Ludwig Glaeser Papers, Box 3, Item 5, Archive of the Canadian Centre for Architecture, Montreal.

34 Interview Ludwig Glaeser with Lilly von Schnitzler, September 6, 1974, transcript, 9, 14. Ludwig Glaeser Papers, Box 3, Item 5, Archive of the Canadian Centre for Architecture, Montreal.

35 Kevin John Heller, *The Nuremberg Military Tribunals and the Origins of International Criminal Law* (Oxford: Oxford University Press 2011), 343.

36 Dietrich Neumann, "Politik und Architektur: Der Bau der Ford Foundation in New York," in *Winfried Nerdinger: Architektur im Museum 1977–2012*, ed. Uwe Kiessler (Munich: Detail Verlag, 2012), 182–95.

37 G.K., "Die Ulmer Hochschule für Gestaltung eröffnet," *Bauwelt* 41 (1955): 809.

38 The most extensive publication about Lilly von Schnitzler to date is Brigitte Salmen and Christian Lenz, eds., *Bereitschaft zum Risiko: Lilly von Schnitzler 1889–1981: Sammlerin und Mäzenin* (Murnau: Schloßmuseum, 2011).

Reconstruction

On January 22, 1957, Mies van der Rohe received a letter from a young Barcelona architect, Oriol Bohigas, who addressed him as "most admired master" and conveyed his profound respect for Mies as "the leader of a whole generation." Spanish architects, he said, felt "sorrow for the disappearance" of the Barcelona Pavilion and proposed that it should be "rebuilt in the Montjuïc Park. [...] If you find the idea practicable, please let us know your requirements in order that you can take up the management of the whole thing yourself. [...] Both the city council and the executives of the fair are quite open to accepting whatever conditions you may wish to establish."[1] Mies responded with uncharacteristic alacrity a week later: "Thank you very much for your letter. It was a surprise and a delight." He pointed out that the original construction drawings had been lost or misplaced in Germany, but that he could do "this work again at cost."[2] Mies confirmed as much, when he was visited shortly after by an emissary from Barcelona, the architect Francesc Bassó Birulés, a friend of Bohigas's who was traveling in the US.[3] Bohigas had been writing about his idea in the popular press since 1954,[4] but now kept the news of Mies's positive response secret in order to gather more support. Finally, in April 1958, he announced the "sensational news" of Mies's offer to rebuild the famous pavilion and urged the mayor of Barcelona to step up to the task: "Those citizens who are aware of the work's transcendence have already spoken and are all behind the idea. [...] Barcelona now has the unique opportunity to do something that is triply interesting: a reconstruction of one of the premier works of art that the country has possessed, a tribute to the great German master who has generously carried our city's name into the artistic circles of the entire world, and the raising of a monument that would be a permanent reminder of the 1929 Exhibition, which today is not even commemorated in Barcelona."[5] Bohigas was careful in selecting the platform for his appeal: *Destino* was a weekly illustrated journal with writers of "the highest intellectual caliber" that had been founded by the Fascist Falange in 1937, and was still the regime's most effective political and cultural platform in Catalonia, designed to "to imbue the Catalan bourgeois soul with the essence of Spain."[6]

Mies's former collaborator, Sergius Ruegenberg, had heard about Bohigas's plans and immediately contacted Mies. He mentioned that he still had a sketchbook with details and a single floor plan of the building: "It would make me very happy to help you rebuild the pavilion."[7] Mies, then in the midst of finishing the Seagram Building in New York, did not reply.

It is worth pausing for a moment to acknowledge the context of Bohigas's initiative. Initially, the Franco regime had tightly controlled the official narrative of Spanish architecture, routinely sidelining progressive organizations such as GATEPAC and GATCPAC,[8] and their members such as Josep Lluís Sert and Sixte

1 Oriol Bohigas to Mies van der Rohe, 20 December1956, LoC, Mies Papers, General Office File, Bohigas folder.

2 Mies van der Rohe to Oriol Bohigas, 30 January 1956, LoC, Mies Papers, General Office File, Bohigas folder.

3 Oriol Bohigas, "Una Noticia Sensacional: Mies van der Rohe se ofrece a reconstruir el famoso Pabellon de 1929," *Destino* 1080 (April 19, 1959): 36–37, http://mdc2.cbuc.cat/cdm/compoundobject/collection/destino/id/256636/rec/4. An English translation appears in Rosa Maria Subirana i Torrent, ed., *Mies van der Rohe's German Pavilion in Barcelona, 1929–1986* (Barcelona: Ajuntament de Barcelona, 1987), 58–59. Francesc Bassó Birulés (1919–2014) was, just like Bohigas, a member of the Grup R of progressive architects in Barcelona, and a professor at the architecture school there.

4 Oriol Bohigas, "A los 25 años. La obra maestra de la Exposición del 29," *Destino*, no. 896 (October 9, 1954), 27–28, http://mdc2.cbuc.cat/cdm/compoundobject/collection/destino/id/246741/show/246592/rec/10. An English translation appears in Subirana i Torrent, *Mies van der Rohe's German Pavilion in Barcelona, 1929–1986*, 56–57 (see note 3). Oriol Bohigas, "La obra barcelonesa de Mies van der Rohe," *Cuadernos de arquitectura* 21 (1955), 17–20.

5 Bohigas, "Una Noticia Sensacional" (see note 3).

6 Francesc Vilanova, "The position of Barcelona's *Destino* group and other regime sympathizers with regard to the Second World War: The example of Britain," *Journal of Catalan Intellectual History* 5 (2013): 35–62, http://revistes.iec.cat/index.php/JOCIH/article/view/72876/72630.

7 Sergius Ruegenberg to Mies van der Rohe, 23 March 1958, LoC, Mies Papers, General Office File, Ruegenberg Folder.

8 Grupo de Artistas y Técnicos Españoles Para la Arquitectura Contemporánea and its Catalan counterpart, Grup d'Arquitectes i Tècnics Catalans per al Progrés de l'Arquitectura Contemporània. Bohigas remembers how "around 1950 he wrote an article for the journal *Destino* about GATCPAC, which was returned to him by the censor with a note: "No. Modern architecture is red and separatistic." Oriol Bohigas, *Modernidad en la Arquitectura de la España republicana* (Barcelona: Tusquets Editores S.A., 1998), 13.

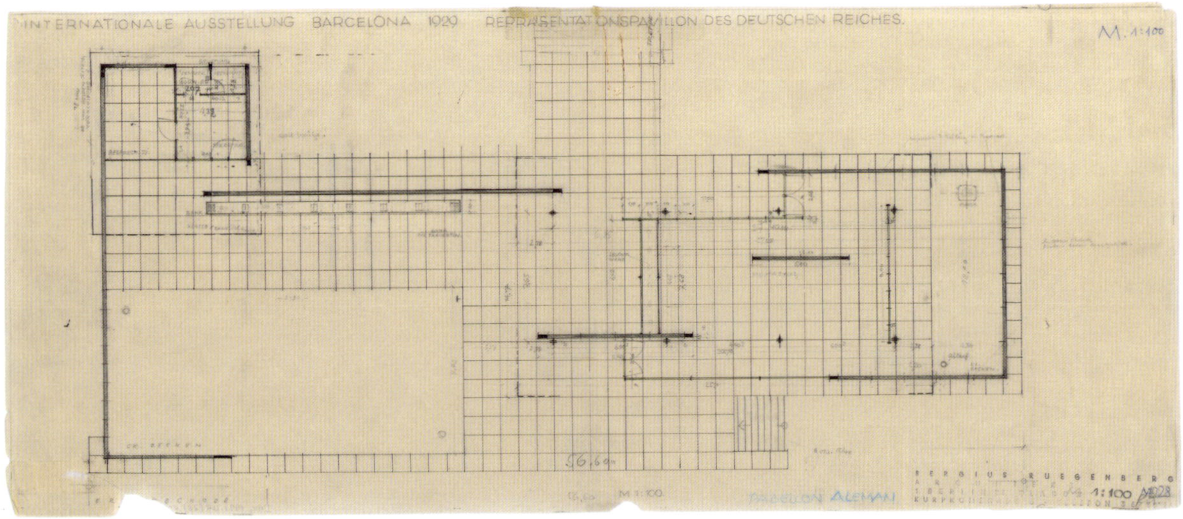

1

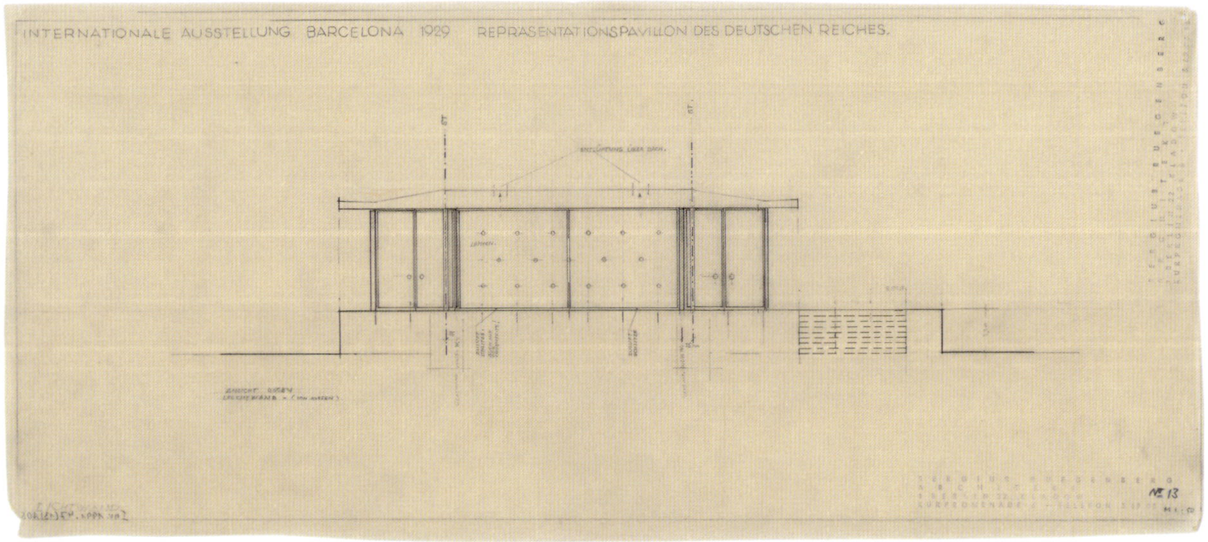

2

Illescas, who had supported the Republicans during the Civil War. But things slowly began to change in the 1950s. Bohigas joined a loose group of Catalan architects, Grup R (Grupo R in Spanish), which between 1951 and 1961 moved the discourse beyond the regime's preferred monumentalism and neoclassicism, advocating instead a rediscovery of the ethics and esthetics of prewar Spanish modernism. Other members included the abovementioned Francesc Bassó Birulés, as well as Josep Antoni Coderch and Manuel Valls, who were all connected with the Escuela Técnica Superior de Arquitectura de Barcelona. In rebuilding Mies's pavilion they hoped not only to restore a significant part of the city's architectural past, but also to resist Francoist cultural politics.

After Mies's initial, and immediate, enthusiastic reply, Bohigas heard nothing more from him. And so in November 1959 Bohigas wrote again, reporting that "a great movement had risen in Spain in favor of a reconstruction of the pavilion," and requested drawings in order to obtain an estimate of the costs. Mies eventually responded in March 1960, saying that he had asked a former collaborator (he was probably referring to Ruegenberg) about the plans, but had not heard back. Mies had indeed contacted Ruegenberg in January. Apparently misremembering Ruegenberg's letter of March 1958, Mies asked to borrow his "complete set of working drawings" for the pavilion.[9] But, of course, all Ruegenberg had were a few sketches and a floor plan. Bohigas then received another letter in October 1960, this time from Mies's collaborator Gene Summers, informing him that since the plans had still not been found, "the only possible way" would be for Mies to recreate the drawings "at cost," for about $55,000–$60,000 (around $450,000 today). As a way of excusing this exorbitant sum, Summers added, "you must know, the building itself is an expensive structure. I am sorry to paint such a bleak picture, but if this building is to be reconstructed it must be done right."[10] It is unclear why Mies decided to demand such a high

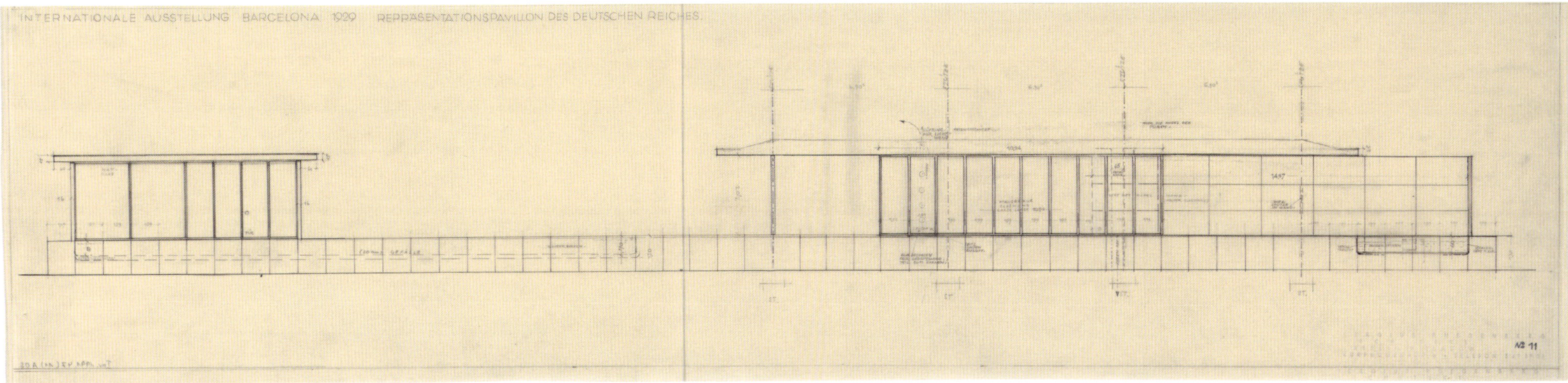

3

1-3 Sergius Ruegenberg, Construction drawings for the Barcelona Pavilion. Redrawn from memory, ca. 1975.

price for recreating his drawings, essentially ending any hope for the pavilion's reconstruction. Perhaps the success of the Seagram Building, which met with widespread international acclaim, had led him to reconsider his status, or perhaps he feared that the building might disappoint the high expectations raised over the years by the iconic photographs. In any event, after this exchange, nothing was heard about the project for a long time. Another Barcelona architect, Joan Bonaventura Bassegoda Nonell (a preservationist and expert on Gaudí), attempted to revive it in 1964 and 1967, but this also came to nothing.[11]

Sergius Ruegenberg, meanwhile, set out to remedy the dearth of surviving plans in his own way by developing a new set based on his recollections, which he promptly tried to sell. "Ruegenberg sits on a stash of working drawings [...] that he wants to sell for roughly a million,"[12] Mies's friend Werner Graef noted with amusement in 1972. After offering his drawings to the Museum of Modern Art in New York, which predictably turned him down, Ruegenberg sold sets of his sketches and blueprints to the Bauhaus archive in Berlin, the drawing collection at the Berlin Kunstbibliothek, the Berliner Galerie, and the architecture school at Tokyo University[13]–apparently as "original" Mies drawings, which led to some consternation among other former members of Mies's office.[14] **FIGS. 1-3** Another set ended up in the hands of Italian engineer Mario Ciamitti, who had approached Ruegenberg in 1977 to sound out the possibility of erecting a replica of the

9 Mies van der Rohe to Sergius Ruegenberg, 15 January 1960, LoC, Mies Papers. See also Mario Ciamitti, "Note sur la construction do Pavillon de Barcelone," in *La Colonne: Nouvelle histoire de la construction*, ed. Roberto Gargiani (Lausanne: Presses polytechniques et universitaires romandes, 2008), 467–71.

10 Gene Summers to Oriol Bohigas October 25, 1960. LoC MvdR Papers, General Office File, Folder Bohigas.

11 See Joan Bonaventura Bassegoda Nonell, "Historia y anécdota de una obra de Mies van der Rohe," *La Vanguardia*, October 6, 1979, 6. See a more detailed overview in Remei Capdevila Werning, "Construing Reconstruction: The Barcelona Pavilion and Nelson Goodman's Aesthetic Philosophy" (Master's thesis, Massachusetts Institute of Technology, 2007), 45, https://dspace.mit.edu/handle/1721.1/39307.

12 Ludwig Glaeser, interview with Werner Graef, Muehlheim, September 17, 1972, Canadian Centre of Architecture, Montréal, Glaeser papers. Willi Kaiser, another collaborator, recalled the sum of $100,000. Ludwig Glaeser, interview with Willi Kaiser in Cologne, July 25, 1978, Canadian Centre of Architecture, Montréal, Glaeser papers.

13 See Hajime Yatsuka, "Mies and Japan," *Cornell Journal of Architecture* 7 (2003): 52–62.

14 Ludwig Glaeser, interview with Willi Kaiser (see note 11).

4 On the left: Instituto Nacional de Industria (INI), 1973.
Architects: Juan Paradinas, Luis Garcia-German, and Jose Ignacio Casanova Fernandez
Photograph: ca. 1990 Robin Evans

5 The reconstructed Barcelona Pavilion nearing completion in 1986.
Photographer: Sergius Ruegenberg

Barcelona Pavilion in Bologna, where Le Corbusier's Pavillon de l'Esprit Nouveau had just been recreated.[15]

The Barcelona Pavilion's fiftieth anniversary in 1979 spawned more interest in the Spanish press and further initiatives such as Ludwig Glaeser's abovementioned traveling exhibition on the pavilion, which originated at the National Gallery of Art in Washington.[16] A year later, when Bohigas became planning director of the city of Barcelona, he immediately returned to his old idea. Both the political and the cultural climate had changed significantly. General Franco had died in 1975, democracy had been restored in a constitutional monarchy under Juan Carlos, and a new generation of Spanish architects probed both international allegiances and their own version of "critical regionalism." A more relaxed attitude to using buildings of the past as sources of inspiration had also recently emerged within architectural discourse, thanks largely to architects and writers such as Aldo Rossi and Robert Venturi.

Bohigas put three of his colleagues in charge of the reconstruction: Cristian Cirici i Alomar, Fernando Ramos Gallino, and Ignasi de Solà-Morales. They had never worked together before, but quickly brought their particular expertise in design, structure, and history to the project.[17] In 1983 a foundation was established to raise funds, and work on site began that year, after a groundbreaking ceremony on October 10.[18] The Spanish press reported regularly on the project's progress.[19] Several Spanish and international firms contributed to the costs of reconstruction, and the German government donated a bronze replica of Kolbe's statue for the inner pool.

By now, Mies himself was dead, and so there was no longer any question of involving him or purchasing a set of drawings from his office. Instead, the Spanish architects relied on a close collaboration with the Museum of Modern Art, although only five versions of the floor plan (in a barely useable 1:100 scale) and a handful of sketches of details could be found among Mies's papers. Ruegenberg's drawings were dismissed as "more properly a personal proposal of a new way of constructing the building than a faithful description of the material characteristics of the building as actually constructed in Barcelona in 1929."[20]

A crucial source of information turned out to be the travertine layout for the floor produced by the marble supplier Köstner & Gottschalk in Berlin. **FIG. 7, P. 74** It revealed slight irregularities in the grid and the fact that the eight columns were not lined up in both directions with the matrix underneath. Luckily, the architects also found the original foundations still in the ground, even stubs of the cruciform columns 50 centimeters below street level, which allowed the pavilion to be placed precisely on its old site. Travertine was selected from two quarries in Tivoli near Rome (a grainier version with a rougher surface for the walls came from the same quarry that had provided stone for the Coliseum, and a less porous version with a finer finish for the floor, steps, and long bench came from the nearby Sibilla quarry); the verde alpi marble came from the Aosta region of the Italian Dolomites; the verde antiqua from Larissa in eastern Greece. The Algerian quarry that supplied the original onyx doré had since closed, but a similar stone was found in another quarry in the Algerian Atlas mountains at Bou Hanifia near Maskara.

The structural system that had led to so much speculation and misunderstanding at the original building became now more solidly a hybrid. The original steel framework for the roof had relied mostly on the eight steel supports, with the ends of the cantilevers lightly supported by the internal wall studs; the new building relied on stronger metal struts inside the marble walls throughout. In the new version, the columns thus play a less significant role for the support of the roof than in the old one. The solid concrete roof (with embedded heating coils) maintains a

4

5

continuous 20 cm thickness, while the old roof was 20 cm at the edges, but grew to 30 cm height in the center. Its original asphalt roofing and plastered undersides were replaced with polyester. Inside the marble walls, six additional drainage points have been installed. All marble cladding has open joints and metal suspension instead of mortar-sealed joints, and it extends to the back and side walls, which were originally only painted. We have no way of telling how close any of the colors come to the original, but we know that the glass had different chemical compositions, probably more imperfections and different hues and probably less transparency, which alters the spatial coherence of the main room. The irregular sizes of the floor slabs were modified to a 1.09-meter grid and their support structure differs to provide better drainage. The window frames and columns are polished stainless steel instead of nickel-covered steel. The light wall was changed from incandescent to fluorescent lights. The Catalan arches under the floor were replaced with a concrete waffle slab, which provides the ceiling for the basement. The Kolbe sculpture (originally a plaster cast, which was damaged on the way back to Germany) was replaced with a new bronze cast. The new pools are shallower than the original, and there are no water lilies in the big pool, nor flower boxes with vines on top of the southern wall. The layout of the small office pavilion in the back was modified, and while railings were added to the rear garden, the path up to the Poble Espanyol was eliminated. There is now a security system with cameras, photoelectric cells, and movement sensors. The two German flags flown at the opening were replaced by a Spanish and a European flag, and neither the inscriptions of the marble supplier, Köstner & Gottschalk (evident at the opening) or *Alemania* (in front and back, applied in October 1929) were reinstated.[21]

The final result is therefore clearly an approximation, but one that is close enough to the original to allow a fairly good sense of the spatial flow, lighting, and material conditions. Luckily, the site had

15 See Mario Ciamitti, "Note sur la construction du Pavillon de Barcelone," in: Roberto Gargiani, *La colonne: Nouvelle histoire de la construction* (Lausanne: Presses polytechniques et universitaires romandes, 2008), 467–71. Together with some related correspondence, the drawings were exhibited during design week in Bologna in the fall of 2015. "Il Padiglione Barcellona a Bologna: Una storia di disegni da Mies van der Rohe a Ruegenberg," *Area* (September 21, 2015), http://www.area-arch.it/it/il-padiglione-barcellona-a-bologna-una-storia-di-disegni-da-mies-van-der-rohe-a-ruegenberg.

16 Franz Schulze, "The Barcelona Pavilion Returns," *Art in America* 67, no. 7 (1979), 98–103. See also Ludwig Glaeser, *Ludwig Mies van der Rohe: The Barcelona Pavilion: Fiftieth Anniversary* (Washington, D.C: National Gallery of Art, 1979), "Para el cincuentenario de la Exposición: Se Pide la reconstrucción del "Pabellón Barcelona," *La Vanguardia* (September 27, 1979), 15.

17 Cristian Cirisi, "Der Barcelona Pavillon," *Der Architekt* 9 (September 1, 1985), 373–75.

18 Jordi Bordas, "Barcelona volverá a tener el pabellón más importante de la Exposición de 1929," *La Vanguardia* (Tuesday, October 11, 1983), 17.

19 Olga Spiegel, "Barcelona celebrará el centenario del nacimiento de Mies van der Rohe inaugurando su pabellón," in *La Vanguardia* (Saturday, September 14, 1985); Ignasi de Solà-Morales, "La reconstrucción del pabellón alemán de Barcelona," *La Vanguardia*, March 2, 1986, 44.

20 Ignasi de Solà-Morales, Christian Cirici and Fernando Ramos, *Mies van der Rohe: El Pabellón de Barcelona* (Barcelona: Gustavo Gili, 1993), 6.

21 At a conference to honor the pavilion's reconstruction thirty years earlier, organized by the Mies van der Rohe Foundation in Barcelona in December 2016, I suggested reinstating the inscriptions in 2019 to mark the fiftieth anniversary of Mies's death. There are currently plans to temporarily restore the pavilion to its original appearance in 2021 by hoisting the two German flags in front and reinstalling the lettering.

7

6 The onyx block for the central freestanding wall in the pavilion before being sliced, ca. 1984
Photographer: Francesc Català-Roca

7-8 The Barcelona Pavilion under construction, ca. 1985
Photographer: Francesc Català-Roca

9 The Pavilion nearing completion, Spring 1986.
Photographer: Sergius Ruegenberg

6

8

remained empty for all those years. Maggi's Bouillon stand had vanished together with the pavilion at the end of the fair, while the eight columns across from it came down in the early 1970s to make room for the exhibition hall of the Instituto Nacional de Industria (INI). **FIGS. 4, 5** This state-owned financing and industrial holding company had been founded in 1941 as part of the Fascist economic regime to support development and national self-sufficiency. In 1973 the architects Juan Paradinas, Luis Garcia-German, and Jose Ignacio Casanova Fernandez created an imposing and expressive 3,000-square-meter Brutalist exhibition hall.[22] Though Spain's return to democracy and a market economy deprived the INI of its original *raison d'être*, the hall continued to be used for exhibition purposes. Thus photographers documenting the new pavilion in 1986 faced a similar problem to their predecessors in 1929: they were prevented from taking orthogonal views of the main facade in its entirety, and mostly refrained from looking east from the pavilion toward the hulking concrete building next to it.[23] At the opening of the new pavilion, one of its architects, Cristian Cirici i Alomar, expressed his hope that the

9

22 "Pabellón de exposiciones del I.N.I. Barcelona," *Informes de la Construcción* 27, no. 267 (January/February 1975), http://informesdelaconstruccion.revistas.csic.es/index.php/informesdelaconstruccion/article/viewFile/2902/3209. I would like to thank Juanjo Romero and architect José Zabala, Barcelona, for kindly providing this information.

23 See, for example, the photographs by Francesc Català-Roca in Solà-Morales, "La reconstrucción del pabellón alemán de Barcelona," 2 (see note 18).

10

10-11 Mies van der Rohe Exhibition at the Miro Foundation in Barcelona, 1986
Photographer: Francesc Català-Roca

11

concrete building would eventually be removed. His wish came true in 1993, after the end of the Olympic Games, whose organizational headquarters it had housed.[24]

The cornerstone for the new pavilion was laid on October 10, 1983, and the board of Trustees of the new Mies van der Rohe Foundation signed the statutes—among them Arthur Drexler of the Museum of Modern Art, Mies's grandson Dirk Lohan and architectural historian Julius Posener. Construction began two months after that.[25] The city of Barcelona commissioned prominent photographer Francesc Català-Roca (1922–1998) to document the building process. We owe many unique and dramatic shots to Català-Roca's campaign, such as the excavation for the basement or the examination of the large onyx block before it was cut into thin slices for the central wall in the pavilion. **FIGS. 6-8** Sergius Ruegenberg, eighty-two years old, also returned to the site and took several photographs of the almost finished building. **FIG. 9**

Nineteen months and 120 million pesetas later, the pavilion was finished in the spring of 1986—some 56 years after the dismantling of the original, 17 years after Mies's death, and 100 years after his birth. A large Mies van der Rohe exhibition was held at the Miró Foundation up on Montjuïc, and a lecture series in mid-April featured, among others, Swiss architect Werner Blaser and German historians Wolf Tegethoff and Julius Posener. **FIGS. 10, 11** The official opening was celebrated on June 2, 1986. After a press conference at the pavilion, invited visitors and dignitaries gathered at City Hall in its famous Saló de Cent, the hall where the city's 100 councilors had met since the fourteenth century. The auspicious location, with the vertical red and gold stripes of the Senyera covering the walls of the room, firmly claimed the event as a success of Catalan culture and independence—in striking contrast to the pavilion's first incarnation under Primo de Rivera's proto-Fascist regime.

Pasqual Maragall, the mayor of Barcelona, architect Oriol Bohigas, Mies's grandson Dirk Lohan, his daughter Georgia van der Rohe, the German ambassador, Guido Brunner, and local dignitaries read statements.[26] The remarks at the opening made it clear that some architects' nostalgia for a lost masterpiece was not the only reason for its recreation. Rather, the rebuilt pavilion fit perfectly into a number of initiatives that set Barcelona on its path to becoming a global tourism destination. The city had hosted the 1982 FIFA World Cup and enjoyed the influx of international visitors that came with it. Under its activist mayor Pasqual Maragall i Mira (in office from 1982–97), Barcelona lobbied successfully to place the work of Antonio Gaudí on the UNESCO World Heritage List (the Casa Milà and the Palau Güell were named in 1984; five more followed later). In this context, the rebuilt Barcelona Pavilion promised to boost cultural tourism, which was increasingly recognized as an important factor of economic growth. Also on January 1, 1986, Spain officially joined the European Union, and in the fall of that year, Barcelona was selected to host the 1992 Olympics. (In their remarks at the pavilion's opening, Mayor Maragall and Josep Figueras, vice president of the foundation, had both expressed their hopes to see the Olympic competitions and celebrations unfold nearby on Montjuïc.)[27] Both events brought an influx of financial support and major infrastructure projects. With its stone from Italy, Greece, and

24 Cristian Cirisi, "Der Barcelona Pavillon," *Der Architekt* 9 (September 1, 1985): 373–75. I am grateful for the information from Juanjo Romero, Barcelona. See also: http://barcelofilia.blogspot.com.es/2011/04/pavello-de-lini-de-la-fira-de-barcelona.html?m=1.

25 Jordi Bordas, "Barcelona volverá a tener el pabellón más importante de la Exposición de 1929," *La Vanguardia*, October 11, 1983, 17; Jordi Bordas, "La reconstrucción del pabellón de Van der Rohe se iniciará en diciembre," *La Vanguardia*, November 17, 1983, 25.

26 Victor A. Amela, "Inaugurado en Barcelona el pabellón alemán de Mies van der Rohe con la presencia de su hija," *La Vanguardia*, June 3, 1986, 52. Rosa Maria Subirana i Torrent, *Mies van der Rohe's German Pavilion in Barcelona, 1929–1986.* (Barcelona: Ajuntament de Barcelona, 1987), 8–21.

27 Subirana i Torrent, *Mies van der Rohe's German Pavilion*, 8–11 (see note 25).

13

12

North Africa, financial contributions from Germany, the E.U., and Spain, one could hardly imagine a more potent symbol for the tides of its time than the new pavilion. Others, however, regretted its instrumentalization. "Was Mies exploited in the name of city marketing?" Rem Koolhaas asked wistfully in 2002.[28]

Koolhaas had critically accompanied the "clone of Mies's pavilion" from its inception and responded to its opening with a two-pronged intervention. He countered the "fiction" of the reconstruction and accompanying narratives about the pavilion's importance with his own fictitious account "in the name of a higher authenticity."[29] A photo novella traced the building parts after the exhibition ends, as they get swept up and tossed around in the political upheavals of the coming decades. At the Milan Triennale of 1986, Koolhaas squeezed a replica of the pavilion into the "curved exedra of the Fascist Triennale building" and then challenged the "lifeless, empty, puritanical, and uninhabitable" modernity of the original with "physical culture in the widest sense," including "projected images, lighting effects," vapor, wind, smell, exercise equipment, and "an abstract soundtrack using the human voice."[30] Koolhaas even included a blurry photograph of himself, on his knees cleaning the small pool in his installation: **FIG. 12** "Yes, I have even cleaned Mies. But, since I do not idolize Mies, his admirers have a hard time with me."[31] Perhaps inspired by Koolhaas's spirited response, the Mies van der Rohe Foundation initiated an ongoing series of interventions by artists and architects a few years later,[32] many of which add surprising depth to the interpretations of the pavilion, as they engage with its history, its experiential qualities, or the ongoing discourse.

Canadian photographer Jeff Wall, for example, picked up on Koolhaas's self-portrait cleaning his pavilion, when he conceived *Morning Cleaning, Mies van der Rohe Foundation, Barcelona 1999*. **FIG. 12a** Like many of Wall's signature images, the photograph was presented as a large (206 by 370 cm) color transparency, housed within a backlit aluminum frame. It shows a man cleaning the glass wall by the small pool with a squeegee on a pole—an act of maintenance required by Mies's precise architecture but usually not witnessed by the public. Briefly the pavilion's inherent order is undermined: the glass is covered in suds, a yellow cleaning bucket on wheels destroys the carefully composed color scheme, the black carpet is dirty and rolled back, and the white leather chairs stand irregularly. In a conversation with the critic Michael Fried, Wall recounted how carefully he planned and timed his photographs over the span of several weeks—there was a very short window in the mornings when the lighting was optimal. The depiction of an apparently unguarded moment before visitors arrive, the quotidian act of cleaning which makes possible the artifice of the pavilion's timeless perfection, turns out to have been a highly staged and elaborate construct, assembled digitally from a number of photographs taken on different days.[33]

Independent from the Mies van der Rohe Foundation's series, other photographers were asked to look at the pavilion afresh, most notably when the Museum of Modern Art in New York held its large Mies van der Rohe exhibition in 2001. The Berlin photographer Kay Fingerle found a vantage point no one else had thought of before. She took a picture from inside the small pool, occupying the opposite corner of Kolbe's sculpture—an image out of kilter, as if taken quickly and furtively with a small, cheap tourist camera. It was the space, where, as Paul Rudolph had put it, "not even fools can tread,"[34] but from where the structure and its spatial depth were most apparent. **FIG. 13**

Counter to convention, the MoMA exhibition interspersed Mies's drawings with large-scale photographs by Thomas Ruff, featuring studies of several of Mies's early projects, some newly taken, others adapting archival material. The most strikingly successful

12a

12 Rem Koolhaas cleaning the replica of the Barcelona Pavilion at the Milan Triennale 1986

12a Jeff Wall *Morning Cleaning*, Mies van der Rohe Foundation, Barcelona 1999
Transparency in lightbox
187 × 351 cm

13 Kay Fingerle, 2001

28 Rem Koolhaas, "Miesverständnisse," *Arch+* 161 (June 2002): 78–83.

29 Rem Koolhaas, "Less is More," in OMA, S,M,L,XL (New York: Monacelli Press, 1995), 48–61.

30 Office for Metropolitan Architecture, "Body-building Home: La Casa Palestra," in Georges Teyssot, *Il Progetto domestico: la casa dell'uomo: archetipi e prototipo* (Milan: Electa, 1986), 52. Office for Metropolitan Architecture, "La Casa Palestra," *AA Files*, 13 (Autumn 1986), 8–12; Koolhaas, "Miesverständnisse" (see note 27).

31 Koolhaas, "Miesverständnisse" (see note 27).

32 Xavier Costa, "Activating the Pavilion," in in OMA, S,M,L,XL (New York: Monacelli Press, 1995), 48–61. *SANAA, Kazuyo Sejima and Ryue Nishizawa: Intervention in the Mies van der Rohe Pavilion, ed. Xavier Costa* (Barcelona: Fundació Mies van der Rohe, 2010), 4–7.

33 See Michael Fried, "Jeff Wall, Wittgenstein, and the Everyday," *Critical Inquiry* 33, no. 3 (Spring 2007), 495–526; and Christine Conley, "Morning Cleaning: Jeff Wall and the Large Glass," *Art History* 32, no. 5 (December 2009), 996–1015.

34 Paul Rudolph, "Conversation at 23 Beekman Place: Interview with Peter Blake (1986)," in *Paul Rudolph: The Late Work*, ed. Roberto de Alba (New York: Princeton Architectural Press, 2003), 203–17.

14

14 Thomas Ruff, d.p.b. 02, 1999
Chromogenic print
51 1/4 x 75 1/4 x 1 1/2 inches
130.2 x 191.1 x 3.8 cm

15 Ai Weiwei, *With Milk __find something everybody can use*
Installation at the Barcelona Pavilion, 2009
Photographer: Anna Mas

was a view of the Barcelona Pavilion—its sky manipulated into the color of pink lemonade—which adorned the catalog cover, announcing the exhibition's irreverent, postmodern approach. **FIG. 14** The image shows the pavilion's front with horizontal blurs, as if the viewer (or even the building) were moving at high speed. "When Mies's German pavilion was built for the 1929 international exposition, it must have looked like a UFO had landed in Barcelona," Ruff mused. "Speed in photography is always blurry, and my picture of the German pavilion looks like a high-speed locomotive—modernity arriving at the train station of the present (albeit the present of 1929)."[35] Here Ruff was tapping into an early-twentieth-century sentiment: in 1910, Mies's most important teacher, Peter Behrens, had written about a future architecture designed with the perception from a moving car in mind: "When we race through the streets of our metropolis in a super-fast vehicle, we can no longer recognize the details of the buildings. [...] Such a way of looking at the world, which has become a constant habit, needs an architecture with forms as coherent and calm as possible."[36] But Ruff, of course, also celebrated the fact that photographers finally had access to the orthogonal view that for so long had eluded them—in 1929 eight columns and a Maggi pavilion were in the way; from 1986 up to its demolition, the INI building blocked the same view. What's more, this view was now available, not just from one carefully placed position, but rather over the full length of the building, to be conquered as if in a "drive-by shooting."

15

Other artists invited by the Mies van der Rohe Foundation have addressed the confusing fact that one is "unable to find the smallest trace of the time that has elapsed, the wear and tear wrought by the passing of the years [...] rust eating away at the chrome surfaces,"[37] an image of timelessness that does not arise naturally, but is the result of continuous maintenance. In December 2009 Chinese conceptual artist Ai Weiwei created *With Milk __ find something everybody can use* by filling the pavilion's large pool with milk and the small one with coffee—liquids whose fast deterioration could be observed and documented over a few days. Whereas the water in the two pools was "replaced all the time, unnoticed to visitors," a "demanding effort" was now required to preserve the condition of the liquids "against light, air, warmth [...] anything [that] encourages growth and change."[38] The "metabolism of a living machine" was thus revealed. **FIG. 15**

35 See Ronald Jones, "A Thousand Words: Thomas Ruff Talks About 'l.m.v.d.r,'" *Artforum* 10 (2001): 159, and Julian Heynen, ed., *Thomas Ruff* (Krefeld: Krefelder Kunstmuseen, 2000), n.p.

36 Peter Behrens, *Kunst und Technik* (1910) quoted in Fritz Neumeyer, ed., *Quellentexte zur Architekturtheorie* (Munich: Prestel, 2002), 358. Siegfried Kracauer similarly comments on the facade of Mies's building for the Weissenhofsiedlung in Stuttgart (1927). See Siegfried Kracauer, "Das neue Bauen: Zur Stuttgarter Werkbund-Ausstellung 'Die Wohnung,'" *Frankfurter Zeitung*, July 31, 1927.

37 Marco de Michelis, "The Smells of History," in *Muntadas: On Translation: Paper BP/MVDR*, ed. Xavier Costa (Barcelona: Fundació Mies van der Rohe, 2010), 28–31.

38 Ai Weiwei, *With Milk__find something everybody can use*, http://miesbcn.com/project/ai-weiwei-intervention.

16 Andrés Jaque / Office for Political Innovation, *Phantom: Mies as Rendered Society*, 2013

17 Andrés Jaque / Office for Political Innovation, *Phantom: Mies as Rendered Society*, 2013
Storage space in the full basement underneath the pavilion

18 SANAA (Kazuyo Sejima and Ryue Nishizawa), 2008
Curved acrylic walls installed at the pavilion, 2008.
Photographer: Anna Mas

16

17

18

39 Ethel Baraona Pohl, "The Value of the Infra-ordinary," *Domus* (January 23, 2013), http://www.domusweb.it/en/architecture/2013/01/23/the-value-of-the-infra-ordinary.html. See also http://miesbcn.com/project/jaque-intervention.

The Spanish architect Andrés Jaque explored a related theme in 2013 with a piece titled *Phantom: Mies as Rendered Society*. All the artifacts necessary for the building's upkeep were on display in the pavilion, be they cleaning devices or chemicals, replacement glass or marble samples—an archaeology documenting the behind-the-scenes stories, actors, and events normally invisible to visitors, and locked away in the storage space beneath the pavilion. This basement was presented as the "Pavilion's ghost (PHANTOM), unknown to most visitors, and deliberately hard to reach, it nevertheless plays an important role facilitating the maintenance and control of the building, holding all the material needed to preserve its pristine, ageless state."[39] **FIGS. 16, 17**

19

19 Luis Martínez Santa-María (Madrid, Spain): *I don't want to change the world. I only want to express it.* Winning entry for the *Fear of Columns* competition at the Barcelona Pavilion, 2016 Photographer: Anna Mas

In 2008 the Japanese architecture firm SANAA (Kazuyo Sejima and Ryue Nishizawa)[40] installed a meandering acrylic wall that induced additional reflections and spatial complexity in the interior of the pavilion, infusing the strict linearity of Mies's structure with his earlier, and rarer, attempts at free-form design. **FIG. 18** Through its curvilinear form the wall referenced the floor plan of Mies's 1922 glass skyscraper, while it also evoked Mies's and Lilly Reich's Café Samt und Seide in Berlin of 1927.

To celebrate the new pavilion's thirtieth birthday, the Mies van der Rohe Foundation held a new competition for another intervention called *Fear of Columns*. Catalan architect Luis Martinez Santa-Maria was selected from a shortlist of 26 architects, designers, and artists, and on June 2, 2016, precisely 30 years after the inauguration of the new pavilion, his installation was unveiled. Eight columns made from 100 discarded industrial steel drums recalled the eight columns that stood in front of the original pavilion, their somewhat worn and aged look the result not of the passage of time but of a high-pressure water treatment. **FIG. 19**

In November 2017 Anna and Eugeni Bach performed the perhaps most radical intervention at the pavilion, *mies missing materiality* when they covered all of its walls with white vinyl sheets for one week. "This simple act turns the pavilion into a 1:1 scale mock-up, a representation of itself that opens the door to multiple interpretations about aspects like the value of the original, the role of the white surface as an image of modernity, and the importance of materiality in the perception of space,"[41] the artists wrote. Thus, the pavilion was deprived of the much discussed preciousness of its materials and their polished reflective surfaces and became a closer sibling to the temporary house that Mies erected at the Berlin Building Exhibition in 1931. **FIG. 20**

In 2018 Spencer Finch related to Mies's often stated affinity to Japanese architecture with a gesture of compelling simplicity: His installation *Fifteen Stones (Ryōan-ji)* turned the large pool into a meditative Zen garden with carefully placed rocks. **FIG. 21** At the Ryōan-ji monastery in Kyoto ("The Temple of the Dragon at Peace"), the garden (*karesansui*) consists of a field of white gravel (its 25 by 10 meter size similar to that of the large pool at the pavilion) in which fifteen stones are placed in such a way that it is not possible to see all of them at the same time. The viewer is compelled to move in order to experience the effect. Finch wrote: "The Ryōan-ji Garden in Kyoto and the Mies van der Rohe Pavilion in Barcelona are two of my favorite places in the world. In spite of their many differences, to me they are incredibly similar, in terms of how they generate thought about being a human seeing and moving through space."[42]

In recognition of the central role that photography had played in the history of the old and new pavilion, German photographer Michael Wesely installed a camera in 2018 that took a single picture over the course of 365 days. The final image, extracted, enlarged to 1:1 scale and installed in the pavilion in the fall of 2019, layers the multitude of movements and light conditions the pavilion encountered during that year. It merges continuity and change, materials and reflections—and reminds us of old and new viewpoints and the seductive power of images.

40 http://miesbcn.com/project/sanaa-intervention.
41 http://miesbcn.com/project/mies-missing-materiality/.
42 "Artist Spencer Finch Evokes Kyoto's Ryoan-ji Garden at the Mies Pavilion," *ArchDaily* (October 3, 2018), https://www.archdaily.com/902857/artist-spencer-finch-evokes-kyotos-ryoan-ji-garden-at-the-mies-pavilion.

20 Anna & Eugeni Bach, *mies missing materiality* Installation at the Barcelona Pavilion, 2017
Photographer: Anna Mas

21 Spencer Finch, *Fifteen Stones (Ryōan-ji)* Installation at the Barcelona Pavilion, 2018
Photographer: Anna Mas

20

21

Impact

If one were to rank modern buildings based on the amount of superlative praise bestowed on them, then Mies van der Rohe's German pavilion at the 1929 Barcelona International Exposition would surely come out somewhere near the top. How did we get from a short-lived exhibition pavilion–compromised and barely finished, unworthy of photography in the eyes of the architect and unnoticed by most visitors–to one of the most influential building of the twentieth century? This book's title points beyond the architectural qualities of the building to the complexities and coincidences surrounding its creation, interpretation and legacy. We place the pavilion within the multiple contexts of its time, as if in the center of the overlapping circles of a Venn diagram. Each context complicates the pavilion's story. Instead of a social democratic government's enlightened representation of the ambitions of the young Weimar Republic, the building was instead initiated, financed, and realized against clear government directives by conservative businessman Georg von Schnitzler, who would soon collaborate with the Nazis and be convicted of war crimes at the Nuremberg trials. The pavilion's much-praised emptiness was more likely the outcome of its particularly messy genesis rather than a deliberate consequence of its design. As a building type, the pavilion fit squarely into the current fashion for inventive trade fair pavilions, but its out-of-placeness as a country pavilion at an international exposition made it a puzzling presence, provoking deep interpretations. While Mies happily made use of Sasha Stone's black-and-white photographs when they appeared, he had had nothing to do with their creation. Georg Kolbe's sculpture was neither called *Morning*, as has often been stated–implying a deliberate reference to the democratic beginnings in Germany–nor was it a careful choice, but rather a hasty, last-minute and accidental decision. The pavilion's existence and critical success depended on many other crucial players besides Mies and Lilly Reich–most prominently on Georg and Lilly von Schnitzler, but also the Marqués de Foronda, who permitted the site to be used; the Spanish dictator, Miguel Primo de Rivera, who personally intervened to reverse the decision to cancel the pavilion; the German economics minister Julius Curtius, who provided an essential loan at the last minute; influential publishers such as Heinrich Simon, who helped to frame the surrounding discourse; Erich Raemisch, a manager in the German silk industry, who commissioned the photography; and Sasha Stone, who created iconic images of such gravitas that they ultimately secured the building's place in the history of modern architecture. Given the constant uncertainties of the design and construction process, one has to acknowledge the steadfastness, even stubbornness with which Mies clung to his vision, as fraught and financially irresponsible as it might have been.

The complexity of this genesis was even surpassed by the picture that emerges from the critical responses that followed, which we document in a complementary volume. Most of the critics and historians surely would have had no qualms calling the pavilion a "masterpiece"–but there seem to be vast disagreements why. Some writers praised its spaces as open, others as closed, some saw embodied movement, others stasis, some discovered frozen music, others silence, some critics saw reflections of the aftermath of the First World War, others a premonition of the Second. Just as one critic observed Mies's "spirited game" with surface qualities that indicated spatial conditions, another was convinced that Mies had set up a didactic demonstration of the structural difference between walls and columns; as one praised its clarity, another experienced it as a "labyrinth." With equal seriousness it was compared to an early modern *Wunderkammer* and to an aquarium. One critic was convinced that the surface reflections were meant to secretly smuggle symmetries into the asymmetrical structure, a second saw a three-dimensional rendering of platonic principles, a third witnessed the drama of the "Holy Grail," and a fourth the "tragedy of modern architecture." The pavilion's political dimension was initially described with the somewhat facile equation that Georg von Schnitzler had proposed at the

1

opening—namely, that the building's clear lines spoke for "clarity" and "sincerity," beckoning a new, less strident and perhaps even humble approach to politics in Germany. In great contrast, Spanish critics at the time saw "the soul of the new Germany," not in its clarity, but in the dizzying reflections from the pavilion's glass and polished surfaces—"a prodigious blending of rays of light which crisscross freely." Reyner Banham, Manfredo Tafuri, and others would find the pavilion inspired by those artistic forces that openly ridiculed Germany's political system, pointing to its Dada-like collage of contradictory materials, or to the juxtaposition of the naturalistic sculpture by Georg Kolbe and its abstract environment. Later critics, again, would see the pavilion as an escapist space, perfectly insulated from the violence and insecurity of the Weimar Republic.[1] How can the same building elicit such different reactions? What does this tell us about the state of architectural criticism or about the modern movement in general? Certainly, the pavilion's emptiness, or programmatic "silence" (as some observers put it) facilitated multiple angles of interpretation and political connotations and offered it as testing ground for different theories.

However, confronting the critical reception with the detailed historical record—pitting the historian against the critic as it were—does not so much produce unambiguous results as raise new sets of questions. For instance, the assumption that the pavilion was intended by the German government to symbolize the country's young democracy and to sanction the modern movement in architecture can clearly be proven wrong. But it should come as no surprise that this narrative survived for so long. After all, the building was the official German pavilion at the fair, even if the delay in adding the word "Alemania" hinted at trouble behind the scenes. At the time, the German government was led by Social Democrats, and von Schnitzler's ambiguously worded speech at the inauguration did not disallow the idea of the building as a piece of state architecture. The affinity of left-leaning politics with modern architecture had a long track record in Weimar Germany—we might think of the Berlin housing projects under Martin Wagner, Mies's Luxemburg/Liebknecht memorial, or Walter Gropius's Monument to the March Dead in Weimar. Thus, the emerging narrative was immediately accepted as entirely convincing and has had a long—and valid—afterlife to this very day, the architect's and client's intentions notwithstanding. Some of the pavilion's influence on other buildings was certainly based on the assumption of such noble lineage, especially in Germany. For its transfer to the United States, the perceived connection of the formal vocabulary to social democracy played no role. Quite the contrary, Philip Johnson thoroughly depoliticized the pavilion in his descriptions. He might have also sensed from his encounters with Mies that in the eyes of those who made it possible, the pavilion stood, as we have seen, for decidedly different political aims than social democracy. Its formal language had become

2

1 Miller House, Palm Springs, California, 1937
Architect: Richard Neutra
Photograph: Julius Shulman

2 A. Conger Goodyear House 3, Old Westbury, New York, 1938
Architect: Edward Durell Stone

acceptable to people like the von Schnitzlers, who were well-to-do, culturally progressive but politically conservative with a distaste for democracy and mass culture, and a strong sense of aristocratic, elitist superiority. The pavilion perfectly served that vision. (Georg von Schnitzler became one of the patrons of Johnson's *Modern Architecture* exhibition of 1932.) The much-noted fact that most visitors at the fair could not relate to it was baked into its concept. It only spoke to those with a very specific knowledge and appreciation of contemporary art and architecture, the "aristocracy of culture" as Pierre Bourdieu aptly put it.[2] This inaccessibility of the aesthetics of the modern movement to those it purportedly served, namely the working class, had been a problem of the avant-garde from the beginning. Now, instead of becoming an officially sanctioned formal language of progressive politics, the modern movement ceased to be political. Thus, one of the most discussed and influential buildings in modern architecture, the movement's "*ur*-hut," or "mother," presents an astonishing paradox, a Freudian return of the repressed. It combined the precise opposite of the attributes the modern movement had stood for: it was functionless, luxurious, structurally ambiguous, formalist, elitist, and unconcerned with a social mission. It perfectly demonstrated Jürgen Habermas's observation that the "qualities of modern buildings result from a consistently applied autonomous system of aesthetic rules" rather than "express the use-functions for which a building is produced."[3] As a result, as Jonathan Hill noted, it implied "contemplation" as the most appropriate response to it, thus affirming "the authority of the architect and denying that of the user."[4] While the pavilion itself was spared much direct criticism due to its exceptional stature and confounding emptiness, how much the political left perceived this turn as a fall from grace, even a betrayal, became obvious soon after, when Mies applied the pavilion's formal language to the Tugendhat House and to his House for a Childless Couple at the Berlin Building Exhibition and was harshly attacked.

Nevertheless, it took Mies more than a decade to move beyond the limited vocabulary that he had developed for the Pavilion—he applied it to the long line of unexecuted projects over the following decade—be they another German Pavilion for the World's Fair in Brussels, several villas and country houses, a golf club and a fictitious museum, even to the first iterations of his IIT masterplan in Chicago. His students at the Bauhaus and in Illinois executed countless version of court houses in his style, and we might speculate that at least some of them noticed the anachronistic nature of these luxurious and generous spaces at a time of economic hardships.

Ultimately, when the war had passed and the economy recovered, a somewhat selective memory of the political associations attached to the original building helped the global spread of its formal language. In 1960 Peter Blake—architect, curator of architecture at MoMA (1948–50), and frequent critic in the pages of *Architectural Forum*—was the first to acknowledge the breadth of the Barcelona Pavilion's impact on practicing architects. He compiled a list of buildings that had been influenced by the pavilion, including Wright's Usonian Houses, I. M. Pei's penthouse office for William Zeckendorf, and Paul Rudolph's early houses in Florida.[5] Indeed, homes that adopted enough of its key elements

1 Robin Evans, "Mies van der Rohe's Paradoxical Symmetries," *AA Files* 19 (1990): 56–68.
2 Pierre Bourdieu, *Distinction: A Social Critique of the Judgment of Taste* (Cambridge, MA: Harvard University Press, 1984), 11–96.
3 Jürgen Habermas, "Modern and Postmodern Architecture" (1982), quoted in Neil Leach, *Rethinking Architecture: A Reader in Cultural Theory* (London: Routledge: 1997), 227–35.
4 Jonathan Hill, "Weather Architecture," in *Architecture: The Subject Is Matter*, ed. Jonathan Hill (London: Routledge, 2001), 58-71.
5 Peter Blake, *The Master Builders* (New York: Alfred A. Knopf, 1960), 208–12.

3

4

3 Jacobs House, Madison, Wisconsin, 1937
Architect: Frank Lloyd Wright

4 Rosenbaum House, Florence, Alabama, 1938–40
Architect: Frank Lloyd Wright

5 New York World's Fair, "Masterpieces of Art" Building
Architects: Harrison & Fouilhoux

7 Revere Quality House, 1948
Architects: Ralph Twitchell, Paul Rudolph

to provide a recognizable likeness (such as its flat roof, wide overhangs, floor-to-ceiling windows, freestanding columns, open spatial connections, etc.) could soon be found in the US and then in Europe, adaptable to an astonishingly wide price range and to regional and cultural differences.

Thomas Hines, for instance, described Richard Neutra's Miller House in Palm Springs (1937) as a "miniature echo of Mies's Barcelona Pavilion."[6] **FIG. 1** A year later, in 1938, Edward Durell Stone's large house in Old Westbury, New York, for A. Conger Goodyear, was an even more overt homage to the pavilion, which Stone had seen on a trip to Europe in 1929. **FIG. 2** And while Frank Lloyd Wright was never one to acknowledge his debts, his Jacobs, Goetsch-Winkler, and Rosenbaum Houses (1939–40) in Michigan and Alabama appeared to be a Usonian translation in wood and brick of Mies's vocabulary, even if Wright avoided the continuous glass panes of the original by employing long sequences of smaller windows expanding from floor to ceiling. **FIGS. 3 AND 4** Perhaps the most obvious imitator of the Barcelona Pavilion in 1930s US, however, was Harrison & Fouilhoux's "Masterpieces of Art" building at the 1939 New York World's Fair, which mirrored not just the form of the original, but also its typology and program. **FIG. 5**

His appetite whetted after the success of the 1932 MoMA show, Philip Johnson decided to study architecture. His first student design in 1940, a seaside house, "looked just like the Barcelona Pavilion," he confessed,[7] and his later projects at Harvard did not progress much beyond that either. His own house at 9 Ash Street in Cambridge, still based on the pavilion, would become his final thesis in 1942. **FIG. 6** Apparently, just like many others, he had taken the columns in the pavilion to be merely decorative, and employed them with enthusiastic abandon. Mies was not impressed: "When ve do this kind of a court house, ve don't put quite so many columns in," Johnson recalled Mies telling him in his heavy German accent. Johnson reduced the number of columns to merely three along the glass front toward the garden, and the house ended up quite elegant. Mies, however, refused to come and see it.[8] Johnson's cylindrical wooden columns had metal sleeves on either end, connecting them to the ceiling and floor construction, and thus giving them a semblance of a simplified base and capital—just what Mies's conservative critics had demanded. Mies's work in Barcelona had quickly become a recognizable modern convention, applicable to both mass-producible, low-cost homes and high-end villas.

5

7

The much publicized Revere Quality House, which Ralph Twitchell designed with his young partner Paul Rudolph in 1948, was meant as an affordable prototype for the Florida Keys. It had been sponsored by *Architectural Forum*, Revere Copper and Brass, and Lamolithic Industries, the builder in charge of the concrete foundation, walls, and roof.[9] **FIG. 7** It was praised as an example of modern regionalism, "especially suited to tropical weather conditions,"[10] its concrete structure proof against mildew, fire, termites, and hurricanes; and its protruding roof provided shelter from the sun.[11] In a similar vein, Donald Wexler's tract of steel houses for a similar climate in Palm Springs for developers George and Robert Alexander (1961–62) also betray a clear debt to Mies.

Richard Neutra's California houses continued to carry references to the building from the late 1930s on, culminating in his Kaufman House in Palm Springs (1946). **FIG. 8** The Case Study House program, initiated in 1945 by the California magazine *Arts & Architecture*, also contains many examples of obvious homages. The most significant is undoubtedly no. 22—Pierre Koenig's Stahl House (1960), where, writes Daniel Dunham:

the most persuasive poetic and pragmatic echoes of the pavilion seem to linger. [...] It is as if the logic of the pavilion was transplanted to a cliff edge, hovering over the city below. Perhaps the only true deviations from the Barcelona prototype are the lack of lavish materials (also true of other Case Study projects in general) and its tectonic muscularity. Mies, of course, designed a project for the world stage, and the materials certainly rose to the occasion of providing a reception space for German diplomats and Spanish royalty. But Mies had always been drawn to the beauty of purity found in stone and wood when their physical qualities were coaxed out through the hand of a skilled craftsperson.[12] **FIG. 9**

6 Thomas S. Hines, *Richard Neutra and the Search for Modern Architecture: A Biography and History* (Berkeley: University of California Press, 1994), 121–23.
7 Kazys Varnelis, ed., *The Philip Johnson Tapes: Interviews by Robert A. M. Stern* (New York: Monacelli Press, 2008), 85.
8 Ibid., 94.
9 See "Cost $18,400: This House Won First Prize in the South," *House and Garden* (August 1949): 76–77, 99; and "Concrete Home in Florida Is One of Eight Prototype Houses Designed to Solve Regional Building Problem," *Architectural Forum* (October 1948): 101–5.
10 "House in Florida," *Architectural Review* (June 1949): 287–90.
11 Other Twitchell/Rudolph buildings would have qualified for Peter Blake's list of Barcelona Pavilion followers as well, such as the Miller Guest House in Casey Keys (1949); the Cocoon House in the Siesta Keys (1950); or the Bennet House in Bradenton, Florida (1950), which would later share a fate similar to that of the pavilion, as a full-scale replica was created in 2015 on the grounds of the Sarasota Architectural Foundation and the Ringling Museum. Peter Blake's own Pinwheel House (1954) in Water Mill, New York, also comes to mind.
12 Daniel Dunham, "Beyond the Red Curtain: Less is More Utopia," *Utopian Studies* 25, no. 1 (2014): 150–73, here 166.

6

8

Similarly striking is the weekend house for civil engineer and contractor Alekos Lanaras, outside Anavissos, in East Attica, south of Athens, designed by Nicos Valsamakis (1961–63). **FIG. 10** Its obvious references to Pierre Koenig's Stahl House and by extension the Barcelona Pavilion signaled a programmatic commitment to the International Style in response to the emergence of a contemporary Greek Regionalism under Dimitris Pikionis, Aris Konstantinidis, and others. In particular Konstantinidis's rustic weekend house nearby, with its stone walls and flat, heavy concrete roof provided a perfect counterpart, as it was built at exactly the same time.[13]

Architectural debates were hardly more fraught with anxiety about repeating mistakes of the past than those in postwar West Germany. Building production under the Nazis was unanimously, vociferously rejected, of course, but there was also no easy agreement about the architectural achievements of the Weimar Republic that had preceded them. The Barcelona Pavilion, though, was the one building that everyone could agree on as a positive model and whenever it was evoked, it was with a clear eye to its assumed political role. Critics praised it as "absolute architecture, a masterpiece," with "a new attitude, a new kind of representation."[14] For others it symbolized "the humane resistance against threats, darkness, and impending chaos."[15] For the Brussels World's Fair of 1958, the architect Hans Schwippert, the artistic director of the German section commissioned a one-story court house from Eduard Ludwig, Mies's last close collaborator before his departure to the US. It evoked the Barcelona Pavilion and Mies's successive court house designs and was modeled on one of the five that Ludwig had built the previous year at the 1957 Interbau exhibition in Berlin.[16] **FIG. 11** Such L-shaped court houses with floor-to-ceiling windows and open spatial connections became a staple of postwar Germany's single-family housing boom.

6 Ash Street House, Cambridge, Massachusetts, 1942
Architect: Philip Johnson

8 Kaufmann House, Palm Springs, California,1946
Architect: Richard Neutra
Photograph: Julius Shulman

Two years later, leftist politician Adolf Arndt praised the pavilion as the only instance of state-sponsored, truly "democratic" architecture so far,[17] and thus set the stage for an "unprecedented debate about modern architecture and political representation"[18] in West Germany's young democracy. The pavilion became the model for the official home of the country's second postwar chancellor, Ludwig Erhard, in Bonn. Architect Sep Ruf's long friendship with Erhard had secured him the commission.[19] The facade of the Kanzlerbungalow, like that of the pavilion, consisted of floor-to-ceiling glass panes under the deep eaves of a flat roof. Ruf provided more livable space inside, developing the floor plan from two overlapping squares—semipublic, representative spaces in the large square, private spaces in the smaller one.[20] **FIG. 12** Structurally, the design had at first featured 32 freestanding cruciform columns (16 in each square), but the final scheme made do without them. Informed architecture critics recognized this "paraphrase" of the pavilion, revealing "at its best a potential image of the twentieth century,"[21] in particular thanks to the "interpenetration of interior and exterior spaces" that Mies had pioneered.[22] Discussions in the popular press and among the general public, were far less generous, however, and showed how little the positive image of Mies's pavilion in architectural circles had trickled down to a generally shared consensus. "Erhard lives like a hedgehog!" proclaimed the mass daily *Bild-Zeitung*, declaring the bedrooms too small and the building not representative enough.[23] Two years later, Erhard resigned as chancellor, and both his predecessor (former chancellor Konrad Adenauer) and his successor (chancellor Kurt Georg Kiesinger) publicly shared humorously disparaging remarks about his official abode.[24] This was followed by polemical statements about modern architecture and representation in all major papers. Architects deplored the ridicule directed at a cultural accomplishment that enjoyed widespread recognition abroad. Egon Eiermann even suggested that the harsh critique indicated a potential return to Nazism.[25] Walter Gropius joined the debate from afar, defending the chancellor's bungalow as representing to the "world the progressive spirit of the German people and its contemporary cultural trend."[26] Meanwhile, Chancellor Kiesinger had the Herman Miller furniture removed and initiated a redesign to make the interior "cozier." His successor, Willy Brandt, refused to move in altogether. Chancellor Helmut Schmidt, finally, moved in and appreciated the modernity of the building and its open connection to the surrounding park.[27] The government's move to Berlin after Germany's unification deprived the building of its original function and today, restored to its original condition, it serves as a museum.

13 Stylianos Giamarelos, "The Art of Building Reception: Aris Konstantinidis behind the Global Published Life of His Weekend House in Anavyssos (1962–2014)," *Architectural Histories* 2, no. 1 (2014), Art. 22. DOI: http://doi.org/10.5334/ah.bx.

14 Ulrich Conrads, "Von ausgestellten Bauten zu Ausstellungsbauten," *Bauwelt* 48, no. 31 (August 5, 1957): 777.

15 Hans Schwippert, lecture manuscript, 1958 (Schwippert Archive), Deutsches Nationalmuseum, Nuremburg. I would like to thank Deborah Ascher Barnstone for kindly supplying this information.

16 Paul Sigel, *Exponiert: Deutsche Pavillons auf Weltausstellungen* (Berlin: Verlag Bauwesen, 2000), 196–97.

17 Adolf Arndt, "Die Demokratie als Bauherr," *Bauwelt* 1 (1961): 7–13. Adolf Arndt also served as president of the German Werkbund between 1964 and 1969.

18 Irene Meissner, *Sep Ruf, 1908–1982* (Berlin: Deutscher Kunstverlag, 2013), 280.

19 Ludwig Erhard had long known Sep Ruf, and shared his architectural taste. Ten years earlier, Ruf had designed a pair of flat-roofed weekend houses (also clearly inspired by Mies's pavilion) for himself and Erhard (then economics minister) in the Bavarian foothills of the Alps. They encountered fierce resistance from conservative members of the local community, who dubbed them "gas stations" and held up the permission for two years. Ibid., 154–69.

20 Burkhard Körner has examined the chancellor's bungalow and its reception in greater detail. See Burkhard Körner, "Der Kanzlerbungalow von Sep Ruf in Bonn," *Bonner Geschichtsblätter* 49/50 (1999/2000): 507–613. I would like to thank Burkhard Körner for kindly providing me with a copy of the manuscript.

21 Hans Wichmann, ed., *Sep Ruf: Bauten und Projekte* (Stuttgart: Deutsche Verlags Anstalt, 1986), 20.

22 Erich Steingräber, in *Der Bungalow: Wohn- und Empfangsgebäude für den Bundeskanzler in Bonn*, ed. Paul Swiridoff (Pfullingen: Neske, 1967), 52.

23 MK, "Erhard wohnt wie ein Maulwurf!" *Bild-Zeitung*, May 21, 1964, 1, 3.

24 Adenauer pitied Kiesinger for now having to live in it, pondering the question if it might possibly be flammable, and suggesting to put the architect behind bars for ten years. Kiesinger compared the bedrooms to a train's sleeper car. Ulrich Kremer, "Der geschmähte Kanzler-Bungalow," *Süddeutsche Zeitung*, January 28/29, 1967. See also Meissner, *Sep Ruf*, 280–81 (see note 18).

25 Meissner, Sep Ruf, 283 (see note 18).

26 Walter Gropius to Günther Neske, 1967, quoted in Körner, "Der Kanzlerbungalow von Sep Ruf in Bonn," 507 (see note 20).

27 Meissner, *Sep Ruf*, 283 (see note 18).

9

9 Case Study House No. 22, Los Angeles, California, 1960 Architect: Pierre Koenig Photograph: Julius Shulman

10 House for Alekos Lanaras, Anavissos, Greece, 1961-63 Architect: Nicos Valsamakis

It would be easy to point to countless other examples of the pavilion's impact on contemporary designers. Two recent examples such as Sarah Waller's Doonan Glass House in Queensland, Australia, or Deborah Berke's North Penn House in Indianapolis, both of 2016, might suffice to demonstrate its continued relevance. **FIGS. 13 AND 14**

Why then (despite occasional misunderstandings and frequent overinterpretation) does the Barcelona Pavilion "continue to fascinate architects and historians? What compels us, after such a long time, to read and write about a work that existed for such a short time and about which its designer seemed apathetic?" George Dodds posed these questions in 2001. We might similarly ask why its key design elements have served as such an easy and frequent model for contemporary architecture. What explains the astonishing staying power of this building and its imagery? For Dodds, the answer lies in the particular role of Sasha Stone's iconic photographs as the main source of information about the short-lived original building and the basis of its reconstruction. Through this representation—which is "as much the image of a building as it is the building of an image [...] the Barcelona Pavilion leads us into the future every time we accept the dream it represents as a part of our present." [28] More broadly, it profits from the accumulation of associations and imagery over time, not just of the pavilion, but also of its followers and imitators, that has again and again evoked notions of luxury, freedom, contemporaneity, and cultural sophistication. Julius Shulman's photographs of Richard Neutra's Kaufman House and Pierre Koenig's Stahl House are just as complicit in this story as Sasha Stone's photographs were thirty years earlier.

The pavilion never quite shirked the elitism that its clients Lilly and Georg von Schnitzler firmly believed in and that several contemporary critics commented on. A recent film, clearly inspired by Pierre Bourdieu's careful examination of taste and its dependence

10

28 George Dodds, "Body in Pieces: Desiring the Barcelona Pavilion," *RES: Anthropology and Aesthetics* 39 (Spring, 2001): 168–91. Four years later, Dodds had enlarged the essay into a substantial book entitled *Building Desire: On the Barcelona Pavilion* (London: Routledge, 2005).

13

14

11

12

11 Patio House, Brussels World's Fair, 1958
Architect: Eduard Ludwig

12 Kanzlerbungalow (Chancellor's bungalow), Bonn, 1963-66
Architect: Sep Ruf

13 Doonan Glass House, in Queensland Australia, 2016
Architect: Sarah Waller

14 North Penn House, Indianapolis, Indiana, 2016
Architect: Deborah Berke

on a viewer's education, gave voice to the accidental tourists walking by. "I hadn't noticed it at all," one said; others commented "It's too modern"; "it doesn't fit in with what's around it"; "I don't understand why it is considered a masterpiece."[29] Catalan philosopher and professor of aesthetics at the Barcelona Polytechnic, Xavier Rubert de Ventós (*1939) noted: "Well, sometimes I have encountered people on tiptoes with Mies, not so they don't leave any dirt, but on cultural tiptoes. Trying to guess it its good. [...] People don't know, because only if they are cultured they can say something about what it resembles, what it contrasts with, what it anticipates. [...] It's hard to see without these kinds of banisters." And we have to acknowledge the fact that of the hundreds of thousands of tourists visiting Antonio Gaudí's almost contemporary buildings nearby, only a few of them find their way to the Barcelona Pavilion.

"Why engage with the mess, the complexity, the compromises, and the downright feebleness of the majority of building practice when yet another reading of the Barcelona Pavilion offers itself?,"[30] historian Iain Boyd Whyte scolded his colleagues for neglecting the vernacular in favor of fruitless interpretations of masterpieces. In answer to Boyd Whyte, the Barcelona Pavilion can and should not be read as a "masterpiece" but as the result of exactly the complexity, compromises, and precariousness of the conditions of architectural production and the political conditions that frame our perception. The result inevitably challenges many of the interpretations the pavilion has provoked over time. But its rich and confounding history of reception will continue to serve as a guide through the uneven terrain of our shifting and competing views of modern architecture, theoretical and political predilections, biases and blinkers. If the past ninety years are any indication, the pavilion will—in its calm and enigmatic way—continue to provoke new critical readings that reflect and challenge our changing discursive landscape.

29 Xavi Campreciós and Pep Martín, dir., *Mies en Scene: Barcelona in Two Acts* (Documentary Film, Spain, 2018).
30 Iain Boyd Whyte, "The Challenge of the Commonplace," *Positions*, no. 0 (Fall 2008): 90-93.

Acknowledgments

The conversation between David Caralt and me about the Barcelona Pavilion began one long afternoon in 2014 in a small café under the shady trees of Plaza de Sant Felip Neri in the heart of Barcelona. David had initiated the contact with an e-mail earlier that year and now we sat with our laptops, comparing photographs and archival documents, and discovered that there was so much important but unknown material about the Barcelona Pavilion that it warranted its own publication. We also realized that we had a very similar approach to research–a fascination with archives, empirical evidence, and context in the broadest sense, and a disinterest in speculative arguments or obscure language. Having been trained as architects, we had also acquired a healthy skepticism vis-à-vis simplifications (or glorifications) of the creative process, authorship, and agency in architecture. Soon after our initial meeting, David accepted a teaching position at the Universidad San Sebastian in Concepción, Chile. The conversation was sustained via countless e-mails, as we sent texts and images back and forth. As often, the project took much longer and ended up looking quite different than initially anticipated, but new archival treasures and new ideas continued to emerge. Not part of our initial concept, a second volume emerged, dedicated to the critical reception of the building over time.

While I am responsible for the text (and its shortcomings), David's research in Catalan archives provided many new details of the Spanish support for Germany's participation, the fair itself, and the reception of the building in Spain, in addition to many unknown photographs. We both had previously published on the nocturnal illumination at the fair[1] and have presented selected aspects of the history of the Barcelona Pavilion while completing this book.[2]

Foremost among the many colleagues who helped during the long process of assembling this book is Helmut Reuter, who on many occasions assisted with information, opinions, and image files. Barbara Buenger provided rare material about Lilly von Schnitzler and Max Beckmann and many spirited discussions about Beckmann's relationship with Mies's clients Georg and Lilly von Schnitzler; the late Thomas Elsaesser surprised the authors by sending, out of the blue, a letter that his grandmother had written about her visit to the pavilion in 1929, when she accompanied her husband Martin Elsaesser to Barcelona. I am particularly grateful to the grandchildren of Georg and Lilly von Schnitzler, Count Seefried and Countess Hoyos. Paul Galloway at the Museum of Modern Art was endlessly patient with many requests for images and archival material, Pamela Popeson at MoMA facilitated access to some of Mies's original drawings, and many people were quick, uncomplicated, and helpful in providing photographic material, granting publication rights, etc. I am thinking of Jeff Wall, for example, Kai Fingerle, Andrés Jaque and Paola Pardo-Castillo at the Office for Political Innovation, and Núria Gil Pujol at the Arxiu Fotogràfic at the Collegi d'Arquitectes de Catalunya. Jean-Louis Cohen, George Dodds, Rudolf Fischer, Lutz Robbers, Matthias Horstmann, Armin Homburg, Phyllis Lambert, the late Detlef Mertins, Wallis Miller, Wolf Tegethoff, Claire Zimmerman, Polly Seidler, Reto Geiser, Birgit Hammers, Hermann Kühn, Deborah Ascher Barnstone, Lynnette Widder, Hans-Georg Lippert, Katherine James-Chakraborty, Robert Wojtowicz, and many others engaged in discussions about the building and offered helpful leads and suggestions. In Barcelona, George Semler shared his love for the city with me during an unforgettable evening. The 2016 conference at the Fundación

Mies van der Rohe about the rebuilt pavilion brought with it intense discussions with generous and engaging colleagues, such as Fritz Neumeyer, Anna Ramos, Fernand Ramos, Juanjo Laherta, Laura Martinez de Guerenu, and Valentín Trillo Martinez. Carol Krinsky read a major section and offered very helpful edits and critique. Barry Bergdoll and Eeva Liisa Pelkonen helped to shape the book's central arguments. Thomas Weaver and Pamela Johnston edited the entire manuscript, adding clarity and the occasional dash of British humor. My sister, Elisabeth Neumann, retrieved many titles from German archives and provided invaluable help with additional research and discussions. Annette Gref and Katharina Kulke at the Birkhäuser Publishing Company have accompanied the project with great patience and much personal engagement. I am grateful for the time I could spend at the American Academies in Berlin and Rome, where large parts of this text were written. Finally, I would like to thank my wife, Vivian, for her patience and unflagging enthusiasm when the book's "imminent" completion took considerably longer than promised.

1 David Caralt's book *Agualuz* (Madrid: Ediciones Siruela, 2010) is the most exhaustive document about this topic. See also Dietrich Neumann, *Architecture of the Night* (Munich: Prestel, 2002), 138–39.

2 Some of Dietrich Neumann's previous research about the Barcelona Pavilion has appeared in William H. Robinson, Jordi Falgas, and Carmen Belen Lord, eds., *Barcelona and Modernity: Picasso, Gaudí, Miró, Dalí*, exh. cat. Metropolitan Museum of Art, New York, and the Cleveland Museum of Art (New Haven: Yale University Press, 2007), 390–99; and a longer German version in Anja Baumhoff and Madgalena Droste, eds., *Mythos Bauhaus* (Berlin: Reimer Verlag, 2009): 227–43. See also Dietrich Neumann, "Mies, Dada, Montage: Notes on a Reception History," in *Mies van der Rohe: Montage = Collage* (Aachen: Ludwig Forum; London: Koenig Books, 2017), 54–67; and Dietrich Neumann, "'What do you mean by a pavilion?' Mies van der Rohe and the Genesis of the Barcelona Pavilion," in *Mies van der Rohe: Barcelona 1929*, ed. Juan José Lahuerta and Celia Marín Vega (Barcelona: Tenov, 2017), 78–101.

Selected Bibliographyv

Adorno, Theodor W. *Negative Dialektik*. Frankfurt: Suhrkamp, 1966.

Amberger, Eva Maria. *Sergius Ruegenberg: Architekt zwischen Mies van der Rohe und Hans Scharoun*. Berlin: Berlinische Galerie, 2000.

Argan, Giulio Carlo. *Walter Gropius und das Bauhaus*. Hamburg: Rowohlt, 1962.

Baldeweg, Juan Navarro. *La Habitación Vacante*, edited by José Muñoz Millanes. Pre-Textos de Arquitectura 400. Girona: COAC, T. G. Ripoll, 1999.

Balza, Eliseo Sanz. *Notas de un visitante*. Barcelona: Imp. Olympia-Pascual Yuste, 1930.

Banham, Reyner. *Theory and Design in the First Machine Age*. London: Architectural Press, 1960.

Barr, Alfred H. *Cubism and Abstract Art*. New York: Museum of Modern Art, 19346.

Baudrillard, Jean. *Simulacra and Simulation*. Ann Arbor: University of Michigan Press, 1994.

Baumhoff, Anja, and Madgalena Droste, eds. *Mythos Bauhaus*. Berlin: Reimer, 2009.

Behne, Adolf. *The Modern Functional Building*. Santa Monica: Getty Research Institute, 1996. Originally published as *Der moderne Zweckbau* (Berlin: Drei Masken Verlag, 1926).

Behrendt, Walter Curt. *Modern Building: Its Nature, Problems and Forms*. New York: Harcourt, Brace and Co., 1937.

Behrendt, Walter Curt. *The Victory of the New Building Style*. Los Angeles: Getty Research Institute, 2000. Originally published as *Der Sieg des neuen Baustils* (Stuttgart: Verlag Dr. Fr. Wedekind and Co., 1927).

Benevolo, Leonardo. *History of Modern Architecture*. London: Routledge and Kegan Paul, 1971. Originally published as *Storia dell'architettura moderna* (Rome: Giuseppe Laterza and Figli, 1960).

Benjamin, Walter. *Illuminations*, edited and with an introduction by Hannah Arendt. New York: Schocken, 1969.

Berger, Ursel, and Josephine Gabler. *Georg Kolbe: Wohn- und Atelierhaus: Architektur und Geschichte*. Berlin: Jovis, 2000.

Berger, Ursel, and Thomas Pavel, eds. *Barcelona Pavilion: Mies van der Rohe & Kolbe: Architecture and Sculpture / Barcelona Pavillon: Mies van der Rohe & Kolbe: Architektur und Plastik*. Berlin: Jovis, 2006.

Bergson, Henri-Louis. *Schöpferische Entwicklung*. Jena: Eugen Diederichs, 1921.

Bertig, Rudolf. *Ein Mies Haus für Emil Nolde*. Aachen: Mies van der Rohe Haus, 2011.

Biege, Bernd. *Helfer unter Hitler*. Hamburg: Kindler, 2000.

Bier, Justus. "Mies van der Rohes Reichspavilion in Barcelona," *Die Form: Zeitschrift für gestaltende Arbeit* 4, no. 16 (August 15, 1929): 423–30.

Blake, Peter. *The Master Builders*. New York: Alfred A. Knopf, 1960.

Blythe, Sarah Ganz, and Andrew Martinez, eds. *Why Art Museums? Alexander Dorner's Unfinished Project*. Cambridge, MA: MIT Press, 2018.

Bohigas, Oriol. *Modernidad en la Arquitectura de la España republican*. Barcelona: Tusquets Editores S.A., 1998.

Bonta, Juan Pablo. *An Anatomy of Architectural Interpretation: A Semiotic Review of the Criticism of Mies van der Rohe's Barcelona Pavilion*. Barcelona: Gustavo Gili, 1975.

Bonta, Juan Pablo. *Architecture and Its Interpretation: A Study of Expressive Systems in Architecture*. London: Lund Humphries, 1979.

Bonta, Juan Pablo. Über Interpretation von Architektur: *Vom Auf und Ab der Formen und die Rolle der Kritik*. Berlin: Archibook, 1982.

Breuer, Robert. *German Arts and Crafts at the Brussels Exhibition 1910*. Stuttgart: Julius Hoffmann, 1910.

Buddensieg, Tilmann. *Industriekultur: Peter Behrens und die AEG 1907–1914*. Berlin: Gebr. Mann, 1979.

Burmeister, Ralf, ed. *Hannah Höch: Aller Anfang ist DADA!* Ostfildern: Hatje Cantz, 2007.

Canales, Jimena. *The Physicist and the Philosopher: Einstein, Bergson, and the Debate That Changed Our Understanding of Time*. Princeton: Princeton University Press, 2015.

Capdevila-Werning, Remei. "Constructing Reconstruction: The Barcelona Pavilion and Nelson Goodman's Aesthetic Philosophy." Master's thesis, Massachusetts Institute of Technology, 2007. https://dspace.mit.edu/handle/1721.1/39307.

Caralt, David. *Agualuz: De Pirotecnias a mundos flotantes: Visiones de Carles Buigas*. Madrid: Ediciones Siruela, 2010.

Carter, Peter. *Mies van der Rohe at Work*. New York: Praeger, 1974.

Casals, Lluís, and Josep M. Rovira. *Mies van der Rohe: Pavilion: Reflections*. Barcelona: Triangle Postals, 2002.

Castillo, José Vela. *(De)gustaciones gratuitas: De la deconstrucción, la fotografía, Mies van der Rohe y el Pabellón de Barcelona*. Madrid: Abada Editores, 2010.

Colomés, Enrique, and Gonazalo Moure. *Café de Terciopelo y Seda Berlin 1927*. Madrid: Editorial Rueda S.L., 2005.

Colomina, Beatriz, ed. *Architectureproduction*. New York: Princeton Architectural Press, 1988.

Colomina, Beatriz. *Manifesto Architecture: The Ghost of Mies*. Berlin: Sternberg Press, 2014.

Colquhoun, Alan. *Modern Architecture*. Oxford: Oxford University Press, 2002.

Conley, Christine. "Morning Cleaning: Jeff Wall and the Large Glass," *Art History* 32, no. 5 (December 2009): 996–1015.

Costa, Xavier, ed. *Muntadas: On Translation: Paper BP/MVDR*. Barcelona: Fundació Mies van der Rohe, 2010.

Curtis, William J. R. *Architecture Since 1900*. Oxford: Phaidon, 1982.

Damisch, Hubert. *Noah's Ark: Essays on Architecture*, edited by Anthony Vidler. Cambridge, MA: MIT Press, 2016.

de Alba, Roberto. *Paul Rudolph: The Late Work*. New York: Princeton Architectural Press, 2003.

de Fries, Heinrich, ed. *Moderne Villen und Landhäuser*. Berlin: Wasmuth Verlag, 1924.

Denk, Andreas, Uwe Schröder, and Rainer Schützeichel, eds. *Architektur, Raum, Theorie: Eine kommentierte Anthologie*. Tübingen: Ernst Wasmuth Verlag, 2016.

Dobson, Andrew. *An Introduction to the Politics and Philosophy of José Orgega y Gasset*. Cambridge: Cambridge University Press, 1989.

Dodds, George. *Building Desire: On the Barcelona Pavilion*. London: Routledge, 2005.

Drexler, Arthur. *Ludwig Mies van der Rohe*. New York: George Braziller Inc., 1960.

Drexler, Arthur, ed. *The Mies van der Rohe Archive*, vol. 2. New York: Garland, 1986.

Durth, Werner, and Paul Sigel, eds. *Baukultur: Spiegel gesellschaftlichen Wandels*. Berlin: Jovis, 2010.

Dvorák, Max. *Katechismus der Denkmalpflege*. Vienna: Anton Schroll, 1918.

Dziewior, Yilmaz. *Mies: Blick durch den Spiegel*. Cologne: Walther König, 2005.

Eddington, Arthur Stanley. *Raum, Zeit und Schwere*. Braunschweig: Vieweg and Teubner, 1923.

Einstein, Carl, and Paul Westheim, eds. *Europa Almanach*. Potsdam: Gustav Kiepenheuer Verlag, 1925.

Elsaesser, Martin. *Bauten und Entwürfe aus den Jahren 1924–1932*. Berlin: *Bauwelt*, 1933.

Evans, Robin. "Mies van der Rohe's Paradoxical Symmetries," *AA Files* 19 (1990): 56–68.

Exposición Internacional Barcelona 1929. Barcelona: Huecograbado, 1929.

Forty, Adrian. *Words and Buildings: A Vocabulary of Modern Architecture*. London: Thames and Hudson, 2000.

Four Great Makers of Modern Architecture: Gropius, Le Corbusier, Mies van der Rohe, Wright: The Verbatim Record of a Symposium Held at the School of Architecture at Columbia University from March to May 1961. New York: Da Capo Press, 1963.

Frampton, Kenneth. *Modern Architecture: A Critical History*. London: Thames and Hudson, 1980.

Fried, Michael. "Jeff Wall, Wittgenstein, and the Everyday," *Critical Inquiry* 33, no. 3 (Spring 2007): 495–526.

Gargiani, Robert, ed. *La Colonne: Nouvelle histoire de la construction*. Lausanne: Presses polytechniques et universitaires romandes, 2008.

Genzmer, Walther. "Der Deutsche Reichspavillon auf der Internationalen Ausstellung in Barcelona," *Die Baugilde* 11, no. 20 (October 1929): 1654–57.

Giedion, Sigfried. *A Decade of New Architecture*. Zurich: Girsberger, 1951.

Giedion, Sigfried. *Gropius: Work and Teamwork*. Zurich: Max E. Neuenschwander, 1954.

Giedion, Sigfried. *Space, Time and Architecture*. Cambridge, MA: Harvard University Press, 1941.

Glaeser, Ludwig. *Ludwig Mies van der Rohe: The Barcelona Pavilion: Fiftieth Anniversary*. Washington: National Gallery of Art, 1979.

Goodman, Nelson. "How Buildings Mean," *Critical Inquiry* 11, no. 4 (June 1985): 642–53.

Granados, J. Oriol, Jordi Calafell, and Rafel Torrella. *Montjuïc 1915, primera mirada*. Barcelona: Arxiu Fotogràfic-Institut de Cultura de Barcelona, 2007.

Hammers, Birgit. *Sasha Stone sieht noch mehr: Ein Fotograf zwischen Kommerz und Kunst*. Petersberg: Michael Imhof, 2014.

Harbers, Guido. *Das freistehende Einfamilienhaus von 10000–30000 Mark und über 30000 Mark*. Munich: Callwey, 1932.

Harbers, Guido. "Deutscher Reichspavillon in Barcelona auf der Internationalen Ausstellung 1929," *Der Baumeister* 27, no. 11 (November 1929): 421–27.

Hartoonian, Gevork. *Time, History and Architecture: Essays on Critical Historiography*. London: Routledge, 2018.

Hays, K. Michael. *Architecture Theory Since 1968*. Cambridge, MA: MIT Press, 1998.

Heine, Jens Ulrich. *Verstand und Schicksal: Die Männer der I.G. Farbenindustrie A.G. (1925–1945) in 161 Kurzbiographien*. Weinheim: VCH, 1990.

Heller, Kevin John. *The Nuremberg Military Tribunals and the Origins of International Criminal Law*. Oxford: Oxford University Press, 2011.

Henderson, Linda Dalrymple. *The Fourth Dimension and Non-Euclidean Geometry in Modern Art*, rev. ed. Cambridge, MA: MIT Press, 2013.

Heynen, Hilde. *Architecture and Modernity*. Cambridge, MA: MIT Press, 1999.

Hilberseimer, Ludwig. *Mies van der Rohe*. Chicago: Paul Theobald and Co., 1956.

Hill, Jonathan, ed. *Architecture: The Subject Is Matter*. London: Routledge, 2001.

Hitchcock, Henry Russell. *19th and 20th Century Architecture*. Harmondsworth: Penguin Books, 1958.

Hochadel, Oliver, and Agustí Nieto-Galan. *Barcelona: An Urban History of Science and Modernity, 1888–1929*. London: Routledge, 2017.

Hochman, Elaine S. *Architects of Fortune: Mies van der Rohe and the Third Reich*. New York: Weidenfeld and Nicolson, 1989.

Horstmann, Matthias. "Der elektrische Barcelona-Pavillon: Bildarchitekturen 1929: Berliner Riesenfotos in Barcelona," *Die Vierte Wand*, no. 7 (May 2017): 80–85.

Hosey, Lance. "The Ship of Theseus: Identity and the Barcelona Pavilion(s)," *Journal of Architectural Education* 72, no. 2 (October 2018): 230–47.

Howe, George. "Abstract Design in Modern Architecture," *Parnassus* 8, no. 5 (October 1936): 29–31.

Huse, Norbert. *Geschichte der Architektur des 20. Jahrhunderts*. Munich: Beck, 2008.

Huse, Norbert. *Neues Bauen 1918–1933: Moderne Architektur in der Weimarer Republik*. Munich: Moos, 1975.

Husserl, Edmund. *Ding und Raum: Vorlesungen 1907*, edited by Ulrich Claesges. Husserliana 16. The Hague: Nijhoff, 1973.

Illescas, Albert, and Manuel Brullet, eds. *Sixte Illescas Arquitecte (1903–1986): De l'avantguarda a l'oblit / de la vanguardia al olvido / From Vanguard to Obscurity*. Barcelona: Collegi d'Arquitectes de Catalunya, 2008.

Ito, Toyo. "Tarzans in the Media Forest," *2G*, no. 2 (January 1997): 121–44.

James, Henry. *The American Scene*. London: Chapman and Hall, 1907.

James, Warren A. "Barcelona: Reconstruction of the Barcelona Pavilion," *Progressive Architecture* 67 (August 1986): 62.

Jencks, Charles. *The Language of Post-Modern Architecture*. London: Academy Editions, 1977.

Jencks, Charles. *Modern Movements in Architecture*. New York: Anchor Press/Doubleday, 1973.

Johnson, Philip C., ed. *Mies van der Rohe*. Exh. cat. Museum of Modern Art, New York. New York: Museum of Modern Art, 1947.

Johnson, Philip C., and Alfred H. Barr. *Modern Architecture: International Exhibition*. Exh. cat. Museum of Modern Art, New York. New York: Museum of Modern Art, 1932.

Jordy, William H. *The Impact of European Modernism in the Mid-Twentieth Century*. American Buildings and Its Architects 5. Oxford: Oxford University Press, 1972.

Julian, Immaculada. *L'Urbanisme a Barcelona entre dues exposicións (1888–1929)*. Barcelona: Els Llibres de la Frontera, 1988.

Kersten, Carl. *Der Eisenhochbau*. Berlin: Wilhelm Ernst und Sohn, 1920.

Kiessler, Uwe, ed. *Winfried Nerdinger: Architektur im Museum 1977–2012*. Munich: Detail, 2012.

Kleinman, Kent, and Leslie Van Duzer. *Mies van der Rohe: The Krefeld Villas*. New York: Princeton Architectural Press, 2005.

Klötzer, Wolfgang, ed. *Frankfurter Biographie*, vol. 2, *M–Z*. Veröffentlichungen der Frankfurter Historischen Kommission 19/2. Frankfurt: Kramer, 1996.

Koenig, Giovanni Klaus. *Architettura e comunicazione*. Florence: Editrice Fiorentina, 1970.

Koenig, Giovanni Klaus. "Gropius or Mies," *Casabella* (November 1969): 34–39.

Koolhaas, Rem. "Miesverständnisse," *Arch+* 161 (June 2002): 78–83.

Koolhaas, Rem, and Bruce Mau. *SMLXL*. New York: Monacelli Press, 1995.

Kracauer, Siegfried. *Schriften*, vol. 5.2, *Aufsätze: 1927–1931*, edited by Inka Mülder-Bach. Frankfurt: Suhrkamp, 1990.

Krauss, Rosalind. "Sculpture in the Expanded Field," *October* 8 (Spring 1979): 30–44.

Lahuerta, Juan José. *Photography or Life: Popular Mies*. Barcelona: Tenov, 2015.

Lahuerta, Juan José, and Celia Marín Vega, eds. *Mies van der Rohe: Barcelona 1929*. Barcelona: Tenov, 2017.

Lammert, Angela, ed. *Topos Raum: Die Aktualität des Raumes in den Künsten der Gegenwart*. Berlin: Akademie der Künste, 2005.

Lange, Christiane. *Ludwig Mies van der Rohe: Architektur für die Seidenindustrie*. Cologne: Nicolaische Verlagsbuchhandlung, 2011.

Lange, Christiane. *Ludwig Mies van der Rohe und Lilly Reich: Möbel und Räume*. Berlin: Hatje Cantz, 2007.

Lange, Christiane, and Robbrecht en Daem architecten, eds. *Mies 1:1 Ludwig Mies van der Rohe The Golfclub Project*. Cologne: Walther König, 2014.

Leach, Neil. *Rethinking Architecture: A Reader in Cultural Theory*. London: Routledge, 1997.

Leatherbarrow, David. *Uncommon Ground: Architecture, Technology and Topography*. Cambridge, MA: MIT Press, 2002.

Le Corbusier. *Kommende Baukunst*. Stuttgart: Deutsche Verlags-Anstalt, 1926.

Le Corbusier. "Neue Gesinnung in der Baukunst," *Europäische Revue* 4, no. 9 (December 1928): 689–700.

Levine, Neil. *Vincent Scully: Modern Architecture and Other Essays*. Princeton: Princeton University Press, 2003.

Lizondo Sevilla, Laura. "Mies's Opaque Cube: The Electric Utilities Pavilion at the 1929 Barcelona International Exposition," *Journal of the Society of Architectural Historians* 76, no. 2 (June 2017): 197–217.

Llorens, Tomás. *Arquitectura, historia y teoria de los signos: El symposium de Castelldefels*. Barcelona: La Gay Ceincia, 1974.

Lorentz, Hendrik A., Albert Einstein, Hermann Minkowski, and Hermann Weyl. *The Principle of Relativity: A Collection of Original Memoirs on the Special and General Theory of Relativity*. London: Methuen, 1923. Originally published as *Das Relativitätsprinzip* (Berlin: B. G. Teubner, 1913).

Maki, Fumihiko. *Nurturing Dreams: Collected Essays on Architecture and the City*. Cambridge, MA: MIT Press, 2008.

Mallgrave, Harry Francis, and David Goodman. *An Introduction to Architectural Theory 1958 to the Present*. Oxford: Wiley Blackwell, 2011.

Mallgrave, Harry Francis, and Eleftherios Ikonomou, eds. *Empathy, Form, and Space: Problems in German Aesthetics, 1873–1893*. Santa Monica: Getty Center for the History of Art and the Humanities, 1994.

Marsà, Ángel, and Luis Marsillach. *La montaña iluminada: Itinerario espiritual de la Exposición de Barcelona 1929–1930*. Barcelona: Ed. Horizonte, 1930.

McGrath, Raymond. *Twentieth-Century Houses*. London: Faber and Faber, 1934.

McQuaid, Matilda. *Lilly Reich, Designer and Architect*. Exh. cat. Museum of Modern Art, New York. New York: Museum of Modern Art, Harry N. Abrams, 1996.

Meier-Graefe, Julius. *Die Weltausstellung in Paris 1900*. Leipzig: Verlag F. Krüger, 1900.

Meissner, Irene. *Sep Ruf, 1908–1982*. Berlin: Deutscher Kunstverlag, 2013.

Mendelson, Jordana. *Documenting Spain: Artists, Exhibition Culture, and the Modern Nation, 1929–1939*. University Park: Pennsylvania State University Press, 2005.

Mertins, Detlef. "Architectures of Becoming: Mies van der Rohe and the Avant-Garde." In Riley and Bergdoll, *Mies in Berlin*, 106–133.

Mertins, Detlef. *Mies*. New York: Phaidon, 2014.

Mertins, Detlef, ed. *The Presence of Mies*. New York: Princeton Architectural Press, 1994.

Mies van der Rohe: Sa carrière, son héritage et ses disciples. Paris: Centre Georges Pompidou, 1987.

Mock, Elizabeth, ed. *Built in U.S.A., 1932–1944*. Exh. cat. Museum of Modern Art, New York. New York: Museum of Modern Art, 1944.

Mock, Elizabeth, and J. M. Richards. *An Introduction to Modern Architecture*. London: Pelican Books, 1940.

Moholy-Nagy, Laszlo. *Von Material zu Architektur*. 1929. Reprint, Berlin: Gebrüder Mann, 2001.

Müller, Guido. *Europäische Gesellschaftsbeziehungen nach dem Ersten Weltkrieg*. Munich: R. Oldenbourg, 2005.

Müller, Ulrich. *Raum, Bewegung und Zeit im Werk von Walter Gropius und Ludwig Mies van der Rohe*. Berlin: Akademie Verlag, 2004.

Nachtlicht, Leo. *Deutsches Kunstgewerbe, St. Louis 1904*. Berlin: Ernst Wasmuth, 1904.

Nerdinger, Winfried, ed. *Geschichte der Rekonstruktion, Rekonstruktion der Geschichte*. Munich: Prestel, 2010.

Nerdinger, Winfried. "Nachlese zum 100. Geburtstag: Neue Literature zu Mies van der Rohe," *Kunstchronik* 41, no. 8 (August 1988): 419–29.

Nesbitt, Kate. *Theorizing a New Agenda for Architecture: An Anthology of Architectural Theory 1965–1995*. New York: Princeton Architectural Press, 1996.

Neufert, Ernst. *Bauentwurfslehre*. Berlin: Bauwelt Verlag, 1936.

Neumann, Dietrich. *Architecture of the Night*. Munich: Prestel, 2002.

Neumann, Dietrich. "The Barcelona Pavilion." In Robinson, Falgas, and Belen Lord, *Barcelona and Modernity*, 390–99.

Neumann, Dietrich. "Der Barcelona Pavilion." In Baumhoff and Droste, *Mythos Bauhaus*, 227–43.

Neumann, Dietrich. Introduction to Trillo Martinez, *Mies en Barcelona*, 13–20.

Neumann, Dietrich. "Mies, Dada, Montage: Notes on a Reception History." In *Mies van der Rohe: Montage = Collage*, edited by Andreas Beitin, Wolf Eiermann, and Brigitte Franzen, 54–67. London: Koenig Books, 2017.

Neumann, Dietrich. "Mies's Concrete Office Building and Its Common Acquaintance," *AA Files* 74 (June 2017): 70–84.

Neumann, Dietrich. "'Wallpaper with Arctic Landscapes': Mies van der Rohe's Patents for Wallpaper Design and Printing Technology 1937–1950." In Reuter and Schulte, *Mies and Modern Living*, 264–79.

Neumann, Dietrich. "'What do you mean by a pavilion?' Mies van der Rohe and the Genesis of the Barcelona Pavilion." In Lahuerta and Marín, *Mies van der Rohe*, 78–101.

Neumeyer, Fritz. *The Artless Word: Mies van der Rohe on the Building Art*. Cambridge, MA: MIT Press, 1991. Originally published as *Mies van der Rohe: Das kunstlose Wort: Gedanken zur Baukunst* (Berlin: Wolf Jobst Siedler Verlag, 1986).

Neumeyer, Fritz, ed. *Quellentexte zur Architekturtheorie*. Munich: Prestel, 2002.

Norberg-Schulz, Christian. *Architecture: Meaning and Place: Selected Essays*. New York: Electa/Rizzoli, 1988.

Ochsendorf, John. *Guastavino Vaulting: The Art of Structural Tile*. New York: Princeton Architectural Press, 2010.

Office for Metropolitan Architecture. "Body-Building Home: La Casa Palestra." In Teyssot, *Il Progetto domestico*, 52.

Papapetros, Spyros, and Julian Rose, eds. *Retracing the Expanded Field: Encounters between Art and Architecture*. Cambridge, MA: MIT Press, 2014.

Paris, William Francklyn. "The Barcelona Exposition: A Splendid but Costly Effort of the Catalan People," *Architectural Forum* (November 1929): 481–96.

Pazaurek, Gustav Edmund. "Ist der Werkbund auf dem richtigen Wege?" *Münchner Neueste Nachrichten* 83, no. 308 (November 12, 1930), 1.

Pevsner, Nikolaus. *An Outline of European Architecture*. London: Pelican Books, 1960.

Piacentini, Marcello. *Architettura d'Oggi*. Rome: Paolo Cremonese, 1930.

Platz, Gustav Adolf. *Die Baukunst der Neuesten Zeit*, 2nd ed. Berlin: Propyläen, 1930.

Plüm, Kerstin, ed. *Mies van der Rohe im Diskurs*. Bielefeld: Transkript, 2013.

Pool, James. *Hitler and His Secret Partners: Contributions, Loot and Rewards, 1933–45*. New York: Pocket Books, 1997.

Puente, Moisés, ed. *Conversations with Mies van der Rohe*. New York: Princeton Architectural Press, 2008.

Quetglas, Josep. *Der gläserne Schrecken: Imágenes del Pabellón de Alemania*. Montreal: Les Editions Section b, 1991.

Quetglas, Josep. *Fear of Glass: Mies van der Rohe's Pavilion in Barcelona*. Basel: Birkhäuser, 2001.

Reed, Peter, and William Kaizen, eds. *The Show to End All Shows: Frank Lloyd Wright and The Museum of Modern Art, 1940*. New York: Museum of Modern Art, 2004.

Rehm, Robin. "Japan–Wright–Mies: Schatten als visuelles Motiv des Barcelona Pavillons," *Figurationen* 5, no. 2 (2004): 67–79.

Reuter, Helmut, and Birgit Schulte, eds. *Mies and Modern Living: Interiors, Furniture, Photography*. Ostfildern: Hatje Cantz, 2008.

Riezler, Walter. "Das neue Raumgefühl in bildender Kunst und Musik." In *Vierter Kongress für Ästhetik und allgemeine Kunstwissenschaft*, Hamburg, October 7–9, 1930, supplement to *Zeitschrift für Ästhetik und allgemeine Kunstwissenschaft* 25 (1931): 179–216.

Riley, Terence. *The International Style: Exhibition 15 and the Museum of Modern Art*. New York: Rizzoli, 1992.

Riley, Terence, and Barry Bergdoll, eds. *Mies in Berlin*. Exh. cat. Museum of Modern Art, New York. New York: Museum of Modern Art, 2001.

Robinson, William H., Jordi Falgas, and Carmen Belen Lord, eds. *Barcelona and Modernity: Picasso, Gaudí, Miró, Dalí*. New Haven: Yale University Press, 2007.

Rorschach, Hermann. *Psychodiagnostics: A Diagnostic Test Based on Perception; including Rorschach's paper "The Application of the Form Interpretation Test."* Bern: H. Huber, 1942. Originally published as *Psychodiagnostik: Methodik und Ergebnisse eines wahrnehmungsdiagnostischen Experiments (Deutenlassen von Zufallsformen)* (Bern: E. Bircher, 1921).

Rovira, Josep M., ed. *Sert 1928–1979: Medio siglo de arquitectura. Obra Completa*. Barcelona: Fundació Joan Miró, 2005.

Rowe, Colin. *The Mathematics of the Ideal Villa and Other Essays*. Cambridge, MA: MIT Press, 1976.

Rubió i Tudurí, Nicolas M. *Actar: Discrimination des Formes de Quiétude, Formes de Mouvement dans la Construction*. Paris: Imp. Union, 1931.

Rubió i Tudurí, Nicolas M. "Le Pavillon de l'Allemagne à l'Exposition de Barcelone par Mies van der Rohe," *Cahiers d'art*, nos. 8/9 (August/September 1929): 408–11.

Ruskin, John. *The Seven Lamps of Architecture*. New York: Wiley and Halsted, 1857.

Salmen, Brigitte, ed. *"Bereitschaft zum Risiko": Lilly von Schnitzler, 1889–1981: Sammlerin und Mäzenin*. Exh. cat. Schlossmuseum Murnau. Murnau: Schlossmuseum, 2011.

Schmarsow, August. *Das Wesen der architektonischen Schöpfung*. Leipzig: Hiersemann, 1894.

Schuldenfrei, Robin. *Luxury and Modernism: Architecture and the Object in Germany 1900–1933*. Princeton: Princeton University Press, 2018.

Schulze, Franz. *Mies van der Rohe: A Critical Biography*. Chicago: University of Chicago Press, 1985.

Schulze, Franz. *Philip Johnson: Life and Work*. Chicago: University of Chicago Press, 1996.

Schulze, Franz, and Edward Windhorst. *Mies van der Rohe: A Critical Biography*, rev. ed. Chicago: University of Chicago Press, 2012.

Schulze, Hagen. *Weimar: Deutschland 1917–1933*. Munich: Siedler Verlag, 1982.

Scully, Vincent, Jr. *Modern Architecture: The Architecture of Democracy*. New York: George Braziller, 1961.

Scully, Vincent, Jr. *The Shingle Style*. New Haven: Yale University Press, 1955.

Segre, Roberto. *Arquitectura y urbanismo modernos: Capitalismo y socialismo*. Havana: Arte y arquitectura, 1988.

Sennott, R. Stephen, ed. *Encyclopedia of Twentieth-Century Architecture*. New York: Fitzroy Dearborn, 2003.

Sigel, Paul. *Exponiert: Deutsche Pavillons auf Weltausstellungen*. Berlin: Verlag Bauwesen, 2000.

Simon, Heinrich. *Barcelona Weltausstellung 1929*. Frankfurt: Frankfurter Zeitung, 1929.

Smith, Kathryn. *Wright on Exhibit: Frank Lloyd Wright's Architectural Exhibitions*. Princeton: Princeton University Press, 2017.

Smithson, Alison, and Peter Smith. *Changing the Art of Inhabitation*. London: Artemis, 1994.

Solà-Morales, Ignasi de. *La Exposición Internacional de Barcelona 1914–1929: Arquitectura y Ciudad*. Barcelona: Feria de Barcelona, 1985.

Solà-Morales, Ignasi de, Cristian Cirici, and Fernando Ramos. *Mies: El Pabellón de Barcelona*. Barcelona: Gustavo Gili, 1993.

Somol, R. E., ed. *Autonomy and Ideology: Positioning an Avant-garde in America*. New York: Monacelli Press, 1997.

Spaeth, David. *Mies van der Rohe*. New York: Rizzoli, 1985.

Speyer, James A. *Mies van der Rohe*. Chicago: Art Institute of Chicago, 1968.

Stead, Naomi, and Cristina Garduño Freeman. "Architecture and 'The Act of Receiving, or the Fact of Being Received': Introduction to a Special Issue on Reception," *Architectural Theory Review* 18, no. 3 (2013): 267–71.

Stern, Robert A. M. "New Directions in American Architecture," *Architectural Association Quarterly* 9, nos. 2 and 3 (1977), 66–71.

Stierli, Martino. "Mies Montage: Mies van der Rohe, Dada, Film und die Kunstgeschichte," *Zeitschrift für Kunstgeschichte* 74, no. 3 (2011): 413.

Stierli, Martino. *Montage and Metropolis*. New Haven: Yale University Press, 2017.

Stone, Sasha. *Berlin in Bildern*, edited by Adolf Behne. Vienna: Dr. Hans Epstein, 1929.

Stumpf, Carl. Über den Psychologischen Ursprung der Raumvorstellung. Leipzig: Verlag von S. Hirzel, 1873.

Subirana i Torrent, Rosa Maria. *Mies van der Rohe's German Pavilion in Barcelona, 1929–1986*. Barcelona: Fundació Pública del Pavelló Alemany de Barcelona de Mies van der Rohe, Ajuntament de Barcelona, 1987.

Sykes, A. Krista, ed. *Constructing a New Agenda: Architectural Theory 1993–2009*. New York: Princeton Architectural Press, 2009.

Tafuri, Manfredo. *The Sphere and the Labyrinth: Avant-Gardes and Architecture from Piranesi to the 1970s*. Cambridge, MA: MIT Press, 1987. Originally published as *La sfera e il labirinto: Avanguardie e architettura da Piranesi agli anni '70* (Turin: Einaudi Editore, 1980).

Tafuri, Manfredo, and Francesco dal Co. *Architettura Contemporanea*. Milan: Electa Editrice, 1976.

Tafuri, Manfredo, and Francesco dal Co. *Modern Architecture*. New York: Harry N. Abrams, 1979.

Tegethoff, Wolf. *Mies: The Villas and Country Houses*. New York: Museum of Modern Art; Cambridge, MA: MIT Press, 1985.

Teige, Karel. *The Minimum Dwelling*. Cambridge, MA: MIT Press, 2002. Originally published as *Nejmenší byt* (Prague: Václav Petr, 1932).

Teyssot, Georges. *Il Progetto domestico: la casa dell'uomo: archetipi e prototipo*. Milan: Electa, 1986.

Torrella, Rafel. *El registre fotogràfic de Montjuïc, 1915–1923: La metamorfosi d'una muntanya*. Barcelona: Arxiu Històric de la Ciutat de Barcelona, 2008.

Trillo Martinez, Valentín. *Mies en Barcelona: Arquitectura, representación y memoria*. Seville: UEUS, Editorial Universidad de, 2017.

Tunnard, Christopher. *Gardens in the Modern Landscape*. London: The Architectural Press, 1938.

van der Rohe, Georgia. *La Donna e mobile: Mein bedingungsloses Leben*. Berlin: Aufbau, 2001.

van Doesburg, Theo. "Die neue Architektur und ihre Folgen." In *De Stijl: Schriften und Manifeste: Zu einem theoretischen Konzept ästhetischer Umweltgestaltung*, edited by Hagen Bächler and Herbert Letsch, 185–88. Leipzig: Kiepenheuer, 1984.

van Doesburg, Theo. *On European Architecture: Complete Essays from Het Boubedrijf, 1924–1931*. Basel: Birkhäuser, 1986.

Varnelis, Kazys, ed. *The Philip Johnson Tapes: Interviews by Robert A. M. Stern*. New York: Monacelli Press, 2008.

Venturi, Robert. *Complexity and Contradiction in Architecture*. New York: Museum of Modern Art, 1966.

von Hildebrand, Adolf. *Das Problem der Form in der bildenden Kunst*. Strasbourg: Heitz and Muendel, 1893.

von Schnitzler, Georg. "Germany and World Trade after the War," *The Atlantic* 165 (June 1940): 817–21.

von Schnitzler, Lilly (L.S.M.). "Marginalien: Die Weltausstellung Barcelona 1929," *Der Querschnitt* 9, no. 8 (August 1929): 582–84.

von Schnitzler, Lilly (L.S.M.). "Weltausstellung Barcelona," *Europäische Revue* 5, no. 4 (July 1929): 286–88.

Washton Long, Rose-Carol, and Maria Makela, eds. *Of "Truths Impossible to Put in Words": Max Beckmann Contextualized*. Bern: Peter Lang, 2009.

Weber, Wolfgang. *Barcelona*. Berlin: Albertus-Verlag, 1929.

Wichmann, Hans, ed. *Sep Ruf: Bauten und Projekte*. Stuttgart: Deutsche Verlags Anstalt, 1986.

Wingler, Hans Maria. *The Bauhaus: Weimar, Dessau, Berlin, Chicago* (Cambridge: MIT Press, 1969). Originally published as *Das Bauhaus, 1919–1933: Weimar, Dessau, Berlin* (Cologne: DuMont Schauberg, 1962).

Yatsuka, Hajime. "Mies and Japan," *Cornell Journal of Architecture* 7 (2003): 52–62.

Zevi, Bruno. *Architecture as Space: How to Look at Architecture*. New York: Horizon Press, 1957.

Zevi, Bruno. *The Modern Language of Architecture*. Seattle: University of Washington Press, 1978.

Zevi, Bruno. *Storia dell'architettura moderna*. Turin: Einaudi, 1955.

Zevi, Bruno. *Towards an Organic Architecture*. London: Faber and Faber, 1950.

Zimmerman, Claire. *Photographic Architecture in the 20th Century*. Minneapolis: University of Minnesota Press, 2014.

Zukowsky, John, ed. *Mies Reconsidered: His Career, Legacy, and Disciples*. Chicago: Art Institute of Chicago; New York: Rizzoli International, 1986.

Zurfluh, Lukas. "Der 'fliessende Raum' des Barcelona-Pavillons: Eine Metamorphose der Interpretation?" *Wolkenkuckucksheim* 13, no. 1 (May 2009), accessed August 1, 2017, http://www.cloud-cuckoo.net/journal1996-2013/inhalt/de/heft/ausgaben/108/Zurfluh/zurfluh.php#_edn7.

Illustration Credits

AC. Documentos de Actividad Contemporanea 4 (1931): **26**: 14; 27: 15;

Alamy Stock Photo: **20**: 1; **151**: 5;

© André Jaque: **166**: 16, 17;

© Anna Mas, Barcelona: **165**: 15; **168**: 19; **170**: 20; **171**: 21;

© Archive Georg-Kolbe-Museum, Berlin: **90**: 1; **91**: 2; **92**: 3, 4; **93**: 5; **94**: 6. **143**: 20;

© Arxiu Fotogràfic de Barcelona: **25**: 11; **36**: 5, 6; **37**: 7; **142**: 19;

© Arxiu Historic de la Ciutat de Barcelona: **101**: 3; **147**: 3.

© Arxiu Històric del Collegi d'Arquitectes de Catalunya: **158**: 6, 7; **159**: 8; **160**: 10, 11;

© Arxiu Nacional de Catalunya: **115**: 2, 3; **116**: 4, 5;

© Bauhaus Archive, Berlin: **33**: 3, 4; **139**: 13; **140**: 17; **154**: 1, 2; **155**: 3;

Bauwelt 12 (1929, Supplement 17/18): **53**: 16;

© Berlinische Galerie, Berlin: **157**: 5; **159**:9;

© Broehan Design Foundation, Berlin: **58:** 7;

D'Aci i D'Alla (Sondernummer zur Weltausstellung Barcelona) December 1929: **27**: 16;

Contemporary illustration or postcard, private collection: **20**: 3; **21**: 4; **23**: 8; **23**: 6, 7, 8; **24**: 9; **25**: 10; **26**: 12; **39**: 8; **56**: 2, 3; **57**: 4, 5; **59**: 8, 9; **60**: 11, 14; **64**: 21, 23; **65**: 25; **68**: 1; **78**: 9; **100**: 1, 2; **126**: 13; **146**: 1.

© Deborah Berke & Partners: **183**: 14;

Diario Oficial: **32**: 2; **62**: 17; **64**: 22; **64**: 22; **65**: 24, 26; **107**: 12; **108**: 13; **132**: 1, 2;

© Ezra Stoller /Esto: **176**: 2; **178**: 6; **178**: 7;

Exposición Internacional Barcelona 1929 (Barcelona: Huecograbado, 1929): **25**: 12; **61**: 16; **63**: 18, 19, 20;

Deutsche Bauzeitung 63, no. 77 (1929): **143**: 22.

© Foto Fayer, Wien: **147**: 2;

© Fundación Mies van der Rohe, Barcelona: **122**: 11.

© Secret State Archive, Preussischer Kulturbesitz, Berlin: **103**: 6.

© Getty Images: **38**: 9;

© Getty Research Institute: **176**, 1; **179**, 8; **180**: 9;

© Glint Studio: **183**: 14.

© Jeff Wall/Jeff Wall Studio: **163**: 12;

© Hassan Bagheri: Tafeln I–VI

© Hoechst Archive: **32**: 1; **114**: 1; **117**: 6, 7; **118**, 8;

Grosse Berliner Kunstausstellung im Landesausstellungsgebäude am Lehrter Bahnhof Ausstellungskatalog (Berlin, 1924): **46**: 6.

© James Steakley: **177**: 3;

© Prof. Juanjo Lahuerta, Barcelona: **143**: 21.

© Kai Fingerle, Berlin: **162**: 13;

© MM Doogie: **177**: 4;

© Nikos Valsamakis: **181**: 10;

© Paul Smith: **183**: 13.

© Picture Alliance / dpa: **183**: 12;

© SANAA: **167**: 18;

© Solomon R. Guggenheim Museum, Licensed by SCALA/Art Resource, NY © 2020/Artists Rights society (ARS), New York/VG Bild-Kunst, Bonn: **148**: 4;

© Thomas Ruff / VG Bild Kunst, Bonn; Courtesy the artist and David Zwirner: **164**: 14;

© Klassik Stiftung Weimar: **44**: 1, 2; **48**: 9; **49**: 11; **50**: 12, 13; **52**: 14, 15; **79**: 12; **101**: 4; **102**: 5; **104**: 7; **105**: 8; **108**: 14; **134**: 3, 4, 5; **135**: 6, 7; **136**: 8, 9; **137**: 10; **138**: 11, 12; **139**: 14, 15; **140**: 16, 17;

© Kunsthalle Mannheim: **46**: 7;

La Vanguardia (October 24, 1929): **120**: 9; **121**: 10;

Museum of Modern Art, Licensed by SCALA/Art Resource, NY © 2020/Artists Rights society (ARS), New York/VG Bild-Kunst, Bonn: **45**: 3, 4, 5; **47**: 8 ; **72**: 4, 5; **73**: 6; **74**: 7; **79**: 10, 11; **82**: 13, 14; **83**: 15, 16; **84**: 17; **85**: 18, 19; **86**: 20, 21;

Public Domain: **20**: 2;

Masterpieces of Art. Official Souvenir Guide and Picture Book (New York: Art News, 1939), back cover: 178: 5;

Meyer Graefe, Julius. *Die Weltausstellung in Paris 1900*. (Paris, Leipzig: F. Krüger Verlag, 1900): **56**: 1.

© Museum für Angewandte Kunst, Wien: **60**: 12;

© Neue Galerie, NY Licensed by SCALA/Art Resource, NY © 2020:

© OMA: 162: 12;

© Paris, Musée des Arts Décoratifs, Pavillon de l'Esprit Nouveau, Fonds Editions Albert Lévy, 1925: **59**, 10.

© Rheinisches Bildarchiv, Cologne: **60**: 13; **61**: 15;

© Robin Evans: **157**: 4;

© Staatliche Museen zu Berlin, Kunstbibliothek, Architektursammlung: **71**: 2; **72**: 3; **74**: 8;

Wasmuth's Monatshefte fuer Baukunst 1 no. 4 (1915), 200: **57**: 6;

Weber, Wolfgang *Barcelona*. (Berlin: Albertus-Verlag, 1928): **22**: 5; **29**: 17;

Wien Museum: **124**: 12;

Copy editing
Keonaona Peterson

Project management
Annette Gref, Katharina Kulke

Production
Amelie Solbrig

Layout, cover design
Severine Mailler

Typesetting
Miriam Bussmann

Paper
Amber Graphic, 150 g/m²

Printing
optimal media GmbH, Röbel/Müritz

Library of Congress Control Number: 2020946079

Bibliographic information published by the German National Library
The German National Library lists this publication in the Deutsche Nationalbibliografie; detailed bibliographic data are available on the Internet at http://dnb.dnb.de.

ISBN 978-3-0356-1986-7
e-ISBN (PDF) 978-3-0356-1997-3

German Print-ISBN 978-3-0356-1979-9

P.O. Box 44, 4009 Basel, Switzerland
Part of Walter de Gruyter GmbH, Berlin/Boston

9 8 7 6 5 4 3 2 1
www.birkhauser.com